MariaDB High Performance

Familiarize yourself with the MariaDB system and
build high-performance applications

Pierre MAVRO

open source*
community experience distilled

BIRMINGHAM - MUMBAI

MariaDB High Performance

First published: September 2014

Production reference: 1190914

Published by Packt Publishing Ltd.
Livery Place
35 Livery Street
Birmingham B3 2PB, UK.

ISBN 978-1-78398-160-1

www.packtpub.com

Credits

Author

Pierre MAVRO

Reviewers

David "DaviXX" CHANIAL

P. R. Karthik

Emilien Kenler

Joffrey MICHAÏE

Daniel Parnell

Dimitri Savineau

Commissioning Editor

Kunal Parikh

Acquisition Editor

Subho Gupta

Content Development Editor

Mohammed Fahad

Technical Editors

Dennis John

Sebastian Rodrigues

Copy Editors

Roshni Banerjee

Sarang Chari

Project Coordinator

Danuta Jones

Proofreaders

Maria Gould

Ameesha Green

Paul Hindle

Kevin McGowan

Elinor Perry-Smith

Indexers

Hemangini Bari

Priya Sane

Tejal Soni

Graphics

Sheetal Aute

Ronak Dhruv

Valentina D'silva

Disha Haria

Production Coordinators

Aparna Bhagat

Manu Joseph

Nitesh Thakur

Cover Work

Aparna Bhagat

About the Author

Pierre MAVRO lives in Joinville-le-Pont (a suburb of Paris). He's an open source software lover and has been working with Linux for more than 10 years now. Today, he works as a Senior DevOps Engineer at Red Hat / eNovance, where he designs and implements solutions for the Web and personal clouds (OpenStack). During the last few years, he has been designing high-availability infrastructures with performance tuning for a high-frequency trading company. He has also built geoclusters and developed tools to fit high-availability requirements for financial companies. He has worked on resolving issues on open source software for the French government. He has also provided training to several IT professionals on subjects such as Linux and MySQL/MariaDB.

I would really like to thank my wife and daughter, who encouraged and helped me to find the time to write this book. I would also like to thank my friend Joffrey and my colleague Dimitri for reviewing the technical part of the book. A big thanks goes to Packt Publishing for approaching me to write this book. And to finish, thanks to the employees of Packt Publishing I worked with (Subho, Neha, and Mohammed); thanks for showing patience. I would also like to thank the technical reviewers Daniel Parnell, P. R. Karthik, Emilien Kenler, and David "DaviXX" CHANIAL, who provided their valuable support and helped me enhance the quality of the content.

Writing this book was my first experience in editing; it was not an easy task, and therefore, thanks a lot to all who helped me in different ways to do so!

About the Reviewers

David "DaviXX" CHANIAL is a French autodidact system administrator and programmer. He has been setting up high-availability hosting solutions for years, especially using Gentoo Linux, Apache/Nginx, PHP, MySQL/MariaDB, and Python/Perl/C.

David sold the French company EuroWeb in 2011, which he had cofounded and managed on a technical level since 2003 (EuroWeb was into hosting, dedicated servers, managed services, and consulting). He spent some time working as a consultant for the company Magic Online that had acquired his old company.

Currently, in addition to working independently with his company DaviXX on projects using Ansible, MariaDB, Django, embedded systems, and some electronic systems, David holds the position of Director of System and Network at Believe Digital Group.

P. R. Karthik has a Bachelor's degree in Engineering in Electronics and Communications. He is an experienced MySQL database administrator and works for one of the Fortune 500 companies providing planning, architecture, and resource management solutions for mission-critical database applications, such as online advertising and e-commerce. He manages one of the biggest MySQL farms. He is a tech enthusiast and is socially connected with MySQL and open source communities, sharing his expertise and learning from other technologists in this field. He is a regular blogger at www.remotemysqldba.blogspot.in.

He has also worked on reviewing the book *Getting Started with MariaDB*, *Packt Publishing*.

> I would like to thank my parents for their support and my colleagues for helping me in reviewing this book.

Emilien Kenler, after working on small web projects, began focusing on game development in 2008 while he was in high school. Until 2011, he worked for different groups and specialized in system administration.

In 2011, he founded a company that sold Minecraft servers while he was completing his engineering in Computer Science. He created a lightweight IaaS based on new technologies such as Node.js and RabbitMQ.

Thereafter, he worked at TaDaweb as a system administrator, building its infrastructure and creating tools to manage deployments and monitoring.

In 2014, he began a new adventure at Wizcorp, Tokyo. He will graduate in 2014 from the University of Technology of Compiègne.

He has also contributed as a reviewer on another book *Learning Nagios 4*, *Packt Publishing* (http://www.packtpub.com/learning-nagios-4/book).

Joffrey MICHAÏE joined MySQL AB / Sun as a consultant in 2009 and quickly became one of the most prominent consultants. He has since joined SkySQL and continues to spread the word as a principal consultant. His common duties include designing architectures, tuning the performance, and troubleshooting or migrating database installations using MariaDB and MySQL. When not in an airplane, Joffrey enjoys the nightlife in Barcelona.

Daniel Parnell has been messing around with computers from a very early age. Starting out with an AIM-65, he has used Commodore VIC-20, Commodore 64, Apple IIe, Commodore Amiga, an ICL Concurrent CP/M-86 machine, Apple Macintosh Plus, and various other PCs and Macs so far.

Recently, Daniel has been working on web applications for the healthcare industry using Ruby on Rails and is building a rich web application using JavaScript as the frontend and Erlang as the backend.

When Daniel is not coding or tinkering with electronic gadgets, he can be found spending time with his family. He lost his 6-year-old son last year to an untreatable neurodegenerative disorder called Batten disease.

www.PacktPub.com

Support files, eBooks, discount offers, and more

For support files and downloads related to your book, please visit www.PacktPub.com.

Did you know that Packt offers eBook versions of every book published, with PDF and ePub files available? You can upgrade to the eBook version at www.PacktPub.com and as a print book customer, you are entitled to a discount on the eBook copy. Get in touch with us at service@packtpub.com for more details.

At www.PacktPub.com, you can also read a collection of free technical articles, sign up for a range of free newsletters and receive exclusive discounts and offers on Packt books and eBooks.

http://PacktLib.PacktPub.com

Do you need instant solutions to your IT questions? PacktLib is Packt's online digital book library. Here, you can search, access, and read Packt's entire library of books.

Why subscribe?

- Fully searchable across every book published by Packt
- Copy and paste, print, and bookmark content
- On demand and accessible via a web browser

Free access for Packt account holders

If you have an account with Packt at www.PacktPub.com, you can use this to access PacktLib today and view 9 entirely free books. Simply use your login credentials for immediate access.

Table of Contents

Preface

What is MariaDB? If you bought this book, it is assumed that you already know a bit; anyways, a quick reminder and a short introduction will help us understand certain things.

MariaDB is a fork (drop-in replacement) of MySQL. MySQL was acquired by Sun Microsystems in 2008. Then, Oracle acquired Sun Microsystems in 2009 with MySQL included.

For several reasons, Michael "Monty" Widenius (founder of MySQL) decided to fork MySQL and to create a company for it called Monty Program AB; that's how MariaDB was born (Maria is the name of the second daughter of Michael Widenius).

In December 2012, the MariaDB foundation was brought into existence to avoid any company acquisition like what had happened in the past for MySQL.

SkySQL is a company formed of ex-MySQL executives and investors who deliver services around MySQL/MariaDB. In April 2013, SkySQL and Monty Program AB were merged, because for a company to switch to MariaDB without support was problematic. But since the merge, it's been possible.

MariaDB has new interesting features, better testing, performance improvements, and bug fixes that unfortunately are not available in MySQL. For example, some optimizations come from Google, Facebook, Twitter, and so on.

Please remember that MariaDB is a full open source project and you're welcome to contribute.

What this book covers

Chapter 1, Performance Introduction, describes common hardware solutions to help you choose the best solution for your needs; furthermore, it introduces system optimization and describes how to migrate from MySQL to MariaDB.

Chapter 2, Performance Analysis, introduces tools to find performance issues and shares basic best practices.

Chapter 3, Performance Optimizations, talks about how to find bottlenecks, how to tune caches, and also introduces some engines.

Chapter 4, MariaDB Replication, explains how to set up MariaDB replications, how to scale with HAProxy, and the benefits of replication.

Chapter 5, WAN Slave Architectures, helps us understand the problems that arise in WAN replications and how to work with them.

Chapter 6, Building a Dual Master Replication, describes what the benefits are of this kind of architecture and how to set it up using DRBD, Pacemaker, PRM, and so on.

Chapter 7, MariaDB Multimaster Slaves, introduces the benefits of using the replication features of MariaDB 10.

Chapter 8, Galera Cluster – Multimaster Replication, describes the benefits and the way to deploy a Galera Cluster.

Chapter 9, Spider – Sharding Your Data, explains how to achieve better performance in sharding your data.

Chapter 10, Monitoring, describes what kind of elements are important to monitor on a single instance, replication, or Galera Cluster.

Chapter 11, Backups, introduces several ways to create backups and helps you choose the best method for your needs.

What you need for this book

As you proceed with this book, you will see a lot of features, solutions, and practical exercises that require technical tests. It's not often easy to test everything in the correct environment.

Many feel that preparing an environment is a waste of time, and they are right! To avoid it and concentrate on the content of the book, we'll use virtual machines. To make it fast and simple, we're going to use VirtualBox and Vagrant. If you are not acquainted with these tools, don't worry, we will show you how to use them here.

These tools will help you test everything very quickly (a few seconds/minutes). The advantages of both tools are:

- They are free
- They can run on Linux, Mac OS X, and Windows
- Fast instance provisioning

To install them, go to the official websites and download and install them on your current infrastructure:

- **VirtualBox**: https://www.virtualbox.org/
- **Vagrant**: http://www.vagrantup.com/

In this book, every exercise will run on Debian GNU/Linux Wheezy amd64 version on a VirtualBox. That's why, after installing both the latest versions of those tools, I suggest you work in a separate folder/box per exercise:

1. Create a folder named `MariaDB` that will contain all the exercises of this book.
2. Inside that folder, create a subfolder named `Chapter X`, where X is the chapter number.
3. Inside the `Chapter X` subfolder, create another subfolder named `Exercise X`, where X is the name of the section.
4. Place the appropriate content of the Vagrantfile in the `Exercise X` folder.
5. Inside that folder, power up machines (you absolutely need to be in to perform actions on the virtual machines):

   ```
   vagrant up
   ```

6. And access them in the following manner:

   ```
   vagrant ssh (for a single machine)
   vagrant ssh machine-name (for multiple machines)
   ```

You're now ready for the exercises. When the exercises finish and you want to get your disk space back, you can stop and remove them with the following command:

```
vagrant halt
vagrant destroy
```

Then, you can remove the current folder.

Who this book is for

This book is for anyone who is already familiar with MariaDB, has good system knowledge, and wants to scale or set up a high availability MariaDB infrastructure. It will be especially useful for system architects, senior system administrators, or DBAs.

Conventions

In this book, you will find a number of styles of text that distinguish between different kinds of information. Here are some examples of these styles, and an explanation of their meaning.

Code words in text, database table names, folder names, filenames, file extensions, pathnames, dummy URLs, user input, and Twitter handles are shown as follows: "This engine is a drop-in replacement for the FEDERATED engine. It uses `libmysql` to talk to an RDBMS."

A block of code is set as follows:

```
# -*- mode: ruby -*-
# vi: set ft=ruby :
ENV['LANG'] = 'C'

# Vagrantfile API/syntax version. Don't touch unless you know what
you're doing!
VAGRANTFILE_API_VERSION = "2"

# Insert all your Vms with configs
boxes = [
    { :name => :mysqlserver },
```

When we wish to draw your attention to a particular part of a code block, the relevant lines or items are set in bold:

```
Replicate_Ignore_Server_Ids:
            Master_Server_Id: 1
             Master_SSL_Crl: /etc/mysql/ssl/cacert.pem
          Master_SSL_Crlpath:
                 Using_Gtid: No
```

Any command-line input or output is written as follows:

```
MariaDB [(none)]> show global variables like 'tmp_table_size';
+-----------------+----------+
| Variable_name   | Value    |
+-----------------+----------+
| tmp_table_size  | 33554432 |
+-----------------+----------+
1 row in set (0.00 sec)
```

New terms and **important words** are shown in bold. Words that you see on the screen, in menus or dialog boxes for example, appear in the text like this: "With HP hardware, a *Ctrl + A* in the BIOS shows an additional **Services Options** menu."

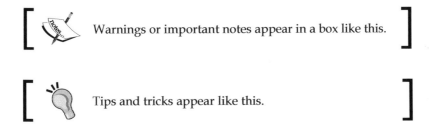

Warnings or important notes appear in a box like this.

Tips and tricks appear like this.

Reader feedback

Feedback from our readers is always welcome. Let us know what you think about this book—what you liked or may have disliked. Reader feedback is important for us to develop titles that you really get the most out of.

To send us general feedback, simply send an e-mail to feedback@packtpub.com, and mention the book title via the subject of your message.

If there is a topic that you have expertise in and you are interested in either writing or contributing to a book, see our author guide on www.packtpub.com/authors.

Customer support

Now that you are the proud owner of a Packt book, we have a number of things to help you to get the most from your purchase.

Downloading the example code

You can download the example code files for all Packt books you have purchased from your account at http://www.packtpub.com. If you purchased this book elsewhere, you can visit http://www.packtpub.com/support and register to have the files e-mailed directly to you.

Errata

Although we have taken every care to ensure the accuracy of our content, mistakes do happen. If you find a mistake in one of our books—maybe a mistake in the text or the code—we would be grateful if you would report this to us. By doing so, you can save other readers from frustration and help us improve subsequent versions of this book. If you find any errata, please report them by visiting http://www.packtpub.com/submit-errata, selecting your book, clicking on the **errata submission form** link, and entering the details of your errata. Once your errata are verified, your submission will be accepted and the errata will be uploaded on our website, or added to any list of existing errata, under the Errata section of that title. Any existing errata can be viewed by selecting your title from http://www.packtpub.com/support.

Piracy

Piracy of copyright material on the Internet is an ongoing problem across all media. At Packt, we take the protection of our copyright and licenses very seriously. If you come across any illegal copies of our works, in any form, on the Internet, please provide us with the location address or website name immediately so that we can pursue a remedy.

Please contact us at copyright@packtpub.com with a link to the suspected pirated material.

We appreciate your help in protecting our authors, and our ability to bring you valuable content.

Questions

You can contact us at questions@packtpub.com if you are having a problem with any aspect of the book, and we will do our best to address it.

1
Performance Introduction

In this chapter, you'll learn about common hardware solutions that you can find on the market, and which ones are slower or faster for MariaDB. You'll be able to properly tune your operating system to optimize your hardware and see how to reserve resources. Finally, you'll learn how to migrate from MySQL to MariaDB and have an overview of the available engines.

MariaDB history

What is MariaDB? If you have bought this book, you probably already know; anyway, a quick reminder and a short introduction helps us to understand certain things.

MariaDB is a fork (drop-in replacement) of MySQL. MySQL was acquired by Sun Microsystems in 2008. Then, Oracle acquired Sun Microsystems in 2010 with MySQL included.

For several reasons, Michael Monty Widenius (the founder of MySQL) decided to fork MySQL and create a company for it called Monty Program AB. Thus, MariaDB (Maria is the name of the second daughter of Michael Monty Widenius) was born.

In December 2012, the MariaDB foundation was created to avoid any company acquisition like what had happened in the past for MySQL.

SkySQL is a company comprising of ex-MySQL executives and investors who deliver services around MySQL/MariaDB. In April 2013, there was a merger between SkySQL and Monty Program AB. For a company that may have wanted to switch to MariaDB without support, it was problematic. However, since the merger, it has been possible.

MariaDB has new interesting features: better testing, performance improvements, and bug fixes that are unfortunately not available in MySQL. For example, some optimizations come from Google, Facebook, Twitter, and so on.

 Please remember that MariaDB is a fully open source project and you're welcome to contribute.

Choosing the appropriate hardware

Choosing the correct hardware is not an easy task. MariaDB has the following hardware requirements:

- Disk performance
- RAID and acceleration cards
- RAM
- CPU

Some types of software do not require so many important resources, but this is not the case for MariaDB. Of course, it depends on what you want to use your MariaDB instance for. For example, for a small website with poor access, you do not really need a huge configuration; a 10-year-old PC should really be enough. However, for a high-load website, requests should be analyzed to know which kind of hardware should be taken into consideration.

Disks

The disk is one of the biggest parts as several kinds of elements should be taken into consideration, and the storage is, in most cases, the bottleneck. Everything will depend on the write access you will need of course. That's why you're going to see several solutions that exist for speedy access to sensitive and reactive requirements.

SATA magnetic drives

SATA **Hard Disk Drives (HDDs)** are the slowest solution that can be commonly found on some servers. Generally, there are two kinds of rotation-per-minute drives:

- **5400 rpms**: These disks have the slowest performances but the highest density
- **7200 rpms**: These are slower drives but they have high density

10K HDDs exist but are not designed for production usages. A good solution to win access time is to have the highest disk cache size.

We can find disk caches with 2,5' and 3,5' sizes on the market. Servers are now generally shipped with 2,5' drives as we could add more than 3,5'. For instance, it's common to see 1U servers with eight arrays plugged to 2,5' disks. On 3U servers, constructors can add up to 25 disks. With **Redundant Array of Independent Disks (RAID)** mechanisms, it becomes interesting to get as many drives as possible to speed up the storage.

SAS magnetic drives

SAS magnetic drives are faster drives than SATA and are generally used with a specific PCI-X RAID card to enhance performance. Like the SATA HDDs, there are two kinds of rotation speeds:

- **10K rpms**: These disks have the highest SAS density but are slower
- **15K rpms**: These disks have the lowest SAS density and are faster but less robust

The disk choice is important, but there is another thing to take into account. Like SATA drives, 3,5' drives exist, but they are hard to find now. Let's stick with 2,5' drives instead.

Hybrid drives

Hybrid drives are more common because their performances are similar to that of **Solid State Drives (SSDs)** with the size of SATA HDDs. This is a real good alternative to the high cost of SSDs. Hybrid drives are bridging the gap between SSDs and SATA drives.

Hybrid drives combine NAND flash drives (SSDs) with HDDs. The NAND flash of the drive is used to store data as cache to quickly deliver often-accessed files. The HDD part of the drive stores all the information, but the access is slower.

The hybrid drives that we can find on the market today have, for example, 1 TB of magnetic storage with 8 GB, 16 GB, or 24 GB of NAND flash.

SSDs

SSDs are the fastest disks on the market! They give the best disk performance that we can find today. However, SSD (NAND flash) drives are expensive, so a storage disk array is really expensive.

SSDs are more expensive and prone to more failures than other disk drives. They have a limited life time, so you should use them with the RAID system.

RAID and acceleration cards

Having an overview of what kinds of disks exist is generally not enough to get maximum fault tolerance and speed performance. That's why additional mechanisms such as RAID and acceleration cards exist. We'll see their pros and cons in the following sections.

RAID cards and levels

I have already talked about PCI-X RAID cards—cards where disks are plugged embed fast cache memory. Today, we can commonly find 512 MB, 1 GB, or 2 GB flash cache. The more flash cache the PCI-X card has, the faster the transactions. You generally, depending on the card model, configure two kinds of cache: read and write caches.

There are two types of read cache:

- **Demand caching**: This helps to quickly serve the same information if requested multiple times. In this case, it significantly improves disk I/O performance.
- **Look-ahead caching**: If the required data is sequentially stored in blocks, this will store the next requested blocks in the cache to serve them faster when they are asked for.

The best performance solution for MariaDB is demand caching, as data is not sequential when reading.

There are two types of write cache:

- **Write-back caching**: When a write request is issued, data is quickly written to the cache and the system is informed about the correct write. When it's free time for the bus or when the buffer does not have enough space to store new data, the data cache is written to the disk.
- **Write-through caching**: This is the same as the write-back caching method, except the data is immediately transferred from the cache to the disk before informing the system.

In the case of a system crash, the write-back caching method is of course the most dangerous option. To avoid losing data, a **Battery Backup Unit (BBU)** is present on the cards to preserve data during a power cut. For example, when the system powers up and the SAS RAID card boots, the battery writes the cache information to disk.

When using BBU, it is recommend to disable the learning cycle. During a learning cycle, the battery is unloaded/reloaded and the write cache method switches from write-back to write-through.

Depending on the card manufacturer, some other options can be configured to customize those cache types.

Regarding the RAID levels, multiple solutions exist, and here are the common ones:

RAID level	Description
0	**Block Level (BL)** striping without parity; this provides fast read and write but no security
1	BL mirroring without parity; this provides security and fast read but slow write access
5	BL striping with distributed parity; this provides more security but slow read and write access
6	This is the same as RAID 5 but with double distributed parity; this is the slowest but it provides high security
10	This is also called 1+0: mirroring without parity but with BL striping; this is fast and provides security

RAID 0 is not really the best solution for production use as there is no security. If a disk crashes, there is no way to recover it. In RAID 1, it's only mirroring! Even if we add more than two disks, the same information will be replicated. So, it is not good to use with MariaDB, but it generally answers OS disk problems. RAID 5 has been a really good solution for several years because of its good security guarantee. But we're losing performance here because of the parity calculation and storage, which corresponds to one disk. It's not recommended to create a very big RAID 5 solution, because if you lose more than one disk, all your data is lost. RAID 6 permits to lose up to two disks at once! However, the parity calculation is double and performance is not what we expect.

RAID 10 is a better solution! RAID 10 stripes mirrors; it's as simple as that! We have security as we could lose more than one disk (with mirroring) and have speed (with striping). The major problem of this solution is the cost, as you would only be able to use half of the total capacity of your disks. For example, if I have 12 disks in a server, you can consider that six disks are mirrored against the other six. Each of the six groups are stripped or they can be divided once again to get smaller (three) stripes.

Fusion-io direct acceleration cards

Fusion-io direct acceleration cards are PCI-X cards that permit the drives to be faster than classic SSD solutions, with a better and consistent I/O throughput to give up to 85 percent more transactions. How? Simply because it requires less hardware components to access data and uses high speed hardware to achieve it.

When you use SSD/HDD SAS drives, CPU transactions need to pass through the RAID card and are then transferred to the disks. This is the bottleneck! On a high load charge on the SAS RAID card, the performance degrades gradually because of the connectivity to the disks.

To avoid it, Fusion-io direct access cards embed NAND flash directly on the PCI-X card to permit the drive to have a big cache system (up to 5 TB per card). The high bus bandwidth of the PCI-X permits the drive to quickly access information from the CPU and reduce a lot of latency.

The Fusion-io company provides other cheaper solutions to speed up server performance, but the fastest solution remains the Fusion-io direct access card anyway. Moreover, MariaDB is a partner with Fusion-io and has created special parameters to double the I/O capacity on those cards (available since MariaDB 5.5.31).

Disk arrays

Disk arrays have been the solution to get maximum performance, and the only way to have a huge data size solution. The information that comes from the server(s) to the disk array (DAS, NAS, and SAN) takes too much time to process requests as it passes through several kinds of components such as networks in the worst case.

Even if it's a good solution in several cases, it's unfortunately not the fastest one. The recommendation for high performance is to store data locally. Multiple solutions exist for replication and high availability, so you don't have to worry about it.

RAM

In MariaDB, RAM availability is very important. The more RAM you have, the more data from your database can be kept in memory. For instance, on the InnoDB/XtraDB engine, to get maximum performance, it's recommended to get the database size equal to the free RAM size. It's also used to store table caches and so on.

Of course, if you have terabits of database data, it will be hard to get that much RAM. However, solutions exist to avoid those problems.

Another important thing is to look at your server architecture. You should take care of the motherboard's bus frequency and keep it as high as possible. In a major case, if you fill all the RAM slots that the motherboard can take, the bus frequency will decrease and the result will be a higher latency communication between the CPU and RAM. If you want to get the maximum RAM capacity of your server without losing any performance, look at the server constructor documentation to fill the correct amount of RAM slots with the highest RAM size per slot.

The latest important thing is not related to MariaDB: the **Error-Correcting Code memory (ECC memory)**. It's a type of RAM that can detect and correct the most common kinds of internal data corruption. You may lower memory performance by around two to three percent. This is not a big performance loss, but you'll be sure that your data will be best protected from corruption.

CPU

Depending on the CPU model and constructor, having a lot of cores is of course interesting for multi-threading operations. A high processor clock speed allows faster calculation.

The L1, L2, and L3 processor cache sizes are very important as well. More memory allocation can be used to store on the processor; the fewer round trips made, faster the transactions will be.

To get maximum dedicated performance, you have to use the Linux `cgroup` feature to bind CPUs/cores to a MariaDB instance. This is also called CPU pinning.

Architecture types and performances

MariaDB is able to run on multiple kinds of operating systems:

- Microsoft Windows x86 and x64
- Oracle Solaris 10 and 11 x64
- Linux x86 and x64

> MariaDB has a special thread-pool implementation that allows it to perform much better than MySQL under heavy loads (lots of connections).

In this book, every exercise will be on Debian GNU/Linux Wheezy amd64 version. Of course, all MariaDB tuning will be portable to any operating system, so you won't be lost. For the operating system performance tuning, we'll focus on Linux amd64 (Debian GNU/Linux), as it's free and open source, and of course MariaDB works very well on it.

To easily test the following parameters, you can use the following Vagrant file that provides you with the necessary virtual machine with MariaDB installed. The requirements are as follows:

- Four cores
- 512 MB of RAM
- 8 GB of disk space

Here is the associated Vagrant file:

```ruby
# -*- mode: ruby -*-
# vi: set ft=ruby :
# Vagrantfile API/syntax version. Don't touch unless you know what
you're doing!
#
VAGRANTFILE_API_VERSION = "2"


# Insert all your Vms with configs
boxes = [
    { :name => :mariadb },
]

$install = <<INSTALL
aptitude update
DEBIAN_FRONTEND=noninteractive aptitude -y -o Dpkg::Options::="--
force-confdef" -o Dpkg::Options::="--force-confold" install python-
software-properties
apt-key adv --recv-keys --keyserver keyserver.ubuntu.com
0xcbcb082a1bb943db
add-apt-repository 'deb http://ftp.igh.cnrs.fr/pub/mariadb/repo/10.0/
debian wheezy main'
aptitude update
DEBIAN_FRONTEND=noninteractive aptitude -y -o Dpkg::Options::="--
force-confdef" -o Dpkg::Options::="--force-confold" install mariadb-
server


INSTALL
```

```
Vagrant::Config.run do |config|
  # Default box OS
  vm_default = proc do |boxcnf|
    boxcnf.vm.box        = "deimosfr/debian-wheezy"
  end

  # For each VM, add a public and private card. Then install Ceph
  boxes.each do |opts|
    vm_default.call(config)
    config.vm.define opts[:name] do |config|
        config.vm.customize ["modifyvm", :id, "--cpus", 4]
        config.vm.host_name = "%s.vm" % opts[:name].to_s
        file_to_disk = 'ext4-journal_' + opts[:name].to_s + '.vdi'
        config.vm.customize ['createhd', '--filename', file_to_disk,
'--size', 250]
        config.vm.customize ['storageattach', :id, '--storagectl',
'SATA Controller', '--port', 1, '--device', 0, '--type', 'hdd',
'--medium', file_to_disk]
        config.vm.provision "shell", inline: $install
    end
  end
end
```

BIOS power management optimization

By default, new servers are configured for low consumption power (green energy). This is a really good point for the environment! However, reducing electric power implies reducing computation power.

The CPU is the main component that directly affects performance because of its wake up time during sleep states. CPU power management should be disabled as much as possible. However, depending on the hardware manufacturer, multiple options may change.

If you're wondering what the effects are of that power management, it's simple. If the activity of the processor is reduced too much, a standard action that takes 1 second could take more than 2 seconds in that period. During this period of 1 or more seconds, CPU power management techniques are changing the CPU state (lowering frequency, lowering voltage, and deactivating some subsystems, and so on).

When the workload increases, subsystems are reactivated, but C-State reactivation implies some latency (milliseconds to seconds) before being at maximum performance.

C-States

C-States are idle CPU states. C0 is the working processor while C1 is the first idle level of the processor. The problem is no instructions are executed during the C1 state, as the CPU manufacturer introduced new C-States to reduce power consumption during an idle period.

P-States

P-States are different levels of the operation state of the processor. Each level differs from the others by different working voltages/frequencies. For example, at P0, a processor can run at 3 GHz, but at P1 it can run at only 1.5 GHz. Voltage is also scaled to reduce power consumption.

In a P-State, the CPU is working, performing operations and executing instructions. This is not an idle state.

Constructor name options

Depending on the CPU constructor, power management technologies do not have the same name. Here is a list of functionalities that should be disabled. For Intel, they are called:

- Speedstep
- Turbo boost
- C1E
- QPI Power Management

For AMD, the functionalities are as follows:

- PowerNow!
- Cooln'Quiet
- Turbo Core

Some constructors have enabled extra power management features that are keyboard tricks (for example, with HP hardware, a *Ctrl + A* in the BIOS shows an additional **Services Options** menu).

 In most cases, it's recommended to look at the BIOS constructor documentation to see what should be turned on or off.

Power management optimization

Most of the following power management commands may not work under virtual machines. So, you should consider having a physical machine to test and run them.

cpufreq

cpufreq allows the OS to control P-States. This means that the OS-based idleness can lower the frequency of the CPU to reduce power consumption.

To get cpufreq information on a specified core, look at the cpufreq folder by running the following command:

```
> ls -1 /sys/devices/system/cpu/cpu0/cpufreq
affected_cpus
bios_limit
cpuinfo_cur_freq
cpuinfo_max_freq
cpuinfo_min_freq
cpuinfo_transition_latency
freqdomain_cpus
related_cpus
scaling_available_frequencies
scaling_available_governors
scaling_cur_freq
scaling_driver
scaling_governor
scaling_max_freq
scaling_min_freq
scaling_setspeed
```

When enabled in the BIOS, cpufreq drivers are loaded and the cpufreq directory in sysfs is available. You can look at the used governor (power management mechanism using the following command):

```
> cat /sys/devices/system/cpu/cpu0/cpufreq/scaling_governor
ondemand
```

If the BIOS settings are disabled, no drivers are loaded and no scaling frequency is allowed. That means your server works at maximum performance. However, you can also tune the scaling governor for performance purposes.

To always get the maximum performance without disabling the options in the BIOS, we'll install a package that will configure all the cores on your machine:

```
aptitude install cpufrequtils
cp
/usr/share/doc/cpufrequtils/examples/cpufrequtils.loadcpufreq.sample
/etc/default/cpufrequtils
```

Then, edit the configuration file (`/etc/default/cpufrequtils`) and set the new configuration:

```
# /etc/default/loadcpufreq sample file
#
# Use this file to override the CPUFreq kernel module to
# be loaded or disable loading at all

ENABLE=true
FREQDRIVER=performance
```

You can get all the available governors with the following command:

```
> cat
/sys/devices/system/cpu/cpu0/cpufreq/scaling_available_governors
ondemand performance
```

Then, you can restart the `cpufrequtils` service and your governors' cores will be updated to `performance`.

cpuidle

`cpuidle` allows the OS to control the CPU C-states (control how the CPU goes into idle/sleep state). Depending on the CPU constructor and model, several C-States are available. Standard ones are C0 and C1. C0 is a running state while C1 is an idle state.

Even if C-States have been disabled in the BIOS settings, the `cpuidle` driver can be loaded and managed. To look at the loaded driver, run the following command:

```
> cat /sys/devices/system/cpu/cpuidle/current_driver
intel_idle
```

The `intel_idle` driver handles more C-States and aggressively puts the CPU into a lower idle mode. Since we have significant latency to wake up from lower C-States, this can affect performance.

When the `intel_idle` driver is loaded, specific `cpuidle` configurations are available for each CPU:

```
> ls -1R /sys/devices/system/cpu/cpu0/cpuidle/
/sys/devices/system/cpu/cpu0/cpuidle/:
state0
state1
state2
state3

/sys/devices/system/cpu/cpu0/cpuidle/state0:
desc
latency
name
power
time
usage
[...]
/sys/devices/system/cpu/cpu0/cpuidle/state3:
desc
latency
name
power
time
usage
```

Each of the C-States are described here with the latency to wake up. To know the time it takes a C-State to wake up and check the `latency` file, run the following command:

```
> cat /sys/devices/system/cpu/cpu0/cpuidle/state3/latency
150
```

In the preceding command, the time for C-State 3 to wake up is 150 ms! To avoid having all the C-States enabled, change the `grub` boot configuration and add the following option (in the `/etc/default/grub` location):

```
GRUB_CMDLINE_LINUX_DEFAULT="quiet intel_idle.max_cstate=0"
```

To make it work, upgrade the `grub` configuration and reboot:

```
update-grub
```

Disk and filesystem optimization

For disks and filesystems, there are multiple factors that can slow down your MariaDB instance:

- Magnetic drives' rotation per minute
- Magnetic drives with data at the beginning of the disk
- Partitions not aligned to the disk
- Small partitions at the end of the disk
- Disk bus speed
- Magnetic drives' seek time
- Active SWAP partitions

Some of these factors can only be resolved by changing the hardware, but others can be changed by tuning the operating system.

Kernel disks' I/O schedulers

The kernel I/O scheduler permits us to change the way we read and write data on the disk. There are three kinds of schedulers. You can select a disk and look at the currently used scheduler using the following command:

```
# cat /sys/block/sda/queue/scheduler
noop deadline [cfq]
```

The I/O scheduler used here is **Completely Fair Queuing (CFQ)**.

The `noop` scheduler queues requests as they are sent to the I/O.

The `deadline` scheduler prevents excessive seek movement by serving I/O requests that are near to the new location on the disk. This is the best solution for SSDs.

The `CFQ` scheduler is the default scheduler on most Linux distributions. The goal of this scheduler is to minimize seek head movements. This is the best solution for magnetic disks if there is no other mechanism above it (such as RAID, Fusion-io, and so on). In the case of SSDs, you have to use the `deadline` scheduler.

To change the disk I/O scheduler with `deadline`, use the following command:

```
echo deadline > /sys/block/device/queue/scheduler
```

You have to replace the device with the device name (such as `sda`).

Another solution to avoid changing the disk I/O scheduler manually is to install `sysfsutils` by using the following command:

```
aptitude install sysfsutils
```

Then, you have to configure it in `/etc/sysfs.conf`:

```
block/sdb/queue/scheduler = deadline
```

Easy to use and understand, `sysfsutils` is a daemon that permits us to make changes in `/sys` automatically (as there is no `sysctl` for `/sys`).

Now, it could be a problem if you have a lot of disks on your machine and want to set the same I/O scheduler on all devices. Simply change the `grub` boot settings (`/etc/default/grub`) with the `elevetor` option:

```
GRUB_CMDLINE_LINUX_DEFAULT="quiet elevator=deadline"
```

To make the preceding setting work, upgrade the `grub` configuration and reboot:

```
update-grub
```

If you want to go ahead, there are several options for each I/O scheduler, and there is no *optimal* configuration. For example, on MyISAM, you need to increase `nr_requests` to multiply the throughput. You have to test them and look at the better solution corresponding to your needs.

In the latest version of CFQ, it automatically detects if it's a magnetic disk and adapts itself to avoid changing the elevator value. You can find all the required information on the Linux kernel website (`http://www.kernel.org`).

Partition alignment

The goal of partition alignment is to match logical block partitions with physical blocks to limit the number of disk operations. You must make the first partition begin from the disk sector 2048. However, it can be done automatically if you're using the `parted` command. First of all, install the package:

```
aptitude install parted
```

Here is an example:

```
device=/dev/sdb
parted -s -a optimal $device mklabel gpt
parted -s -a optimal $device mkpart primary ext4 0% 100%
```

In the preceding example, we set /dev/sdb as the disk device, then created a gpt table partition, and finally created a single partition that takes the full disk size. 0% means the beginning of the disk (which in fact starts at 2M) and goes to the end (100%). The optimal option means we want the best partition alignment to get the best performance.

SSD optimization

From the 2.6.33 version of kernel, you can enable TRIM support. Btrfs, Ext4, JFS, and XFS are optimized for TRIM when you activate this option. The TRIM feature blocks data that is no longer considered in use and that can be wiped internally. It allows the SSDs to handle garbage collection overhead that otherwise slows down future operations on the blocks.

Ext4 is one of the best solutions for high performance. To enable TRIM on it, modify your fstab (/etc/fstab) configuration to add the discard option:

```
/dev/sda2 / ext4 rw,discard,errors=remount-ro 0 1
```

Now, remount your partition to enable TRIM support for Ext4:

```
mount -o remount /
```

On LVM, you can also enable TRIM for all the logical volumes by changing the issue_discards option in your LVM configuration file (/etc/lvm/lvm.conf):

```
issue_discards = 1
```

Finally, we want to limit needless utilization of SSD, and this can be done by setting temporary folders in the RAM using the tmpfs filesystem. To achieve this, edit the fstab file at /etc/fstab and add the following three lines:

```
tmpfs /tmp tmpfs defaults,noatime,mode=1777 0 0
tmpfs /var/lock tmpfs defaults,noatime,mode=1777 0 0
tmpfs /var/run tmpfs defaults,noatime,mode=1777 0 0
```

Mount the preceding partitions to make them active.

> On Debian, you do not need to change /etc/fstab, and you can make add tmpfs is /etc/default/tmpfs instead.

Filesystem options

Several kinds of filesystems exist and their performances generally depend on their usage. For MariaDB, I've performed several tests against XFS. My conclusion is the same as what we can find on most of the specialized websites on the Internet: XFS is a good solution but Ext4 is slightly faster.

On Ext4, you can add several interesting options to limit write access on the disk. You can, for example, disable the access time on all files and folders. This will avoid writing the last access time information to any acceded files on partition. As MariaDB often needs to access the same files, they are updated on each MariaDB modification (insert/update/delete), which is disk I/O consuming.

This could be a problem in some cases (for example, if you absolutely need these updates), but most of the time, it can be disabled by adding the following options in the `fstab` configuration (`/etc/fstab`):

```
/dev/sda2 / ext4 rw,noatime,nodiratime,data=writeback,discard 0 1
```

On a high disk I/O system, you will reduce the disk's access significantly.

You've also noticed that we used `data=writeback`. This option means that only metadata writes are journalized. It works well with InnoDB and is safe. Why? Because InnoDB has its own transaction logs, there is no need to duplicate the same action. This is the fastest solution, but if you prefer a safer one, you can use `data=ordered` instead to get data written before metadata.

Another interesting filesystem performance solution is to separate the Ext4 journal from the data disk (as in journaling, the filesystem writes data twice). Place the journal on a separate fast drive such as SSD. By default, the journal occupies between 2.5 percent and 5 percent of the filesystem size. It's suggested to keep the size at minimum for performance (it could be reduced on a very large data size).

First of all, check your current filesystem block size (here `/dev/mapper/vg-home`):

```
> dumpe2fs /dev/mapper/vg-home | grep "^Block"
dumpe2fs 1.42.5 (29-Jul-2012)
Block count:           1327104
Block size:               4096
Blocks per group:        32768
```

Here, we've got a `4096` block size and the journal needs to have the same block size as well.

To dedicate a journal to a current partition, we need to unmount it. To be sure that there is no access, remove the current journal from the partition, create the journal partition on the dedicated device (*partition size * 5 / 100*), attach it to the wished partition, and then remount it:

```
> umount /home
> dumpe2fs /dev/mapper/vg-home | grep "Journal"
Journal inode:              8
Journal backup:             inode blocks
Journal features:           (none)
Journal size:               128M
Journal length:             32768
Journal sequence:           0x0000002f
Journal start:              0
> tune2fs -f -O ^has_journal /dev/mapper/vg-home
> mke2fs -O journal_dev -b 4096 /dev/sdb1
> tune2fs -j -J device=/dev/sdb1 /dev/mapper/vg-home
> mount /home
```

Now, you check on your partition to see whether the journal is located on another partition:

```
> dumpe2fs /dev/mapper/vg-home | grep "Journal"
Journal UUID:               8a3c6cec-2d45-4aa9-ac2f-4a181093a92e
Journal device:             0x0811
Journal backup:             inode blocks
```

To locate it, use the following command:

```
> blkid | grep 8a3c6cec-2d45-4aa9-ac2f-4a181093a92e
/dev/mapper/vg-home: UUID="6b8f2604-e1ac-4bea-a5c9-e7acf08cec8c"
TYPE="ext4" EXT_JOURNAL="8a3c6cec-2d45-4aa9-ac2f-4a181093a92e"
/dev/sdb1: UUID="8a3c6cec-2d45-4aa9-ac2f-4a181093a92e" TYPE="jbd"
```

As you now have a dedicated journal for your partition, add two other options to /etc/fstab (journal_async_commit). The advantage is that the commit block can be written to disk without waiting for the descriptor blocks. This option will boost performance. The code is as follows:

```
/dev/mapper/vg-home /home ext4
rw,noatime,nodiratime,data=writeback,discard,journal_async_commit
0 2
```

Another option exists for Ext4: `barrier=0`. It will boost performance as well. Do not use it if you have a standalone server, because it will delay journal data writes and you may not be able to recover your data if your system crashes. You only have to use `barrier=0` if you're using a RAID car with a BBU.

 The Linux kernel evolves very quickly. XFS has new options, new filesystems appear, and Ext4 may not be the best solution in all cases. You should stay in touch with all the kernel-related news and test your usage cases yourself.

SWAP

As SWAP is used on a physical disk (magnetic or SSD), it's slower than RAM. Linux, by default, likes swapping for several reasons. To avoid your MariaDB data being SWAP instead of RAM, you have to play with a kernel parameter called `swappiness`.

A `swappiness` value is used to change the balance between swapping out runtime memory and dropping pages from the system page cache. The higher the value, the more the system will swap. The lower the value, the less the system will swap. The maximum value is `100`, the minimum is `0`, and `60` is the default. To change this parameter in the persistence mode, add this line to your `sysctl.conf` file in `/etc/sysctl.conf`:

```
vm.swappiness = 0
```

To avoid a system reboot to get this value set on the running system, you can launch the following command:

```
sysctl -w vm.swappiness=0
```

And now check the value to be sure it has been applied:

```
> sysctl vm.swappiness
vm.swappiness = 0
```

Dedicating hardware with cgroups

Linux kernel brings features that permit the isolation of a process from others, called `cgroups` (since version 2.6.24). If we want to dedicate CPU, RAM, or disk I/O, we can use `cgroups` to do it (it also provides other interesting features if you want to go ahead). With this solution, you can be sure to dedicate hardware to your MariaDB instance.

To start using cgroups, we must start preparing the environment. In fact, cgroups needs a specific folder hierarchy to work, but you'll see the advantages when we use it. So, edit the fstab file in /etc/fstab to mount cgroups at each machine startup, and add the following line:

```
cgroup  /sys/fs/cgroup  cgroup  defaults  0   0
```

Mount cgroup now to make cgroups available:

```
mount /sys/fs/cgroup
```

To get all the CPU and memory features enabled, you need to change the grub configuration by adding two new features in /etc/default/grub (cgroup_enable and swapaccount):

```
GRUB_CMDLINE_LINUX_DEFAULT="quiet cgroup_enable=memory
swapaccount=1"
```

Then, upgrade your grub settings and reboot:

```
update-grub
```

After the machine has rebooted, you can check whether your cgroup hierarchy exists:

```
> mount | grep ^cgroup
cgroup on /sys/fs/cgroup type cgroup
(rw,relatime,perf_event,blkio,net_cls,freezer,devices,memory,cpuacct,
cpu,cpuset)
```

Manual solution

Let's create our first cgroup, the MariaDB one! Create a folder with a name of your choice in the cgroup folder:

```
mkdir /sys/fs/cgroup/mariadb_cgroup
```

If we now look at the mariadb_cgroup content, you can see all the limitations that the cgroup features are able to offer:

```
> ls -1 /sys/fs/cgroup/mariadb_cgroup/
[...]
cpuset.cpu_exclusive
cpuset.cpus
cpuset.mem_exclusive
cpuset.mem_hardwall
```

```
cpuset.memory_migrate
cpuset.memory_pressure
cpuset.memory_spread_page
cpuset.memory_spread_slab
cpuset.mems
[...]
tasks
```

You can see that there's a lot of stuff! Ok, now let's look at your processor information to see how many cores you've got:

```
> cat /proc/cpuinfo | grep ^processor
processor   : 0
processor   : 1
processor   : 2
processor   : 3
```

I can see that I've got four cores available on this machine. For example, let's say I want to dedicate two cores to my MariaDB instance. The first thing to do is to assign two cores to the `mariadb_cgroup` cgroup:

```
echo 2,3 > /sys/fs/cgroup/mariadb_cgroup/cpuset.cpus
```

You can set multiple cores separated by commas or with the minus character if you want a CPU range (0-3 to set from C0 to C3).

In case of multiple cores, I've just asked the cgroup to be bound to the last two cores. That means this `cgroup` is only able to use those two cores and that doesn't mean it is the only one able to use them. Those cores are still sharable with other processes. To make them dedicated to this `cgroup`, simply use the following command:

```
echo 1 > /sys/fs/cgroup/mariadb_cgroup/cpuset.cpu_exclusive
```

You can check the configuration of your `cgroup` simply with `cat`:

```
> cat /sys/fs/cgroup/mariadb_cgroup/cpuset.cpu*
1
2-3
```

We also need to specify the memory nodes that the tasks will be allowed to access. First, let's get a look at the available memory nodes:

```
> numactl --hardware | grep ^available
available: 1 nodes (0)
```

Then, set to the wished memory node (here 0):

```
echo 0 > /sys/fs/cgroup/mariadb_cgroup/cpuset.mems
```

Now, the cgroup is ready to dedicate cores to a process ID:

```
echo $(pidof mysqld) > /sys/fs/cgroup/mariadb_cgroup/tasks
```

That is it! If you want to be sure that you've correctly configured your cgroups, you can add another PID in that cgroup that will burst the two cores and check with the top or htop command, for example.

You can check your configuration using a PID in the following way:

```
> cat /proc/$(pidof mysqld)/status | grep _allowed
Cpus_allowed:   c
Cpus_allowed_list:   2-3
Mems_allowed:   00000000,00000001
Mems_allowed_list:   0
```

Automatic solution using the cgconfig daemon

It's preferable to be able to manage the manual solution before the automatic solution to check whether your configuration works as expected.

Now, if you want to have it enabled on boot and automatically configured correctly, you will need to use the cgconfig daemon. It will load a configuration and then watch all the launched processes. If one matches its set configuration, it will automatically apply the defined rules.

To get cgconfig, you'll need to install the following package:

```
aptitude install cgroup-bin daemon
```

The cgroup-bin package in Debian wheezy is a little bit young, so we need to manually set up the init file and the configuration from the package documentation.

Unfortunately, you need to do a little hack with the init skeleton file to be able to use the update-rc.d command for the cgconfig services because the original init files are not 100 percent Debian-compliant yet:

```
cd /etc/init.d
cp skeleton cgconfig
cp skeleton cgred
chmod 755 cgconfig cgred
```

```
sed -i 's/skeleton/cgconfig/' cgconfig
sed -i 's/skeleton/cgred/' cgred
update-rc.d cgconfig defaults
update-rc.d cgred defaults
cd /usr/share/doc/cgroup-bin/examples/
cp cgred.conf /etc/default/
cp cgconfig.conf cgrules.conf /etc/
gzip -d cgconfig.gz
cp cgconfig cgred /etc/init.d/
cd /etc/init.d/
sed -i 's/sysconfig/defaults/' cgred cgconfig
sed -i 's/\/etc\/rc.d\/init.d\/functions/\/lib\/init\/vars.sh/' cgred
sed -i 's/--check/--name/' cgred
sed -i 's/killproc.*/kill $(cat $pidfile)/' cgred
sed -i 's/touch "$lockfile"/test -d \/var\/lock\/subsys || mkdir
\/var\/lock\/subsys\n\t&/' cgconfig
chmod 755 cgconfig cgred
```

In the meantime, we've updated a Red Hat path to a Debian one (**sysconfig | defaults**), modified the folder to store the lock file of the daemon, and changed the default cgred init to correct some bugs.

Regarding the configuration files, let's start with /etc/cgconfig.conf:

```
#
#   Copyright IBM Corporation. 2007
#
#   Authors:     Balbir Singh <balbir@linux.vnet.ibm.com>
#   This program is free software; you can redistribute it and/or
modify it
#   under the terms of version 2.1 of the GNU Lesser General Public
License
#   as published by the Free Software Foundation.
#
#   This program is distributed in the hope that it would be
useful, but
#   WITHOUT ANY WARRANTY; without even the implied warranty of
#   MERCHANTABILITY or FITNESS FOR A PARTICULAR PURPOSE.
#
group mariadb_cgroup {
    perm {
        admin {
```

```
            uid = mysql;
        }
        task {
            uid = mysql;
        }
    }

    cpuset {
            cpuset.mems = 0;
            cpuset.cpus = "2,3";
            cpuset.cpu_exclusive = 1;
    }
}
```

Here, we've got the cgroup name mariadb_cgroup. When a user, mysql, launches an operation, the cpuset configuration will be applied. In the same way as in the manual method, we've limited the mysql user process to the second and third cores.

The last thing to configure is the cgrules.conf file in /etc/cgrules.conf, which will indicate which process belongs to which cgroup. You need to add the user mysql to modify the cpu information and the cgroup folder name where it should be placed:

```
    mysql              cpu           mariadb_cgroup/
```

Of course, you can check your configuration in /sys/fs/cgroup when you want.

When you've finished configuring your cgroup and want the new configuration to be active, restart the services in the following order:

- /etc/init.d/cgred stop
- /etc/init.d/cgconfig stop
- umount /sys/fs/cgroup 2>/dev/null
- rmdir /sys/fs/cgroup/* /sys/fs/cgroup 2>/dev/null
- mount /sys/fs/cgroup
- /etc/init.d/cgconfig start
- /etc/init.d/cgred start

Dedicating hardware optimization with NUMA

With large InnoDB databases (~ >32G), it becomes important to take a look at this kind of optimization.

In old/classic **Uniform Memory Architecture (UMA)**, all the memory was shared among all the processors with equal access. There wasn't any affinity and performances were equal among all cores to the memory bank. With the **Non-Uniform Memory Access (NUMA)** architecture (starting with Intel Nehalem and AMD Opteron), this is totally different:

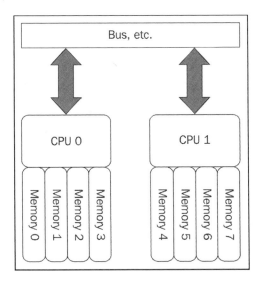

Each core has a local memory bank that gives closer access and thus reduces the latency. Of course, the whole system is visible as one unit, but optimization can be done to restrict a processor to its local memory bank. If there is no NUMA optimization, a core can ask for memory outside its local memory, which will increase the latency and lower the global performances.

By default, Linux automatically knows when it runs on a NUMA architecture and performs the following kind of operations natively:

- Collects hardware information to understand the running architecture
- Binds the correct memory module to the local core it belongs to
- Splits physical processors to nodes
- Collects cost information regarding inter-node communication

To look at the NUMA hardware on a running system, you can use the `numactl` command (install it first if not present):

```
> numactl --hardware
available: 2 nodes (0-1)
node 0 cpus: 0 2 4 6 8 10 12 14 16 18 20 22 24 26 28 30
node 0 size: 65490 MB
node 0 free: 56085 MB
node 1 cpus: 1 3 5 7 9 11 13 15 17 19 21 23 25 27 29 31
node 1 size: 65536 MB
node 1 free: 35150 MB
node distances:
node 0 1
0: 10 20
1: 20 10
```

We can see two different nodes here that indicate two different physical CPUs and the physical allocated RAM.

The node distances represent the cost of interconnect access. The weight for `node 0` to access its local bank is `10`, and for `node 1`, it's `20`. This is the same constraint for `node 1` to access `node 0`.

You can see the NUMA policy and information using the following command:

```
> numactl --show
policy: default
preferred node: current
physcpubind: 0 1 2 3 4 5 6 7 8 9 10 11 12 13 14 15 16 17 18 19 20 21 22
23 24 25 26 27 28 29 30 31
cpubind: 0 1
nodebind: 0 1
membind: 0 1
```

Now, if you want to bind a process to a CPU, use the following command:

```
numactl -physcpubind=0,1 <PID>
```

To allocate the local memory of a NUMA node, use the following command:

```
numactl --physcpubind=0 --localalloc <PID>
```

Now, if you want to get stats and see how your NUMA system works when the interleave has been hit and so on, use the `numastat` command:

```
> numastat
node0 node1
numa_hit 407467513 656867541
numa_miss 0 0
```

```
numa_foreign 0 0
interleave_hit 32442 32470
local_node 407037248 656824235
other_node 430265 43306
```

Migrating from MySQL to MariaDB

First of all, MariaDB is a fork of MySQL. So, if you're using a version from 5.1 to 5.5, the migration will be really easy. To make it clear and simple, if you're running a MySQL version under 5.1, upgrade it first to 5.1 at least and 5.5 at max.

Then, it will be easy to migrate. First of all, you need to understand the best compatibility version, as shown in the following table:

MySQL version	MariaDB version
5.1	5.1, 5.2, 5.3
5.5	5.5
5.6	10

It is recommended, for example, to switch from the 5.1 version of MySQL to the 5.1 version of MariaDB. Then test it, see if everything is fine, and then you can upgrade to a higher version of MariaDB.

There is something that you should consider: starting from the 5.6 version of MySQL, MariaDB will start to number the version from 10. Why? Because MariaDB developers want to be clear on the features portability from MySQL to MariaDB. All the features won't be ported in version 10. They may be done later or not at all. Some features will be fully rewritten for several reasons, and MariaDB developers will try to keep compatibility with MySQL. That's why for a migration, it's preferable to migrate a MySQL version from 5.1 to 5.5. If you don't use advanced features, it shouldn't be a problem as incompatibilities are very low.

Since 5.5 is really stable, you can skip the upgrade to 5.3 (the latest branch of MariaDB based on 5.1) and go straight to 5.5. Of course, complete regression testing of the application is recommended.

To get more information on the compatibility list from one version to another, I strongly recommend following the official MariaDB compatibility information page available on the main site: `https://mariadb.com/kb/en/mariadb-versus-mysql-compatibility/`.

Now that you've understood how to migrate, we'll perform a migration using a virtual machine. You'll need the following:

- 1 CPU
- 512 MB of RAM
- 8 GB of disk space

This is the code you need to run:

```ruby
# -*- mode: ruby -*-
# vi: set ft=ruby :
ENV['LANG'] = 'C'

# Vagrantfile API/syntax version. Don't touch unless you know what
you're doing!
VAGRANTFILE_API_VERSION = "2"

# Insert all your Vms with configs
boxes = [
    { :name => :mysqlserver },
]

$install = <<INSTALL
aptitude update
DEBIAN_FRONTEND=noninteractive aptitude -y -o Dpkg::Options::="--
force-confdef" -o Dpkg::Options::="--force-confold" install mysql-
server
INSTALL

Vagrant::Config.run do |config|
  # Default box OS
  vm_default = proc do |boxcnf|
    boxcnf.vm.box        = "deimosfr/debian-wheezy"
  end

  # For each VM, add a public and private card. Then install Ceph
  boxes.each do |opts|
    vm_default.call(config)
    config.vm.define opts[:name] do |config|
        config.vm.host_name = "%s.vm" % opts[:name].to_s
        config.vm.provision "shell", inline: $install
    end
  end
end
```

Install on this virtual machine the application of your choice (WordPress, MediaWiki, and so on) to confirm the migration doesn't break anything.

You will see that the migration is an easy step. First of all, remove the current MySQL version, but keep the data:

```
apt-get remove mysql-server
```

Then, your database will still be available in the data directory (`/var/lib/mysql` by default) but no binary will be present.

It's time to install MariaDB. First add the MariaDB repository (for version 5.5 here):

```
apt-get install python-software-properties

apt-key adv --recv-keys --keyserver keyserver.ubuntu.com
0xcbcb082a1bb943db

add-apt-repository 'deb
http://mirrors.linsrv.net/mariadb/repo/5.5/debian wheezy main'
```

Now install MariaDB:

```
apt-get update

apt-get install mariadb-server
```

It should have started without any issues. Take a look at the logs in `/var/log/syslog` if this is not the case.

Introduction to MariaDB engines

When you use MariaDB, you may not know all of the engines, what they can do, which one is more efficient, and in which situation, and so on.

Comparing all the available engines of MariaDB could take a whole book. So, we're going to cover them here, but just an introduction with some additional information to help you to choose some of them for testing.

The classic engines that can also be found on MySQL are as follows:

Engine	Description
MyISAM	This is a light and nontransactional engine. It has good performance and a small data footprint. MyISAM has good performances for small database access.
InnoDB	InnoDB gets very high performance when the database size is less or equal to the RAM size to be used as cache. It's unfortunately not as efficient as MyISAM if there is not enough RAM memory.

Engine	Description
BLACKHOLE	The BLACKHOLE engines accept data but they are immediately dropped and a zero result is returned by the engine. This engine is generally used for complex replication filtering on very high load databases.
CSV	The CVS engine is able to read and write CSV (comma-separated-values) format files.
MEMORY	The MEMORY engine stores data in memory to perform very fast queries. Generally used for read-only cache or temporary access, it's the fastest engine but with some limitations, such as no support for blob or text columns. As a result, it's a nonpersistent engine because all data is in the RAM.
ARCHIVE	The ARCHIVE engine is a good solution for minimal disk space occupation with small footprint. It compresses rows with the `zlib` algorithm. It's one of the slowest solutions (no index + compression) but it's perfect to store a huge amount of data without specific performance requirements.
MERGE	The MERGE engine is a collection of identical MyISAM tables that can be used as one table.

MariaDB introduces several new engines and is still adding some more for different usages and performances:

Engine	Available version	Description
Aria	>= 5.1	This engine is a crash-safe alternative to MyISAM. It's able to be a transactional and nontransactional storage.
XtraDB	>= 5.1	The Percona XtraDB engine is a drop-in replacement for InnoDB. It's more scalable with many cores and also gets highest performances and more metrics.
PBXT	< 5.5	The **PrimeBase XT (PBXT)** engine is designed for a high concurrency environment. It's unfortunately not maintained anymore.
FederatedX	>= 5.1	This engine is a drop-in replacement of the FEDERATED engine. It uses `libmysql` to talk to an RDBMS. The idea is to use other RDBMS as data sources.
SphinxSE	>= 5.2	The **Sphinx Search Engine (SphinxSE)** is a built-in client to talk directly to the searchd daemon and run search queries. It doesn't store data at all.
IBMDB2I	< 5.5	This engine is able to store its data in a DB2 table running on IBM.

Engine	Available version	Description
TokuDB	>= 5.5	This is a highly scalable engine with indexing-based query acceleration, no slave lag performance, unparalleled compression, and hot schema modification. It has better performances compared to XtraDB, when you do not have enough RAM. In that case, performances are quite similar to MyISAM.
Cassandra	>= 10	This engine allows direct access to a Cassandra cluster from MariaDB.
Connect	>= 10	This engine permits access to local or remote data when defining tables based on different data types.
Sequence	>= 10	This engine permits the creation of ascending or descending number sequences using a starting and ending value and increment.
Spider	>= 10	This is a built-in sharding features engine that supports xa transactions, partitioning, and allows table links to the table on a remote server.
HandlerSocket	>=5.3	This is a NoSQL plugin. It doesn't support SQL queries but supports **CRUD (Create/Update/Delete)** operations on tables. It accepts direct TCP connections.

In the future, more and more NoSQL engines will be integrated.

Summary

This chapter gave you an overview of the hardware that exists for MariaDB and which one is better than the others. You also now know how to take advantage of some hardware and operating systems for MariaDB. You've seen a quick overview of which MariaDB engines are available and which ones are faster. Selecting the correct hardware is a very important thing, and to know how it works is a completely different topic. Take time to understand how to optimize and how your environment works to avoid misunderstood slowdowns. As a rule, try to keep yourself updated on the new CPU features / power management and how Linux evolves with it.

2
Performance Analysis

In this chapter, you'll get recommendations for how to achieve good performance, what tools to use, and MariaDB internal presentations for analyses purposes. The goal of this chapter is to help you find where a performance issue comes from.

The performance goal takes time and requires a lot of tests to make things as performant as possible. There are many situations, many possibilities, and different architectures, and all these complex things need to be answered with many tools. These tools will help you diagnose performance issues as fast as possible to find complex issues.

Tools are not the only solutions. You can do many other things to optimize your databases:

- Use good index types when it's necessary. Too many indexes will slow down your databases.
- Set the best column data type. For example, do not use a `char` column data type if it stores only integers.
- Avoid duplicated keys.
- Optimize your SQL queries as much as possible.

If these points are correctly taken into account, the number of performance issues can be minimized.

For this chapter, some features are only available from MariaDB 10. That's why you need to change your repository information. In addition, we're going to use Percona tools and the Percona repositories need to be set up. So, here is the `Vagrantfile` for it:

```ruby
# -*- mode: ruby -*-
# vi: set ft=ruby :
# Vagrantfile API/syntax version. Don't touch unless you know what
you're doing!
```

```
#
VAGRANTFILE_API_VERSION = "2"

# Insert all your Vms with configs
boxes = [
    { :name => :mariadb },
]


$install = <<INSTALL
aptitude update
DEBIAN_FRONTEND=noninteractive aptitude -y -o Dpkg::Options::="--
force-confdef" -o Dpkg::Options::="--force-confold" install python-
software-properties
apt-key adv --recv-keys --keyserver keyserver.ubuntu.com
0xcbcb082a1bb943db
apt-key adv --keyserver keys.gnupg.net --recv-keys 1C4CBDCDCD2EFD2A
add-apt-repository 'deb http://ftp.igh.cnrs.fr/pub/mariadb/repo/10.0/
debian wheezy main'
add-apt-repository 'deb http://repo.percona.com/apt wheezy main'
echo 'Package: *
Pin: release o=Percona Development Team
Pin-Priority: 100' > /etc/apt/preferences.d/00percona.pref
aptitude update
DEBIAN_FRONTEND=noninteractive aptitude -y -o Dpkg::Options::="--
force-confdef" -o Dpkg::Options::="--force-confold" install mariadb-
server percona-toolkit bzr
INSTALL


Vagrant::Config.run do |config|
  # Default box OS
  vm_default = proc do |boxcnf|
    boxcnf.vm.box       = "deimosfr/debian-wheezy"
  end

  # For each VM, add a public and private card. Then install Ceph
  boxes.each do |opts|
    vm_default.call(config)
    config.vm.define opts[:name] do |config|
        config.vm.customize ["modifyvm", :id, "--cpus", 2]
        config.vm.host_name = "%s.vm" % opts[:name].to_s
        config.vm.provision "shell", inline: $install
    end
  end
end
```

In addition, in some of this chapter's examples, free and open source software will be taken for their database analysis, such as MediaWiki (http://www.mediawiki.org) and Tiny Tiny RSS (http://tt-rss.org).

Slow queries

The slow query log feature gives the possibility to log queries that take more than *x* seconds to be executed. This is the first step when investigating a performance issue. To look at the current status, connect to your MariaDB instance and launch it:

```
MariaDB [(none)]> SHOW GLOBAL VARIABLES LIKE '%SLOW_QUERY%';
+---------------------+----------------------------------+
| Variable_name       | Value                            |
+---------------------+----------------------------------+
| slow_query_log      | OFF                              |
| slow_query_log_file | /var/log/mysql/mariadb-slow.log  |
+---------------------+----------------------------------+
2 rows in set (0.00 sec)
```

Here, we can see the path of the slow query logs. To activate this on the fly, run that SQL command:

```
MariaDB [(none)]> SET GLOBAL SLOW_QUERY_LOG=1;
Query OK, 0 rows affected (0.00 sec)
```

The other option is to set in seconds the query delay to mark it as a long query. These long queries will be logged as follows:

```
MariaDB [(none)]> SHOW GLOBAL VARIABLES LIKE '%LONG_QUERY%';
+-----------------+----------+
| Variable_name   | Value    |
+-----------------+----------+
| long_query_time | 1.000000 |
+-----------------+----------+
1 row in set (0.00 sec)
```

This is the default setting; the long query is set to 10 seconds. You can change this setting on the fly as well:

```
MariaDB [(none)]> SET GLOBAL LONG_QUERY_TIME=1;
Query OK, 0 rows affected (0.00 sec)
```

Now, you've set global status variables on the fly. This prevents MariaDB from rebooting, and this is good news. However, only new connections will be affected by these changes. The problem will occur during the next start boot of MariaDB, as it will lose those settings. To avoid this, you have to set the MariaDB configuration file settings (/etc/mysql/my.cnf):

```
[mysqld]
slow_query_log=1
slow_query_log_file = /var/log/mysql/mariadb-slow.log
long_query_time=1
```

You're now ready to look at the slow logs in the mariadb-slow.log file at /var/log/mysql/mariadb-slow.log. You will find all the slow queries, the query time, the lock time, and other interesting information in these queries. This is the first step to looking into your application and performing changes on the code part generating those requests. This could involve a lot of things, such as requests being too long, missing indexes, and so on, but the good thing is you now know which queries are slow and which ones make your application look slow.

The explain command

The explain SQL command provides information for a specific request. Most of the time, we get a query from the slow query logs to analyze the request. The explain command won't return the classical output of the query but will provide some information concerning the related SQL query.

The explain command can only be applied on a SELECT query. UPDATE and DELETE are supported in Version 10.0.5!

Let's take a query that you can have in your slow query logs. Here is an example with a working version of MediaWiki:

```
MariaDB [mediawiki]> explain select page_id, page_title,
page_namespace, page_is_redirect, old_id, old_text from wiki_page,
wiki_revision, wiki_text where rev_id=page_latest and
old_id=rev_text_id\g;
*************************** 1. row ***************************
           id: 1
  select_type: SIMPLE
        table: wiki_page
         type: ALL
```

```
possible_keys: NULL
          key: NULL
      key_len: NULL
          ref: NULL
         rows: 2005
        Extra:
*************************** 2. row ***************************
           id: 1
  select_type: SIMPLE
        table: wiki_revision
         type: eq_ref
possible_keys: rev_id
          key: rev_id
      key_len: 4
          ref: mediawiki.wiki_page.page_latest
         rows: 1
        Extra:
...
3 rows in set (0.00 sec)
```

The `explain` feature lists two rows here. If you examine the first one, `ALL` means there is a full scan done on the `wiki_page` table. Then, in the `type` section, you can see how the table is accessed. Here, there is no index type. That's why `2005` rows were scanned and that's why it's slow.

If you now look at the second row, it's better. There is an index (`eq_ref`), which means this is the best possible plan to find the row. In addition, the number of scanned rows is `1`, so it's perfect!

Slow query logs

Since you can directly have the query log the output of the `explain` command in MariaDB 10.0.5, this will help you save time. To make it active, you need to add this line in your MariaDB configuration file (`/etc/mysql/my.cnf`):

```
[mysqld]
log_slow_verbosity      = query_plan,explain
```

Then, restart MariaDB. To test it, simply force the creation of a long query. Here is a SQL script with a loop. Adapt the first line if the default time is not enough:

```
-- Change this value to a higher one if you need more time
-- This will insert x lines number in your database
SET @MAX_INSERT = 100000;

-- Vars
SET SQL_MODE="NO_AUTO_VALUE_ON_ZERO";
SET time_zone = "+00:00";

-- Create database
DROP DATABASE IF EXISTS chapter2;
CREATE DATABASE chapter2;
USE chapter2;

-- Create table and add index
CREATE TABLE IF NOT EXISTS `s_explain` (
   `id` int(11) DEFAULT NULL,
   `ts` timestamp NOT NULL DEFAULT '0000-00-00 00:00:00' ON UPDATE
CURRENT_TIMESTAMP
) ENGINE=InnoDB DEFAULT CHARSET=latin1;
ALTER TABLE `s_explain` ADD INDEX ( `id` );

-- Create a procedure to insert lines
DELIMITER $$
DROP PROCEDURE IF EXISTS proc_name$$
CREATE PROCEDURE proc_name()
BEGIN
 DECLARE count INT DEFAULT 0;
 WHILE count < @MAX_INSERT DO
    SET count = count + 1;
    INSERT INTO `s_explain`(`id`, `ts`) VALUES (FLOOR(RAND() *
@MAX_INSERT), NOW());
 END WHILE;
END$$
DELIMITER ;

-- Call procedure
call proc_name();
```

You can now simply call this script by slowing down the `long_query_time`, calling the `loop.sql` script, and running a SELECT command on it:

```
mysql < loop.sql
```

Here is the result you will find in your slow query logs:

```
# Time: 140113 23:02:57
# User@Host: root[root] @ localhost []
# Thread_id: 65  Schema: chapter2  QC_hit: No
# Query_time: 0.254088  Lock_time: 0.000090  Rows_sent: 60000
Rows_examined: 60000
# Full_scan: Yes  Full_join: No  Tmp_table: No  Tmp_table_on_disk: No
# Filesort: No  Filesort_on_disk: No  Merge_passes: 0
#
# explain: id    select_type    table    type    possible_keys    key
key_len ref    rows    Extra
# explain: 1    SIMPLE  s_explain    ALL    NULL    NULL    NULL
NULL    60249
#
SET timestamp=1389654177;
select * from s_explain;
```

Here is some more information:

- `Query_time`: This indicates the time taken for the query to run. It's important to check the `Lock_time` value as well to avoid table locking, which then could block other requests. The query time should be much bigger than the lock time.

- `Rows_examined`: The lesser the rows examined, the shorter the time the query will take. You can use an index to reduce this time. `Rows_examined` should be much bigger than `Rows_sent` in most cases.

- `Query_plan`: This gives the information from `Full_scan` to `Merge_passes`. It should also give important information that helps you understand where a query spends too much time.

This information is just the first step for investigation. You need to dive more into your SQL query or the application that creates the SQL query.

The show explain command

The show explain feature is only available in MariaDB 10. It allows you to get an explanation directly from a running process, for example, if you use the loop.sql script once again. At the time of insertion, execute a show processlist command:

```
MariaDB [chapter2]> SHOW PROCESSLIST\G;
[...]
*************************** 2. row ***************************
      Id: 81
    User: root
    Host: localhost
      db: chapter2
 Command: Query
    Time: 0
   State: query end
    Info: INSERT INTO `s_explain`(`id`, `ts`) VALUES (FLOOR(RAND() *
@MAX_INSERT), NOW())
Progress: 0.000
2 rows in set (0.00 sec)
```

We can see here the 81 ID, which is the INSERT command in the loop.sql script. We're going to analyze it with the show explain command:

```
MariaDB [chapter2]> SHOW EXPLAIN FOR 81\G;
*************************** 1. row ***************************
           id: 1
  select_type: INSERT
        table: s_explain
         type: ALL
possible_keys: NULL
          key: NULL
      key_len: NULL
          ref: NULL
         rows: NULL
        Extra:
1 row in set, 1 warning (0.01 sec)
```

This could be very interesting on a really long slow query, without having to wait till the end of it to perform an explain analysis.

Profiling

Profiling permits you to benchmark information that indicates resource usages during a session. This is used when we want to get information on a specified query. Here are the types of information:

- Block I/O
- Context switches
- CPU
- IPC
- Memory
- Page faults
- Source
- Swaps
- All

First of all, you need to know that profiling on a production server is not recommended because of the performance degradation it can cause.

To enable profiling, use the following command:

```
MariaDB [none]> SET PROFILING=1;
```

Perform all the query tasks you want to profile and then list them:

```
MariaDB [none]> SHOW PROFILES;
```

Query_ID	Duration	Query
1	0.30798532	select * from s_explain
2	0.25341312	select * from s_explain

In the preceding command-line output, you can see that we've two query IDs. To get information related to the first `Query_ID`, with extra columns for the CPU, use the following command:

```
MariaDB [none]> SHOW PROFILE CPU FOR QUERY 1;
```

Status	Duration	CPU_user	CPU_system

```
| starting                      | 0.000034 | 0.000000 |   0.000000 |
| Waiting for query cache lock  | 0.000009 | 0.000000 |   0.000000 |
| init                          | 0.000008 | 0.000000 |   0.000000 |
[...]
| init                          | 0.000016 | 0.000000 |   0.000000 |
| optimizing                    | 0.000011 | 0.000000 |   0.000000 |
| statistics                    | 0.000050 | 0.000000 |   0.000000 |
| preparing                     | 0.000017 | 0.000000 |   0.000000 |
| executing                     | 0.000008 | 0.000000 |   0.000000 |
| Sending data                  | 0.007369 | 0.004001 |   0.000000 |
| Waiting for query cache lock  | 0.000020 | 0.000000 |   0.000000 |
| Sending data                  | 0.003420 | 0.004000 |   0.000000 |
[...]
| Sending data                  | 0.271156 | 0.272017 |   0.000000 |
| end                           | 0.000020 | 0.000000 |   0.000000 |
| query end                     | 0.000010 | 0.000000 |   0.000000 |
| closing tables                | 0.000015 | 0.000000 |   0.000000 |
| freeing items                 | 0.000009 | 0.000000 |   0.000000 |
| updating status               | 0.000041 | 0.000000 |   0.000000 |
| cleaning up                   | 0.000029 | 0.000000 |   0.000000 |
+-------------------------------+----------+----------+------------+
```

You will find a lot of interesting information in the preceding command-line output. Here is an overview:

- `init`: This gives information of the starting process for the storage engine
- `optimizing`: This gives the query plan information as given in the slow query logs
- `statistics`: This shows the engine locking and optimization
- `executing`: This shows the execution time (as in `Query_plan`)

In the preceding command line, we've just specified the CPU type and got all the extra columns related to it. If we want maximum information, replace `CPU` with `ALL`.

So, now you're able to compare multiple requests, see their evolution, and track the used resources with them.

Performance schema

In Version 5.5.3, you can use the `performance_schema` monitoring feature of MariaDB to monitor performance. It has been implemented as an engine (that's why you can see it on a `show engines` command) with a database that stores data performance.

To activate the performance schema, add this line to your `my.cnf` configuration file:

```
performance_schema=on
```

You can then check whether it has been correctly activated:

```
MariaDB [(none)]> SHOW VARIABLES LIKE 'performance_schema';
+--------------------+-------+
| Variable_name      | Value |
+--------------------+-------+
| performance_schema | ON    |
+--------------------+-------+
1 row in set (0.00 sec)
```

You can now list the complete table list to see the available monitoring features:

```
MariaDB [(none)]> USE PERFORMANCE_SCHEMA;
MariaDB [performance_schema]> show tables;
+---------------------------------------------------+
| Tables_in_performance_schema                      |
+---------------------------------------------------+
| accounts                                          |
| cond_instances                                    |
| events_stages_current                             |
[...]
| table_lock_waits_summary_by_table                 |
| threads                                           |
| users                                             |
+---------------------------------------------------+
52 rows in set (0.00 sec)
```

You can get a complete list of all the features in the MariaDB documentation at https://mariadb.com/kb/en/list-of-performance-schema-tables/.

User statistics

Since MariaDB 5.2, a patch from Google, Percona, and other companies has been implemented, which permits you to view the user statistics, client statistics, index statistics (and usage), and table statistics.

You can activate it on the fly using the following command:

```
MariaDB [(none)]> SET GLOBAL userstat=1;
```

Alternatively, you can make it persistent in the MariaDB configuration (my.cnf) using the following code:

```
[mysqld]
userstat = 1
```

You now have access to the new FLUSH and SHOW commands:

```
MariaDB [(none)]> FLUSH TABLE_STATISTICS
MariaDB [(none)]> FLUSH INDEX_STATISTICS
MariaDB [(none)]> FLUSH USER_STATISTICS
MariaDB [(none)]> FLUSH CLIENT_STATISTICS
MariaDB [(none)]> SHOW CLIENT_STATISTICS
MariaDB [(none)]> SHOW USER_STATISTICS
MariaDB [(none)]> SHOW INDEX_STATISTICS
MariaDB [(none)]> SHOW TABLE_STATISTICS
```

Here is an example of what the user statistics look like:

```
MariaDB [(none)]> SHOW USER_STATISTICS\G;
*************************** 1. row ***************************
                    User: root
       Total_connections: 2
  Concurrent_connections: 0
          Connected_time: 23
               Busy_time: 0.002942
                Cpu_time: 0.0024703
          Bytes_received: 96
              Bytes_sent: 5147
    Binlog_bytes_written: 0
               Rows_read: 0
               Rows_sent: 3
```

```
        Rows_deleted: 0
       Rows_inserted: 0
        Rows_updated: 0
      Select_commands: 1
     Update_commands: 0
      Other_commands: 0
  Commit_transactions: 0
Rollback_transactions: 0
   Denied_connections: 0
     Lost_connections: 0
        Access_denied: 0
        Empty_queries: 0
1 row in set (0.00 sec)
```

You can get the fine statistics about a user through the preceding command.

Sysbench

Sysbench is a benchmarking tool that has several modes to bench:

- - `fileio`: This performs the file I/O test
- - `cpu`: This performs the CPU performance test
- - `memory`: This performs the memory functions speed test
- - `threads`: This performs the thread subsystem performance test
- - `mutex`: This performs the mutex performance test
- - `oltp`: This performs the OLTP test

To install it, run this command:

```
> aptitude install sysbench
```

The common test is to use the **Online Transaction Processing (OLTP)** scenario with small transactions to hit an optimized database. We will pass arguments to the command to simulate application threads (the `--num-threads` argument).

You can run this OLTP test with two kinds of scenarios:

- Read only (14 SELECT queries per transaction)
- Read/Write (14 SELECT, 1 INSERT, 1 UPDATE, and 1 DELETE queries per transaction)

The available version in Debian Wheezy is 0.4. A newer version exists with more interesting results such as a reporting interval every *x* sec. In addition, you can also find a complete set of tests from the sysbench repository. That's why we're not going to use the sysbench version from the MariaDB repository. To install it, you need to proceed as follows:

```
> aptitude install automake libtool libmariadbclient-dev bzr
> bzr branch lp:sysbench
> cd sysbench
> ./autogen.sh
> ./configure
> make
```

The `sysbench` binary is now available in the `sysbench` folder. We can now test it! First of all, you need to prepare your instance. This will create a dedicated username and database for the tests (`sbtest`):

```
> cd sysbench
> ./sysbench --test=tests/db/oltp.lua --num-threads=4 --max-time=30 --mysql-user=root prepare
sysbench 0.5:  multi-threaded system evaluation benchmark


Creating table 'sbtest1'...
Inserting 10000 records into 'sbtest1'
```

You can now run the test:

```
> ./sysbench --test=tests/db/oltp.lua --num-threads=4 --max-time=30 --mysql-user=root --report-interval=5 run
sysbench 0.5:  multi-threaded system evaluation benchmark


Running the test with following options:
Number of threads: 4
Report intermediate results every 5 second(s)
Random number generator seed is 0 and will be ignored
    Threads started!
[   5s] threads: 4, tps: 267.47, reads/s: 3751.99, writes/s: 1069.88, response time: 23.65ms (95%)
[  10s] threads: 4, tps: 271.20, reads/s: 3796.78, writes/s: 1085.59, response time: 23.06ms (95%)
```

```
[ 15s] threads: 4, tps: 270.20, reads/s: 3785.20, writes/s: 1080.80,
response time: 21.80ms (95%)
[ 20s] threads: 4, tps: 243.80, reads/s: 3412.38, writes/s: 975.19,
response time: 23.80ms (95%)
[ 25s] threads: 4, tps: 265.00, reads/s: 3709.83, writes/s: 1060.81,
response time: 22.29ms (95%)
[ 30s] threads: 4, tps: 257.60, reads/s: 3607.19, writes/s: 1029.60,
response time: 24.05ms (95%)
OLTP test statistics:
    queries performed:
        read:                      110320
        write:                     31520
        other:                     15760
        total:                     157600
    transactions:                  7880      (262.55 per sec.)
    deadlocks:                     0         (0.00 per sec.)
    read/write requests:           141840    (4725.92 per sec.)
    other operations:              15760     (525.10 per sec.)


    General statistics:
    total time:                    30.0132s
    total number of events:        7880
    total time taken by event execution: 119.9270s
    response time:
        min:                                5.68ms
        avg:                               15.22ms
        max:                              110.65ms
        approx.  95 percentile:            23.15ms


    Threads fairness:
    events (avg/stddev):           1970.0000/10.32
    execution time (avg/stddev):   29.9817/0.01
```

We can see here how many operations this instance is able to handle with its configuration. In this case, we've seen the basic test with OLTP processing.

You can find other tests in the `tests/db/` location. Sysbench is an old and common tool to perform tests against MariaDB.

You are now able to perform changes and see the benefits of them with sysbench.

Percona Toolkits

Percona Toolkits is a suite of tools for MySQL and MariaDB. They are very useful in many situations and well documented (the main website is `http://www.percona.com/software/percona-toolkit`). To install them, you can add the repository:

```
> aptitude install python-software-properties
> apt-key adv --keyserver keys.gnupg.net --recv-keys 1C4CBDCDCD2EFD2A
> add-apt-repository 'deb http://repo.percona.com/apt wheezy main'
```

Then, configure APT-Pining to avoid the Percona repository overriding MariaDB's repository and conflict some packages. So, create this file at `/etc/apt/preferences.d/00percona.pref` and add the following content to it:

```
Package: *
Pin: release o=Percona Development Team
Pin-Priority: 100
```

You're now ready for the installation of the package:

```
> aptitude update
> aptitude install percona-toolkit
```

That's it! Several binaries starting with `pt-` are now available on your system.

pt-query-digest

The `pt-query-digest` tool will help you analyze the MariaDB slow queries and binary logfiles. To get a report on slow queries, run `pt-query-digest` directly on them:

```
> pt-query-digest /var/log/mysql/mariadb-slow.log
# Rank Query ID              Response time Calls R/Call Apdx V/M    Item
# ==== ================== ============= ===== ====== ==== =====
==========
#    1 0x1CB7FFA97DE5F579  1.7216 23.9%     6 0.2869 1.00  0.00
DELETE SELECT ttrss_entries ttrss_user_entries
#    2 0xB44E823E1547F193  1.1306 15.7%     6 0.1884 1.00  0.00
SELECT ttrss_feeds
```

```
#     3 0x813031B8BBC3B329   0.9622 13.4%   3194 0.0003 1.00   0.00
COMMIT
#     4 0x8DB6A7CBF78AD7EA   0.5197  7.2%    108 0.0048 1.00   0.01
SELECT ttrss_user_entries
#     5 0x559EB525379A2B6B   0.4575  6.4%   1941 0.0002 1.00   0.00
SELECT ttrss_entries ttrss_user_entries
```

Here is the summary of the five slowest queries and the first query (rank 1) takes `23.9%` of the total response time.

You also have the analysis of all the queries to help you more. There are other interesting options if you have a huge slow query logfile: `--since` and `-until`. These options will help you have a better filter. Another one is `-limit` to display the 90 percent or the top 30 worst queries:

```
> pt-query-digest -limit 90%:30
```

More than that, you can have a report from `tcpdump` or through the MariaDB `process list` command.

pt-stalk

The `pt-stalk` tool can save you a lot of time. When you're facing random performance issues, happening during a short period of time, it's very hard to analyze. `pt-stalk` will help you gather data when a trigger condition occurs.

Let's say we want to start data gathering as soon as (`cycles=1`) there are five more (threshold) connected threads (variables):

```
> pt-stalk --threshold=5 --variable=connected --cycles=1 -- -u<user>
--p<passoword>
2014_01_11_07_29_58 Starting /usr/bin/pt-stalk --function=status --
variable=connected --threshold=5 --match= --cycles=1 --interval=1 --
iterations= --run-time=30 --sleep=300 --dest=/var/lib/pt-stalk --
prefix= --notify-by-email= --log=/var/log/pt-stalk.log --
pid=/var/run/pt-stalk.pid
2014_01_11_07_29_59 Check results: connected=5, matched=no,
cycles_true=0
2014_01_11_07_30_00 Check results: connected=5, matched=no,
cycles_true=0
2014_01_11_07_30_01 Check results: connected=5, matched=no,
cycles_true=0
2014_01_11_07_30_02 Check results: connected=6, matched=yes,
cycles_true=1
```

```
2014_01_11_07_30_02 Collect triggered
2014_01_11_07_30_02 Collector PID 8008
2014_01_11_07_30_02 Sleeping 300 seconds after collect
```

You can also run it as a daemon, change the default destination, and be notified by e-mail. The gathering of data is not only on the MariaDB side, but the system side as well.

Here is the list of what kind of result you get from `pt-stalk`:

```
> ls /var/lib/pt-stalk | sed 's/2014_01_11.*-//' | column
df              processlist   lsof         trigger        opentables1
space           procstat      meminfo      variables      opentables2
diskstats       procvmstat    status1      vmstat         output
hostname        ps            status2      overall        pmap
innodbstatus1   slabinfo      mysqladmin   df             processlist
innodbstatus2   sysctl        netstat      space          procstat
interrupts      top           netstat_s    diskstats      procvmstat
lsof            trigger       opentables1  hostname       ps
meminfo         variables     opentables2  innodbstatus1  slabinfo
status1         vmstat        output       innodbstatus2  sysctl
status2         overall       pmap         interrupts     top
mysqladmin      df            processlist  lsof           trigger
netstat         space         procstat     meminfo        variables
netstat_s       diskstats     procvmstat   status1        vmstat
opentables1     hostname      ps           status2        overall
opentables2     innodbstatus1 slabinfo     mysqladmin
output          innodbstatus2 sysctl       netstat
pmap            interrupts    top          netstat_s
```

Also, another interesting option if you're located on the server and the problem occurs at this moment is that you can collect data with no delay by using the `--no-stalk` option.

pt-summary

The `pt-summary` tool provides information related to the system. It could help to see the basic issues related to the system side:

```
> pt-summary
# Percona Toolkit System Summary Report #####################
```

```
         Date | 2014-06-15 11:41:04 UTC (local TZ: UTC +0000)
     Hostname | mariadb
       Uptime | 1 min,  1 user,   load average: 0.27, 0.09, 0.03
       System | innotek GmbH; VirtualBox; v1.2 (Other)
  Service Tag | 0
     Platform | Linux
      Release | Debian GNU/Linux 7.5 (wheezy) (wheezy)
       Kernel | 3.2.0-4-amd64
 Architecture | CPU = 64-bit, OS = 64-bit
    Threading | NPTL 2.13
      SELinux | No SELinux detected
  Virtualized | VirtualBox
# Processor ##############################################
   Processors | physical = 1, cores = 2, virtual = 2, hyperthreading =
no
       Speeds | 2x2388.297
       Models | 2xIntel(R) Core(TM) i5-4258U CPU @ 2.40GHz
       Caches | 2x6144 KB
# Memory #################################################
        Total | 496.8M
         Free | 166.5M
         Used | physical = 330.3M, swap allocated = 300.0M, swap used
= 0.0, virtual = 330.3M
      Buffers | 18.9M
       Caches | 231.5M
```

pt-mysql-summary

The pt-mysql-summary tool will give you a summary of your MariaDB instance with schema and databases (this will require a dump). This is just a tool to summarize all the information of your instance and it gives you an overview of the health of your database instance:

```
> pt-mysql-summary
# Percona Toolkit MySQL Summary Report ######################
            System time | 2014-01-11 07:11:13 UTC (local TZ: UTC
+0000)
# Instances #############################################
```

```
   Port  Data Directory              Nice OOM Socket

   =====  ========================== ==== === ======
   3306 /var/lib/mysql                  0    0   /var/run/mysqld/mysqld.sock
# MySQL Executable #######################################
      Path to executable | /usr/sbin/mysqld
           Has symbols | No
# Report On Port 3306 ###################################
                  User | root@localhost
                  Time | 2014-01-11 07:11:13 (UTC)
              Hostname | mariadb
               Version | 5.5.34-MariaDB-1~wheezy-log mariadb.org
binary distribution
              Built On | debian-linux-gnu x86_64
               Started | 2014-01-11 05:59 (up 0+01:11:51)
             Databases | 3
                Datadir | /var/lib/mysql/
             Processes | 1 connected, 1 running
           Replication | Is not a slave, has 0 slaves connected
               Pidfile | /var/run/mysqld/mysqld.pid (exists)
```

It's usually good to be sure your configuration is conformed to your wishes. It's recommended to take care of the configuration information, if your instance has not been running with at least 24 hours of a normal load.

pt-duplicate-key-checker

The `pt-duplicate-key-checker` tool will find duplicate indexes and foreign keys for you in your database tables. It reads the result of the `show create table` commands and related queries to find suspicious indexes. The result is really explicit:

```
> pt-duplicate-key-checker
# ######################################################################
##
# tinyrss.ttrss_prefs
# ######################################################################
##

# ttrss_prefs_pref_name_idx is a duplicate of PRIMARY
# Key definitions:
```

```
#    KEY `ttrss_prefs_pref_name_idx` (`pref_name`),
#    PRIMARY KEY (`pref_name`),
# Column types:
#         `pref_name` varchar(250) not null
# To remove this duplicate index, execute:
ALTER TABLE `tinyrss`.`ttrss_prefs` DROP INDEX
`ttrss_prefs_pref_name_idx`;


# ######################################################################
##
# Summary of indexes
# ######################################################################
##


# Size Duplicate Indexes    73241117
# Total Duplicate Indexes    17
# Total Indexes             819
```

You directly got the SQL queries to remove the duplicated index and a summary of the whole analysis. The duplicate index could really slow down your write queries, so you should be sure that your index is correctly placed. The same information could be shown for the foreign keys.

You can directly apply the changes suggested by `pt-duplicate-key-checker` as follows:

```
> pt-duplicate-key-checker | mysql
```

pt-index-usage

The `pt-index-usage` tool will use the slow query logs to analyze which indexes are unused. Removing those indexes will speed up the specified queries. However, the listed indexes may be used by other queries to make them faster. For example, if the `long_query_time` index is set to `10s` and `pt-index-usage` reports some unused indexes, this doesn't mean you have to remove them as they can be used on other slow queries with an execution time lower than `10s`. So, you absolutely need to be sure it won't affect other requests before deleting an index.

The `pt-index-usage` tool can also do other interesting things, such as check for queries that have unstable plans or which indexes have alternatives that were never used, and so on. The following command analyzes the slow query logs:

```
> pt-index-usage /var/log/mysql/mariadb-slow.log
ALTER TABLE `tinyrss`.`ttrss_enclosures` DROP KEY `post_id`, DROP KEY
`ttrss_enclosures_post_id_idx`; -- type:non-unique

ALTER TABLE `tinyrss`.`ttrss_entries` DROP KEY
`ttrss_entries_date_entered_index`, DROP KEY
`ttrss_entries_guid_index`, DROP KEY `ttrss_entries_updated_idx`; --
type:non-unique

ALTER TABLE `tinyrss`.`ttrss_user_entries` DROP KEY `feed_id`, DROP
KEY `orig_feed_id`, DROP KEY `owner_uid`, DROP KEY
`ttrss_user_entries_feed_id`, DROP KEY
`ttrss_user_entries_owner_uid_index`, DROP KEY
`ttrss_user_entries_ref_id_index`, DROP KEY
`ttrss_user_entries_unread_idx`; -- type:non-unique
```

Process list progression

You certainly know the `show process list` command that shows you the current list of running queries on your MariaDB instance. Since the Version 5.3 of MariaDB, another option is available that shows you the progression of certain long tasks such as the following:

- ALTER TABLE
- CREATE INDEX
- DROP INDEX
- LOAD DATA IN FILE
- CHECK TABLE
- REPAIR TABLE
- ANALYZE TABLE
- OPTIMIZE TABLE

By default, it's enabled in MariaDB, but your client or driver should be recent enough to support this feature. MariaDB sends back the information to the client every 5 seconds by default.

Here is an example of changing the storage engine of a table:

```
MariaDB [chapter2]> ALTER TABLE s_explain ENGINE = Aria;
Stage: 1 of 2 'copy to tmp table' 9.09e+03% of stage done
```

You can see the progression simply by running the ALTER TABLE command. The progression is also available from the processlist command:

```
MariaDB [(none)]> SHOW PROCESSLIST\G;
[...]
*************************** 2. row ***************************
      Id: 70
    User: root
    Host: localhost
      db: chapter2
 Command: Query
    Time: 0
   State: copy to tmp table
    Info: ALTER TABLE s_explain ENGINE = Aria
Progress: 22.767
2 rows in set (0.00 sec)
```

Then, when it's finished, it returns the information:

```
ALTER TABLE s_explain ENGINE = Aria;
Query OK, 100000 rows affected (0.85 sec)
Records: 100000  Duplicates: 0  Warnings: 0
```

With the MariaDB built-in commands, the progression is supported. However, if you are using a MariaDB driver, you can change the default update values directly from the driver connection process.

mytop

mytop was a powerful tool for MySQL, which is now deprecated. Fortunately, the MariaDB project has continued this tool and included advanced features, such as progression as described in the preceding section. It permits us to show the current running queries and update often using the top command. As this is an interactive command, several options exist. To download it, get it from the MariaDB source code and add it to your binary PATH environment:

```
wget -O /usr/bin/mytop "http://bazaar.launchpad.net/~maria-
captains/maria/10.0-base/download/sergii%40pisem.net-20121017170408-
6g093t8gm948zore/mytop.sh-20110627161159-12i6t8if6e5q5v6c-1/mytop.sh"
chmod 755 /usr/bin/mytop
```

Once `mytop` is installed, you can call it with extra parameters to connect to the MariaDB instance. You can also use the `~/.mytop` file to set your default parameters. With the current VirtualBox configuration, you only need to define the selected database (here, it is not specified, so all databases are matched), as shown in the following screenshot:

```
> mytop
MariaDB on localhost (10.0.7-MariaDB-1~wheezy-log)
up 0+01:03:39 [19:48:08]
 Queries: 623.0  qps:   0 Slow:    9.0      Se/In/Up/De(%):   22/49219/00/00
 Sorts:    0 qps now:   1 Slow qps: 0.0 Threads:   2 (  2/  1) 00/00/00/00
 Cache Hits: 11.0  Hits/s: 0.0 Hits now:  0.0  Ratio: 7.9%  Ratio now: 0.0%
 Handler: (R/W/U/D) 19876/39492/  0/  0      Tmp: R/W/U:   78/  78/  0
 ISAM Key Efficiency: 96.8%  Bps in/out: 10.1/217.2   Now in/out:  38.6/ 2.6k


Id    User      Host/IP     DB   Time   %   Cmd        State Query
--    ----      -------     --   ----   -   ---        ----- ----------
85    root      localhost chapter2   1 35.9  Query copy to tmp tab alter table s_explain engine=InnoDB
86    root      localhost            0  0.0  Query          init show full processlist
```

You can see the current list of running processes. As `mytop` is interactive, you can type ? to get the full list of available options.

One of the most used features is killing a process with the k key. It's the solution to stop a query that locks tables and slows down all your applications. Of course, most of the time, it's preferable to know why some queries were running before killing them.

innotop

`innotop` is an InnoDB transaction/status monitor. It is more advanced than `mytop` as it knows how to monitor several kinds of things. Several modes exist, and they basically perform the following operations:

- Replication and Galera cluster monitoring
- Query monitoring
- Transaction monitoring

The `innotop` command works like the `top` command and refreshes its data periodically. Here is an example:

```
> innotop

When   Load   QPS     Slow   QCacheHit   KCacheHit   BpsIn    BpsOut

Now    0.00   254.85    0    19.00%      100.00%   35.10k   66.42k

Total  0.00   89.87     3    42.63%       98.21%   14.41k   86.21k


Cmd    ID      State   User    Host          DB        Time     Query
```

You can monitor multiple servers at the same time. There are a lot of options and hotkeys. You can set a configuration file if you always want something specific or with a lot of servers to connect to.

mysqlsla

`mysqlsla` is a parser of MySQL/MariaDB slow, binary, and microslow logs. It filters and analyzes logs in order to create a custom report from the desired logs and their meta-property values.

To install mysqlsla, get the latest version, install it, and create a symbolic link in order to get it in your classic PATH environment:

```
> wget http://hackmysql.com/scripts/mysqlsla
> chmod +x mysqlsla
```

You're now ready to make a report from the slow query logs; for example:

```
> mysqlsla -lt slow /var/log/mysql/mariadb-slow.log
Report for msl logs: /var/log/mysql/mariadb-slow.log
183 queries total, 31 unique
Sorted by 't_sum'
Grand Totals: Time 559 s, Lock 0 s, Rows sent 460, Rows Examined 0



001 ___

Count       : 11   (6.01%)
Time        : 558.794256 s total, 50.799478 s avg, 13.793118 s to
59.643728 s max   (99.98%)
  95% of Time : 499.150528 s total, 49.915053 s avg, 13.793118 s to
58.413305 s max
```

```
Lock Time (s) : 462 ms total, 42 ms avg, 26 ms to 155 ms max   (1.03%)
  95% of Lock : 307 ms total, 31 ms avg, 26 ms to 36 ms max
Rows sent     : 0 avg, 0 to 0 max   (0.00%)
Rows examined : 0 avg, 0 to 0 max   (0.00%)
Database      : chapter2
Users         :
  root@localhost  : 100.00% (11) of query, 66.12% (121) of all users


Query abstract:
SET timestamp=N; CALL proc_name();


Query sample:
SET timestamp=1389652094;
call proc_name();
```

You can see here a nice report that is easy to analyze. You can also check the man for advanced sorting filters and usages.

Summary

In this chapter, you saw some tools and solutions to find where slowdowns and bottlenecks are located. In some cases, SQL queries are correctly optimized and the hardware should be enough to get your database working correctly. In other cases, other solutions exist such as the choice of the storage engine or the optimization. That's what we're going to see in the next chapter.

Performance Optimizations

3

In this chapter, you will see how to choose the engine depending on your needs, how to optimize them, and how to optimize your operating system for MariaDB.

Checking all the requests passed to your MariaDB database can be a long quest. When you're facing slowdown issues on an application, some other elements should be taken into consideration before auditing all your application code. For example, there is a lot of engine optimization that can be checked and adjusted before diving into the code. There are also several engines that can answer your needs. We'll see here a few things that you need to check, and that can be easily verified.

In this chapter, a lot of MariaDB global variables will be seen and configured. Some of them are simply counters. Before taking them into account, it's recommended that you run a MariaDB instance for at least 24 hours with a normal load. If you set new environment variables and want to reset those counters, it's recommended that you restart the instance.

Just as with any kind of optimization test, if you want to make optimization changes, try them one by one to be sure that they have the desired effect. Of course, even if the optimizations mentioned in this chapter are powerful, some of them depend on your hardware. It's strongly recommended that you perform a test on a pre-production server before applying changes to production.

Also, you'll see how to set (without restarting the MariaDB instance) global values on the fly and how to set them permanently.

You can use the `Vagrantfile` from the previous chapter for the tests mentioned in this chapter.

Resetting statistics

In this chapter, we'll play with the MariaDB statistics. Sometimes, you'll need to reset them. You have two choices to do so:

- Do it on the fly
- Make the change on the configuration file and restart the MariaDB instance

We'll see here how to flush the statistics on the fly with the `mysqladmin` command as follows:

```
> mysqladmin flush-all-statistics
```

If you prefer using a classical command, here's one:

```
MariaDB [(none)]> FLUSH STATUS;
```

That's it!

Global statistics

Here is an easy but often-forgotten command to quickly see the status of your MariaDB instance:

```
> mysqladmin status
Uptime: 22  Threads: 1  Questions: 88  Slow queries: 0  Opens: 99
Flush tables: 1  Open tables: 78  Queries per second avg: 4.000
```

Here, you've got one of the most important pieces of information. In this chapter, we'll see what all this information means.

DNS connections

Here is a basic option that can reduce the connection time.

 It's preferable to use an IP connection instead of DNS if you want to reduce latency. More than that, this will prevent your database server from going down when your DNS is down or responding slowly.

There is a configuration option that denies naming the connection that you can add to your MariaDB configuration file (`my.cnf`):

[mysqld]

skip_name_resolve

Before going ahead, you need to check the current configuration of your user with the allowed hostname. You need to check that no hostnames are present and check for wildcard hostnames as well:

```
MariaDB [(none)]> SELECT USER,HOST FROM mysql.user;
+------------------+-----------+
| USER             | HOST      |
+------------------+-----------+
| root             | 127.0.0.1 |
| root             | ::1       |
| debian-sys-maint | localhost |
| root             | localhost |
| root             | mariadb   |
+------------------+-----------+
```

In the HOST table, only the IP address should remain!

You now need to restart your MariaDB instance and check out the logs! It's preferable to validate that all your applications are correctly configured before making this change in production!

The DNS cache server

We covered the fastest solution in the previous sections. However, you may want to keep (for several reasons) the usage of the DNS.

If you do not care about latency, you can also add a local DNS cache server (on the same host as your MariaDB instance). For example, we can use a Bind9 server. Here is how to set one up:

```
> aptitude install bind9
```

Edit the `named.conf.options` file in `/etc/bind/`, and add your DNS servers in the `forwarders` brackets like this:

```
forwarders {
    8.8.8.8;
    8.8.4.4;
};
```

Then, start the Bind9 service. To finish, add a short `timeout` parameter in your `resolv.conf` file (in `/etc`) to quickly switch to another server in the event of a problem (here, 1 second):

```
domain example.com
search example.com
options timeout:1
nameserver 127.0.0.1
nameserver 8.8.8.8
nameserver 8.8.4.4
```

Now, to test the request, you can use the `dig` command and see where it goes if the bind server is either up or down:

```
> dig A mariadb.org
...
;; Query time: 59 msec
;; SERVER: 127.0.0.1#53(127.0.0.1)
;; WHEN: Tue Jun 17 11:38:00 2014
;; MSG SIZE  rcvd: 256
```

With the local DNS server, you will see a DNS request the first time, which could take up to several hundreds of milliseconds to resolve (depending on your network speed and DNS server availability).

The next time you need to access the record, it will take less than 10 milliseconds as it is in the cache (the cache will depend on the TTL of the record you're targeting).

Maximum connections

By default, MariaDB is configured for 150 connections plus one for root access if not already used (so 151 connections). In most cases, 150 is really enough, but it might not be in your case if you've got a lot of connection errors on your application.

The recommended action to change this value is the persistent way and then restarting MariaDB (of course, this will kill all the current persistent connections). So, change this value in the configuration file:

```
[mysqld]
max_connections = 200
```

After rebooting MariaDB, you should be able to see the new value:

```
MariaDB [(none)]> select @@global.max_connections;
+--------------------------+
| @@global.max_connections |
+--------------------------+
|                      200 |
+--------------------------+
```

You can change the number of connections on the fly like this:

```
MariaDB [(none)]> SET GLOBAL max_connections=1000;
```

However, you may be in a situation where no connections are available for you to connect. That's why there's a trick using gdb (the C debugger), and you need to have it installed on your server. This solution is not really recommended in production; anyway, if you really do not have the choice and prefer doing it this way instead of waiting for a reboot, here is the solution:

```
> gdb -p $(cat /var/run/mysqld/mysqld.pid) -ex "set
max_connections=1000" -batch
[Thread debugging using libthread_db enabled]
Using host libthread_db library "/lib/x86_64-linux-
gnu/libthread_db.so.1".
[New Thread 0x7f346abb4700 (LWP 3043)]
[New Thread 0x7f346b3fe700 (LWP 3035)]
[...]
[New Thread 0x7f34777fe700 (LWP 3003)]
[New Thread 0x7f3477fff700 (LWP 3002)]
[New Thread 0x7f34a2bff700 (LWP 3001)]
0x00007f34a3860e33 in poll () from /lib/x86_64-linux-gnu/libc.so.6
```

Now, if you look at the @@global.max_connections value, it will be set to 1000. This command will catch the PID of MariaDB, find the maximum_connections value in the memory, and change it to the one you've set.

You shouldn't go over 1,000 connections (threads) per instance, as the server may not be as responsive as it should be due to context switching, contention for hot locks, or bad CPU cache localities. The best way to avoid that is to change the way your application uses your MariaDB instance. Several solutions exist, such as using a connection pool or a thread pool, allowing you to have more than 15,000 connected threads.

The binlogs cache

The binlogs cache has been split into two versions, which are as follows:

- Transactional cache
- Nontransactional cache (introduced in version 5.5)

Both caches can be tuned, and their usage depends on the engine you're using. For example, InnoDB/XtraDB are transactional engines, while MyISAM is a nontransactional engine. There is, of course, no sense in tuning a transactional cache if you're only using the MyISAM engine, and vice versa. By the way, the transactional cache shouldn't move if you're not using it.

Binlogs are mandatory for replication systems. If the cache is not correctly used, the disk will be used and slowdowns are felt. So, the first thing to do is to check the correct usage of that cache.

Binlogs for transactional caches

For transactional caches, you need to check the global values:

```
MariaDB [(none)]> show global status like 'Binlog_cache%';
+-----------------------+-------+
| Variable_name         | Value |
+-----------------------+-------+
| Binlog_cache_disk_use | 0     |
| Binlog_cache_use      | 128   |
+-----------------------+-------+
2 rows in set (0.00 sec)
```

This cache is the transactional cache. This corresponds to the following:

- `Binlog_cache_use`: This value should grow to get maximum performance. This indicates how many transactions have been written to the cache. So, if it's growing, it means that the cache is used, and this is good.
- `Binlog_cache_disk_use`: This value should stay at `0`. If this value grows, it means that transactions were too big to enter into the cache (more than 32 K). So, the disk has to be used, which reduces the performance.

You can dynamically change the default size of the binlog cache (to 64 K for example) as follows:

```
MariaDB [(none)]> SET global binlog_cache_size=64*1024;
```

And you can set it in your configuration file (my.cnf) to be persistent as follows:

```
[mysqld]
binlog_cache_size = 64k
```

Do not go over 4 G of binlog cache to avoid performance degradation.

Binlogs for nontransactional caches

For nontransactional (statement) caches, it works exactly as it does for transactional caches. Here are the nontransactional binlog values:

```
MariaDB [(none)]> show global status like 'Binlog_stmt%';
+----------------------------+-------+
| Variable_name              | Value |
+----------------------------+-------+
| Binlog_stmt_cache_disk_use | 0     |
| Binlog_stmt_cache_use      | 68    |
+----------------------------+-------+
2 rows in set (0.00 sec)
```

To change the default size of the cache (32 K) to 64 K, the code is as follows:

```
MariaDB [(none)]> SET global binlog_stmt_cache_size=64*1024;
```

And to make it persistent, add this line to the configuration file:

```
[mysqld]
binlog_stmt_cache_size=64k;
```

Temporary tables

Temporary tables show you how many temporary files are created in the disk because they couldn't be set in memory. To show them, you can use the global status information:

```
MariaDB [(none)]> show global status like 'Created_tmp%';
+------------------------+--------+
| Variable_name          | Value  |
```

```
+------------------------+--------+
| Created_tmp_disk_tables | 13363  |
| Created_tmp_files       | 6      |
| Created_tmp_tables      | 107681 |
+------------------------+--------+
3 rows in set (0.00 sec)
```

You can see all the temporarily created disk tables, files, and tables here. Here is a description of them to better understand how they work:

- Created_tmp_disk_tables: This value should stay at 0 instead of getting BLOB or TEXT columns in your databases. They are used when the in-memory tables become too large.

- Created_tmp_files: This is how many temporary files were created. When Created_tmp_disk_tables is not enough, disk files are created, and the counter increments.

- Created_tmp_tables: This is the number of internal temporary tables created.

If the Created_tmp_disk_tables value becomes too big, you need to adjust the tmp_table_size or max_heap_table_size values. The maximum Created_tmp_disk_tables size is the minimum of tmp_table_size.

If you absolutely need BLOB or TEXT columns and want to have better performance, you should consider thinking about tmpfs as the temporary directory.

You can check these values in the global status values:

```
MariaDB [(none)]> show global variables like 'tmp_table_size';
+-----------------+----------+
| Variable_name   | Value    |
+-----------------+----------+
| tmp_table_size  | 33554432 |
+-----------------+----------+
1 row in set (0.00 sec)
MariaDB [(none)]> show global variables like 'max_heap_table_size';
+---------------------+----------+
| Variable_name       | Value    |
+---------------------+----------+
| max_heap_table_size | 33554432 |
+---------------------+----------+
1 row in set (0.00 sec)
```

The default value is 32 M. To set a new size, add the following lines in your MariaDB configuration file (`my.cnf`):

```
[mysqld]
tmp_table_size = 64M
max_heap_table_size = 64M
```

And if you want those new values to be applicable without restarting, here's how you can go about it:

```
MariaDB [(none)]> SET global tmp_table_size=64*1024*1024;

MariaDB [(none)]> SET global max_heap_table_size=64*1024*1024;
```

Open tables

Some tables can't be cached, and there are also statistics for them. In MySQL versions older than 5.1.3, the option was called `table_cache`. It's now called `table_open_cache` in MariaDB.

To view the current status, enter the following command:

```
MariaDB [(none)]> SHOW global STATUS LIKE 'Open%';
```

Variable_name	Value
Open_files	288
Open_streams	0
Open_table_definitions	329
Open_tables	222
Opened_files	767
Opened_table_definitions	296
Opened_tables	525
Opened_views	0

```
8 rows in set (0.00 sec)
```

We can see here the number of currently opening tables (222) and those already opened (525). Check regularly that the opened tables are not growing too fast. If this is the case, you should consider increasing the allocated memory for the table cache.

To see the current settings, run the following command:

```
MariaDB [(none)]> select @@table_open_cache;
+--------------------+
| @@table_open_cache |
+--------------------+
|                400 |
+--------------------+
1 row in set (0.00 sec)
```

Here, 400 is the default size for MariaDB 10.

Try to grow this value to get better performance. You should also take care about setting too high a value, which could result in a nonstarting MariaDB instance. This is generally because of the file descriptor limitation from your operating system.

If you want to get an idea of what the table_open_cache size should be, it's approximately max_connections * X. X represents the maximum number of tables per join of any executed queries.

Another important thing is that you shouldn't change this value on the fly to avoid side effects. So, to change this value, add the following line in your MariaDB configuration file:

```
[mysqld]
table_open_cache = 1024
```

Then, restart MariaDB to apply the new configuration.

 Do not set the table_open_cache value greater than 4096, or your performance could be degraded.

The table_definition_cache value speeds up table opening if there are a large number of tables increasing the cache size (the default is 400). So, if you have a lot of open tables, you should increase this value.

To optimize performance, add similar lines in your configuration file as follows:

```
[mysqld]
table_definition_cache = 16384
```

The query cache

The query cache stores the results of the previously executed `select` statements so that they may be reused if the same query is issued again. If data is updated/added to a table, the query cache is flushed, and the data should be retrieved once again from the disk on the next `SELECT` query.

When there are too many concurrencies, the query cache could be a bottleneck. Depending on the size of the database and the requested access, here are two scenarios:

- **Smaller database, no high load traffic, no money**: The query cache should help you to get fast database access
- **Huge database, high load traffic, money**: Disable the query cache, optimize your indexes, spread the read load across several read-only replicas, and use a better caching mechanism, such as Memcache/Redis

A lot of common rules exist, but that doesn't mean they should always be applied. If you do not encounter slowdown due to the query cache, it's fine! You can even tune it to make it faster.

Understanding the query cache

To check whether the query cache is enabled, run the following command:

```
MariaDB [(none)]> SHOW VARIABLES LIKE 'query_cache_type';
+------------------+-------+
| Variable_name    | Value |
+------------------+-------+
| query_cache_type | ON    |
+------------------+-------+
1 row in set (0.01 sec)
```

Here it is! If this is not the case, you can enable it by adding the following line in your MariaDB configuration file (`my.cnf`):

```
[mysqld]
query_cache_type = 1
```

You unfortunately can't set it dynamically if it was disabled at the start, but you can disable it if it was enabled at start. The `query_cache_type` parameters can have three different values:

- **0/disabled**: No queries are cached
- **1/enabled**: All the queries are cached instead of only those that contain the `SQL_NO_CACHE` clause
- **2/demand**: No queries are cached instead of only those that contain the `SQL_CACHE` clause

To look at the query cache values, enter the following command:

```
MariaDB [(none)]> SHOW global STATUS LIKE 'Qc%';
+-------------------------+-----------+
| Variable_name           | Value     |
+-------------------------+-----------+
| Qcache_free_blocks      | 1158      |
| Qcache_free_memory      | 225271912 |
| Qcache_hits             | 12206713  |
| Qcache_inserts          | 8989093   |
| Qcache_lowmem_prunes    | 0         |
| Qcache_not_cached       | 2696299   |
| Qcache_queries_in_cache | 90748     |
| Qcache_total_blocks     | 183057    |
+-------------------------+-----------+
8 rows in set (0.00 sec)
```

Here is an explanation of those variables:

- `Qcache_free_memory`: This is the available memory to store queries (SQL request and results queries).
- `Qcache_hits`: This value corresponds to the number of times the cache has been hit.
- `Qcache_inserts`: This is the number of queries that have entered the cache. To get the correct performance and validate whether the Qcache is finely used, the `Qcache_hits` value should be greater than that of `Qcache_inserts`.
- `Qcache_lowmem_prunes`: If there is not enough space in the cache, the oldest requests will be replaced by new ones.

- Qcache_not_cached: This represents the queries that were not cached. This value is important to know whether you have changed the query_cache_type value to force queries to be cached or if you have disabled Qcache because queries couldn't be cached.

Depending on the applications that are using your databases, the query cache may not be as efficient as it should be in some cases. Here are the important items that you should take into consideration to know whether you have to keep the query cache or not:

- If the Qcache_hits value is less than Qcache_inserts, you should consider disabling the query cache in most cases. This is not true if you have one query hitting 100 percent of the query cache, and removing it can cause disastrous performance.
- MariaDB has a feature to list the queries in the query cache.
- If the Qcache_not_cached value is less than the addition of the Qcache_hits and Qcache_inserts values, try to grow the query cache size and the per-query cache size. Then, if Qcache_not_cached is still growing, disable the query cache.
- If the Qcache_lowmem_prunes value is growing, add more memory to the Qcache.

Modifying the query cache

To get the current set memory for the query cache, run the following command:

```
MariaDB [(none)]> SHOW global VARIABLES LIKE 'query_cache%';
+-----------------------------+----------+
| Variable_name               | Value    |
+-----------------------------+----------+
| query_cache_limit           | 131072   |
| query_cache_min_res_unit    | 4096     |
| query_cache_size            | 67108864 |
| query_cache_strip_comments  | OFF      |
| query_cache_type            | ON       |
| query_cache_wlock_invalidate | OFF     |
+-----------------------------+----------+
6 rows in set (0.00 sec)
```

The important new information here is as follows:

- `query_cache_size`: This is the dedicated memory size for Qcache. Here, we've got 64 MB.

- `query_cache_limit`: This is the size of the maximum cache size per query.

To change those settings on the fly with 2 MB per query and 128 MB for the query cache, use the following commands:

```
MariaDB [(none)]> SET global query_cache_limit = 2*1024*1024;
MariaDB [(none)]> SET global query_cache_size = 128*1024*1024;
```

> You should avoid having a query cache with more than 256 MB to avoid performance issues.

To set it as persistent, add the following lines to your MariaDB configuration file:

```
[mysqld]
query_cache_limit = 2M
query_cache_size = 128M
```

Optimizing storage engines

In this section, you will learn how to get maximum benefit from using the storage engines. They are all working differently and all have different kinds of optimizations.

Entering each engine and seeing all the advanced features really goes beyond the scope of this book. So, here we will see the most common engines optimizations that can enhance performance. In addition, as some MariaDB engines are still not fully implemented, we'll cover the most used engines that you generally have in production.

Summarizing your databases

To get your database, index, and table sizes, run the following command:

```
MariaDB [(none)]> SELECT
TABLE_SCHEMA,ENGINE,SUM(TABLE_ROWS),SUM(DATA_LENGTH),SUM(INDEX_LENGTH
) FROM INFORMATION_SCHEMA.TABLES GROUP BY ENGINE,TABLE_SCHEMA ORDER
BY TABLE_SCHEMA;
```

The output of this command is shown in the following screenshot:

```
+--------------------+--------------------+----------------+-------------------+--------------------+
| TABLE_SCHEMA       | ENGINE             | SUM(TABLE_ROWS) | SUM(DATA_LENGTH) | SUM(INDEX_LENGTH)  |
+--------------------+--------------------+----------------+-------------------+--------------------+
| chapter2           | InnoDB             |          10157 |            393216 |             278528 |
| information_schema | MEMORY             |           NULL |                 0 |                  0 |
| information_schema | Aria               |           NULL |             81920 |              81920 |
| mysql              | CSV                |              4 |                 0 |                  0 |
| mysql              | MyISAM             |           2047 |            555990 |             120832 |
| mysql              | InnoDB             |             21 |             49152 |                  0 |
| performance_schema | PERFORMANCE_SCHEMA |          74026 |                 0 |                  0 |
+--------------------+--------------------+----------------+-------------------+--------------------+
7 rows in set (0.01 sec)
```

As you can see here, we've got a lot of different engines and interesting information:

- SUM(DATA_LENGTH): Data size without indexes
- SUM(INDEX_LENGTH): Index size without data

> Running this kind of query is resource expensive. It may freeze the server for several minutes if you have a large number of tables. You can easily count 10 minutes if you have 10,000 tables and 1 minute if you disable innodb_stats_on_metadata:
>
> **MariaDB [(none)]> SET innodb_stats_on_metadata = 0;**

InnoDB/XtraDB

The InnoDB storage engine is one of the most used engines for high load traffic after memory. Why? Because it is able to cache in RAM data and indexes.

But there is a cost for that performance! The cost is you need to have more than enough free RAM available than the database size. This is because indexes are cached as well. Typical values for InnoDB are shown in the following table:

Database size	RAM available for InnoDB
5 to 6 GB	8 GB
20 to 25 GB	32 GB
110 to 120 GB	128 GB

These are typical values, but what really counts is the size of the active working set. You can find this information by looking at the buffer pool hit ratio in the status variables. That's why it's important to have enough RAM! If you do not, your performance will be slower than MyISAM, and you may think about using another storage engine, such as TokuDB.

XtraDB (Percona) is an enhanced version of InnoDB to scale better and get better performance. It's backward compatible and is named as InnoDB (ENGINE=InnoDB) on MariaDB. So, you'll never see XtraDB as the storage engine but InnoDB instead, even if XtraDB is being used. You can see the XtraDB engine loading in the MariaDB logs. In fact, it's a drop-in replacement for InnoDB.

Pool size and statistics

The best way to know exactly how much RAM you should reserve for the engine is to show the engine statistics by running the following command:

```
MariaDB [(none)]> SHOW engine innodb STATUS\G;
*************************** 1. row ***************************
  Type: InnoDB
[...]
---------------------
BUFFER POOL AND MEMORY
---------------------
Total memory allocated 826540032; in additional pool allocated 0
Total memory allocated by read views 112
Internal hash tables (constant factor + variable factor)
    Adaptive hash index 18423648    (12750568 + 5673080)
    Page hash           797656 (buffer pool 0 only)
    Dictionary cache    4132069    (3189008 + 943061)
    File system         171664    (82672 + 88992)
    Lock system         1993392    (1993016 + 376)
    Recovery system     0    (0 + 0)
Dictionary memory allocated 943061
Buffer pool size         49151
Buffer pool size, bytes 805289984
Free buffers             18830
Database pages           29975
Old database pages       11052
```

```
Modified db pages        0
Pending reads 0
Pending writes: LRU 0, flush list 0, single page 0
Pages made young 50, not young 0
0.00 youngs/s, 0.00 non-youngs/s
Pages read 28131, created 1844, written 281524
0.00 reads/s, 0.00 creates/s, 16.12 writes/s
Buffer pool hit rate 1000 / 1000, young-making rate 0 / 1000 not 0 /
1000
Pages read ahead 0.00/s, evicted without access 0.00/s, Random read
ahead 0.00/s
LRU len: 29975, unzip_LRU len: 0
I/O sum[0]:cur[0], unzip sum[0]:cur[0]
[...]
1 row in set (0.00 sec)
```

Here, we can see a lot of interesting information:

- `Buffer pool size`: 49151 * 16 * 1024 = 768 MB
- `Free buffers`: 18830 * 16 * 1024 = 294 MB

We can see here that the dedicated space for the InnoDB cache is enough. If this isn't the case, you can set a higher value to the buffer pool size in your MariaDB configuration file using the following command:

```
[mysqld]
innodb_buffer_pool_size = 1024M
```

Then, you need to restart your MariaDB instance for the changes to take effect.

Redo logs

Redo logs are used to make sure that your data is safe and that recovery is possible after a crash. Since MariaDB 5.5, the performance of redo logs has been good, so you should consider keeping them to get better security for your data even if you have a little lower performance on very intensive writes.

You can change the size of the redo logs, but this will involve removing the current ones to avoid errors on the next boot. Here is the procedure:

1. Change the size of the redo logs per file (2 by default) in your configuration file:

    ```
    [mysqld]
    innodb_log_file_size = 512M
    ```

2. Force the syncing data to the redo logs:

    ```
    MariaDB [(none)]> SET GLOBAL innodb_fast_shutdown = 0;
    ```

3. Stop the MariaDB instance:

    ```
    service mysql stop
    ```

4. Remove the current redo logs:

    ```
    rm -f /var/lib/mysql/ib_logfile*
    ```

5. Start MariaDB:

    ```
    service mysql start
    ```

Here, the dedicated size for the redo logs is set to 512 MB.

To calculate the right size of the redo logs, you have to calculate how much data is written in 1 hour. If the server writes 95 MB, you should set it to 64 MB (because there are two redo log files by default). The bigger the redo log files, the more the recovery time will be.

But if you get intensive writes on your databases, you can grow this value up to a maximum of 64 GB.

Transaction commits and logs

There is an option that can affect performance that is called `innodb_flush_log_at_trx_commit`. You can see the current value of it using the following command:

```
MariaDB [(none)]> SHOW SESSION VARIABLES LIKE
'innodb_flush_log_at_trx_commit';
+---------------------------------+-------+
| Variable_name                   | Value |
+---------------------------------+-------+
| innodb_flush_log_at_trx_commit  | 1     |
+---------------------------------+-------+
1 row in set (0.00 sec)
```

There are several options for it:

- 1: InnoDB is Atomicity, Consistency, Isolation, Durability (**ACID**) compliant. This is the best choice when you are searching for the safest solution for your data. But you can get an overhead if you have slow disks as an `fsync` is made to flush each change to the redo logs.

- 2: This solution is less safe as the transactions are only flushed to the disk (to the redo logs) once per second. This would not be a problem if you're using replication.

- 0: This is the fastest solution, and you can set this value only if you're in a full sync replica situation, or data may be lost. This is the most dangerous of the three as it can lead to complete database corruption, and it can be impossible to start. Use this only on slaves.

To change the value, modify it in your configuration file to make it permanent:

```
[mysqld]
innodb_flush_log_at_trx_commit = 2
sync_binlog=0
```

Another important setting is the `sync_binlog` value. Setting this value to 1, MariaDB will synchronize the binary logs to disk after every `sync_binlog` write, so this is the best solution for safe data. But the best solution for performance is to set this value to 0. It's preferable to get get a RAID card with battery protection if you choose the 0 value.

If you're using replication and want to also have good performance, you can use a group commit as follows:

```
[mysqld]
flush_log_at_trx_commit =1
sync_binlog =1
```

You can check the value using the following command:

```
MariaDB [(none)]> SHOW SESSION VARIABLES LIKE 'sync_binlog';
+---------------+-------+
| Variable_name | Value |
+---------------+-------+
| sync_binlog   | 1     |
+---------------+-------+
1 row in set (0.00 sec)
```

And to change it on the fly, the command is as follows:

```
MariaDB [(none)]> SET global sync_binlog=0;

MariaDB [(none)]> SET GLOBAL innodb_flush_log_at_trx_commit=2;
```

There are other options that can permit us to change the checkpoint value (writing modified pages in memory to table files). By default, the value is 200, but you can change it if you have RAID 10, SSD, or Fusion IO cards.

For instance, here are the basic values that you can set to the innodb_io_capacity· parameter:

Storage type	The innodb_io_capacity value
HDD	200
RAID 10 HDD	1,000
SSD	5,000
Fusion IO	10,000

Of course, these values may change a little depending on your hardware. You should consider benchmarking your hardware I/O capacity before setting a value to be sure that it can handle it well.

The last important option is innodb_max_dirty_pages_pct. This is the percentage of the maximum dirty pages contained in the InnoDB/XtraDB buffer pool size you've set.

For example, if you've set a buffer pool size equal to 100 GB and your redo logs are set to 2 GB, by default, you will allow only 75 percent of the modified data in RAM. But the redo logs' (ib_logfile) size is only 2 GB! Reducing the percentage of innodb_max_dirty_pages_pct will make InnoDB/XtraDB flush more often, and you'll be better protected against a crashing system.

So, you can set a lower value in your MariaDB configuration file (my.cnf) as follows:

```
[mysqld]
innodb_io_capacity = 1000
innodb_max_dirty_pages_pct = 85
```

Buffer pool instances

The innodb_buffer_pool_instances parameter is used when the innodb_buffer_pool_size value is greater than 1 GB. It divides the buffer pool size into a number of instances (the default value is 1).

But if the buffer pool size is too high, you need to change this value to reduce contention concurrency. This is done by having several instances. Each one will have its own data structures. Here is the formula:

instance size = innodb_buffer_pool_size / innodb_buffer_pool_instance

You shouldn't have less than 1 GB per instance to get good performance. To get the current value, use the following command:

```
MariaDB [(none)]> show variables like 'innodb_buffer_pool_instances';
+------------------------------+-------+
| Variable_name                | Value |
+------------------------------+-------+
| innodb_buffer_pool_instances | 1     |
+------------------------------+-------+
1 row in set (0.00 sec)
```

And to set this value permanently, update your configuration file as follows:

```
[mysqld]
innodb_buffer_pool_instances = 4
```

The flush method

The flush method mechanism permits you to control how your data and logs are going to be flushed to disk. If you have the RAID hardware with battery protection on the write-back cache and fdatasync, you can set the value to O_DIRECT. It is made to avoid double cache buffering between the filesystem cache and InnoDB cache (which is a waste).

To check the current value, run the following commands:

```
MariaDB [(none)]> SHOW SESSION VARIABLES LIKE 'innodb_flush_method';
+---------------------+----------+
| Variable_name       | Value    |
+---------------------+----------+
| innodb_flush_method | O_DIRECT |
+---------------------+----------+
1 row in set (0.00 sec)
```

To set it permanently, add the following line in your MariaDB configuration file:

```
[mysqld]
innodb_flush_method = O_DIRECT
```

You have just changed this value on the fly and now need to reboot your instance to apply your changes.

The other possibility, if you do not have a RAID card, is to set the value to O_DSYNC. It's strongly recommended to test both the scenarios and choose the best solution depending on your hardware.

TokuDB

TokuDB is a highly scalable engine provided by Tokutek (http://www.tokutek.com). It provides good performance for any database size (marketed as a big data engine). Here are some benefits of this engine:

- Up to 20 times more improvement in insertions and indexing
- No replication slave lags
- High compression (LZMA)
- Fast schema changes (hot indexes, hot column addition)
- Fractal trees (no fragmentation)
- Less memory usage (compared to InnoDB)

To get good performance, it's recommended to get at least 2 GB of main memory on your system.

Installation

TokuDB is available in MariaDB 5.5.33 and MariaDB 10.0.5. The official TokuDB version differs from the MariaDB integrated version because MariaDB developers don't want to add too much code in the stable version. The full features will be added in the next stages.

Even if TokuDB is present in MariaDB, it's not activated by default. To enable it, you need to uncomment the plugin line in the tokudb.cnf file at /etc/mysql/conf.d/:

```
[mariadb]
# See https://mariadb.com/kb/en/how-to-enable-tokudb-in-mariadb/
# for instructions how to enable TokuDB
#
# See https://mariadb.com/kb/en/tokudb-differences/ for
differences
```

```
# between TokuDB in MariaDB and TokuDB from
http://www.tokutek.com/

# For MariaDB 10
plugin-load-add=ha_tokudb.so
# For MariaDB 5.5
# plugin-load=ha_tokudb.so
```

On the Linux kernel, when transparent hugepages are enabled, TokuKV
(transactional key-value) counters problems for the memory usage tracking
calculation. This can lead to memory overcommit and TokuKV won't start.

To check the current value, use the following command:

```
> cat /sys/kernel/mm/transparent_hugepage/enabled
[always] madvise never
```

If it's not disabled (the never value), you have to add an option to Grub to enable it
on boot (/etc/default/grub):

```
GRUB_CMDLINE_LINUX_DEFAULT="quiet transparent_hugepage=never"
```

Then, update your Grub to make the transparent hugepages active on the next reboot:

```
> update-grub2
```

So now, you have to reboot your machine to get the transparent hugepages disabled.

To check whether the transparent hugepages have been correctly enabled, run the
following command:

```
MariaDB [(none)]> show engines\G;
[...]
*************************** 6. row ***************************
      Engine: TokuDB
     Support: YES
     Comment: Tokutek TokuDB Storage Engine with Fractal Tree(tm)
Technology
Transactions: YES
          XA: YES
  Savepoints: YES
*************************** 7. row ***************************
[...]
11 rows in set (0.00 sec)
```

Performance Optimizations

The flush method

The flush method works like the InnoDB engine. You have the choice to get either direct I/O or buffered I/O caching. By default, it is set to buffer, but you can have better performance with direct I/O caching (depending on your hardware). Do not forget to get a RAID card with battery protection on the write-back cache.

As you can't change this value on the fly, you need to add it in the configuration file of MariaDB and then restart the process:

```
[mariadb]
tokudb_directio = 1
```

Another important point is that if you choose direct I/O, you will need to change the default cache size!

Cache size

By default, the cache size is automatically set when TokuDB is loaded, and it depends on the memory hardware size. It will take half of the system memory.

You do not need to allow more than the automatic calculated size as the OS cache is getting data in a compressed form inside its cache. And as the TokuDB cache gets data in an uncompressed form, you allow the OS cache to be bigger, which means more data (as compressed) in memory!

 If you're using the direct I/O flush method, you will have to take 80 percent of the main memory!

Anyway, you can check the cache size if you really want to. To check this value, run the following command:

```
MariaDB [(none)]> show global variables like 'tokudb_cache%';
+--------------------+-----------+
| Variable_name      | Value     |
+--------------------+-----------+
| tokudb_cache_size  | 260491264 |
+--------------------+-----------+
1 row in set (0.00 sec)
```

This value unfortunately cannot be updated on the fly. So, if you want to change it, you have to set it in the MariaDB configuration file:

```
[mariadb]
tokudb_cache_size = 512M
```

As explained, you now need to reboot your MariaDB instance to change this value.

Transaction commits and logs

Like the `innodb_flush_log_at_trx_commit` InnoDB option, TokuDB can change the way it writes data to disk.

TokuDB provides an option called `tokudb_commit_sync`, and here are the possible values:

- 1: The logfile is `fsynced` at each transaction commit. This is safe but is the slowest method.
- 0: This disables fsync on each commit but not fsync on each checkpoint. This is less safe, but is the faster method.

To get the current status of the commit sync, use the following command:

```
MariaDB [(none)]> show global variables like '%tokudb_commit%';
+---------------------+-------+
| Variable_name       | Value |
+---------------------+-------+
| tokudb_commit_sync  | ON    |
+---------------------+-------+
1 row in set (0.00 sec)
```

Here, it is enabled. But if we want to be faster, then allow up to 1 second of data loss in the case of a crash:

```
[mariadb]
tokudb_commit_sync = 0
tokudb_fsync_log_period = 1000
```

And if you want to do it on the fly, run the following commands:

```
MariaDB [(none)]> SET global tokudb_commit_sync = 0
MariaDB [(none)]> SET global tokudb_fsync_log_period = 1000
```

Temporary directory

If you've set the temporary directory as a `tmpfs` filesystem, you can update the TokuDB configuration as well to take advantage of it:

```
[mariadb]
tokudb_tmp_dir = /var/tmp
```

It won't have a big performance impact, but this will be the fastest solution for temporary files.

Compression

One of the most interesting features of TokuDB is compression. It is always enabled, uses ZLIB by default, and you can use a different algorithm per table. It saves you disk space and money. Four types of compression exist, which are as follows:

- **UNCOMPRESSED**: This type has no compression
- **QUICKLZ**: This type has light compression but less CPU usage
- **ZLIB**: This type has medium compression but more CPU usage than QUICKLZ
- **LZMA**: This type has the best compression, but it is CPU intensive

Compression is done in the background and doesn't affect your database performance. Anyways, it takes more CPU than uncompressed tables and requirements exist, as follows:

- If your server runs more than six cores, you can use LZMA.
- If your server runs less than six cores, it's recommended to use QUICKLZ or ZLIB.
- To look at the default compression algorithm when you create a new table, use the following code:

```
MariaDB [(none)]> show global variables like '%tokudb_row%';
+--------------------+-------------+
| Variable_name      | Value       |
+--------------------+-------------+
| tokudb_row_format  | tokudb_zlib |
+--------------------+-------------+
1 row in set (0.00 sec)
```

As you can see, this is ZLIB.

- To change it, simply prefix the algorithm with `tokudb_`:

```
MariaDB [(none)]> set global tokudb_row_format=tokudb_lzma;
```

- And if you want to make it persistent, add it to your MariaDB configuration file:

```
[mariadb]
tokudb_row_format = tokudb_lzma
```

MyISAM

For the past several years, MyISAM has been the default storage for MySQL (since 3.23). It has also been the default engine up to the 5.5 version of MariaDB.

It has a small data footprint, has good performance, and it is light, but it is nontransactional. If you don't want to do a lot of modification on your applications that use MyISAM and absolutely need some MyISAM features, you should consider moving to the Aria engine. Aria will have better performance and provide interesting features such as transactions. Aria has been designed to replace the MyISAM engine.

By default, on MariaDB, all the temporary tables created on the disk use the Aria storage engine. To reverse the change to MyISAM, you will need to recompile.

Key buffer

The MyISAM storage engine uses a key buffer to cache indexes on the disk. To check the current state of the key buffer cache, use the following command:

```
MariaDB [(none)]> SHOW global STATUS LIKE 'key%';
+------------------------+---------+
| Variable_name          | VALUE   |
+------------------------+---------+
| Key_blocks_not_flushed | 0       |
| Key_blocks_unused      | 14497   |
| Key_blocks_used        | 12268   |
| Key_blocks_warm        | 3214    |
| Key_read_requests      | 2413795 |
| Key_reads              | 67366   |
| Key_write_requests     | 106173  |
| Key_writes             | 104947  |
+------------------------+---------+
8 ROWS IN SET (0.00 sec)
```

Here is the explanation of some of these variables:

- `Key_reads_requests`: This represents the number of requests to read a key block from the cache

- `Key_reads`: This represents the number of physical reads of a key block from the disk

- `Key_writes_requests`: This represents the number of requests to write a key block from the cache

- `Key_writes`: This represents the number of requests to write a key block from the cache

To know whether your read cache is set correctly, use the following formulas:

Read cache efficiency = key_reads_requests/ key_reads

Write cache efficiency = key_writes_requests/key_writes

You can consider that if the read and write cache efficiency is more than 10, you don't really need to adjust it.

You can check the current buffer size value using the following command:

```
MariaDB [(none)]> SHOW variables LIKE 'key_buffer%';
+------------------+-----------+
| Variable_name    | Value     |
+------------------+-----------+
| key_buffer_size  | 134217728 |
+------------------+-----------+
1 row in set (0.00 sec)
```

You can change this value in the MariaDB configuration file using the following code:

```
[mysql]
key_buffer_size          = 128M
```

Then, restart the MariaDB instance.

Index

This chapter cannot end without discussing indexes. Entering into the details of indexes could be long drawn out and is out of the scope of this book. Anyway, we'll talk about them a bit and see what you should take care about.

Most of the time, indexes are the way to get very good query result performances. But if they are badly used, they could have an inverted effect.

Let's say your application makes a search on several columns. First of all, run an `explain` command on the desired query and see what the explanation recommends. Maybe it will recommend to add some specific indexes to the columns. Do not add too many indexes only on the most used columns, or you'll waste resources.

If your application uses small tables, indexes won't make performance better. Indexes are useful on large tables.

Engines

First, you have to know that there exist three kinds of index engines in the default MariaDB installation, as follows:

- **BTREE**: This is the most commonly used index engine, which is used for column comparison (only for InnoDB/XtraDB)
- **RTREE**: This is used for spacial columns, such as geographical coordinates, rectangles, or polygons (only for MyISAM/Aria)
- **HASH**: This is used for equal comparison (only in memory) and also internally in an InnoDB-adaptive Hash index (you cannot control it but only enable or disable it)

Types

There are four kinds of indexes in MariaDB:

- Primary key
- Unique index
- Plain index
- Full-text index

If the desired query is using `LIKE` with a `%` sign, it's recommended to use a full-text index, or your table will be analyzed each time. This will result in a big slowdown. Unfortunately, some storage engines do not support the use of a full-text index, and you should check this before trying to apply it.

Better full-text search engines, such as Sphinx, Elasticsearch, Lucene, and Solr, are suited for full-text searching and can each be a very good complement to MariaDB.

If you have a huge table with high read and write loads, you should consider delaying the writes by using `batch`. This will reduce the number of I/O disks.

mysqltuner

`mysqltuner` is a tool that helps you quickly analyze a running MariaDB instance and gives you basic information to optimize it. Take care about the suggestions; the tool doesn't really know what you're doing with your application. However, it's generally a good way to start the first analysis.

The current Debian version (available in the default Debian repository) is unfortunately not yet MariaDB 10 compatible. That's why you should take the latest version, which is partially MariaDB 10 compatible, for the moment (version 1.3.0). To install it, run the following commands:

```
> wget -O /usr/bin/mysqltuner
https://raw.githubusercontent.com/major/MySQLTuner-perl/master/
mysqltuner.pl

> chmod 755 /usr/bin/mysqltuner
```

Now, you can launch it and see the recommendations made by the tool. Run the following commands:

```
> mysqltuner

  >>  MySQLTuner 1.3.0 - Major Hayden <major@mhtx.net>

  >>  Bug reports, feature requests, and downloads at
http://mysqltuner.com/

  >>  Run with '--help' for additional options and output filtering

[OK] Logged in using credentials from debian maintenance account.

[!!] Currently running unsupported MySQL version 10.0.12-MariaDB-
1~wheezy-log

[OK] Operating on 64-bit architecture


-------- Storage Engine Statistics -------------------------------------
-----

[--] Status: +ARCHIVE +Aria +BLACKHOLE +CSV +FEDERATED +InnoDB
+MRG_MyISAM

[--] Data in MyISAM tables: 166M (Tables: 84)

[--] Data in InnoDB tables: 763M (Tables: 293)

[--] Data in PERFORMANCE_SCHEMA tables: 0B (Tables: 52)

[--] Data in MEMORY tables: 0B (Tables: 1)

[!!] Total fragmented tables: 49
```

-------- Security Recommendations ---------------------------------------
-----

[OK] All database users have passwords assigned

-------- Performance Metrics ---

[--] Up for: 9d 2h 43m 31s (37M q [47.313 qps], 291K conn, TX:
42B, RX: 6B)

[--] Reads / Writes: 88% / 12%

[--] Total buffers: 1.3G global + 23.3M per thread (100 max
threads)

[OK] Maximum possible memory usage: 3.6G (11% of installed RAM)

[OK] Slow queries: 0% (325/37M)

[OK] Highest usage of available connections: 33% (33/100)

[OK] Key buffer size / total MyISAM indexes: 128.0M/35.9M

[OK] Key buffer hit rate: 97.9% (22M cached / 464K reads)

[OK] Query cache efficiency: 36.3% (15M cached / 42M selects)

[!!] Query cache prunes per day: 127508

[OK] Sorts requiring temporary tables: 0% (0 temp sorts / 253K
sorts)

[!!] Joins performed without indexes: 3127

[OK] Temporary tables created on disk: 15% (133K on disk / 851K
total)

[OK] Thread cache hit rate: 99% (33 created / 291K connections)

[!!] Table cache hit rate: 0% (457 open / 2M opened)

[OK] Open file limit used: 22% (229/1K)

[OK] Table locks acquired immediately: 99% (16M immediate / 16M
locks)

[OK] InnoDB buffer pool / data size: 768.0M/763.6M

[OK] InnoDB log waits: 0

-------- Recommendations ---

General recommendations:

    Run OPTIMIZE TABLE to defragment tables for better performance

    Increasing the query_cache size over 128M may reduce
performance

    Adjust your join queries to always utilize indexes

    Increase table_open_cache gradually to avoid file descriptor
limits

```
    Read this before increasing table_open_cache over 64:
http://bit.ly/1mi7c4C
Variables to adjust:
    query_cache_size (> 384M) [see warning above]
    join_buffer_size (> 16.0M, or always use indexes with joins)
    table_open_cache (> 457)
```

You can now see the suggested variables to adjust. Be sure that you've ran MariaDB for at least 24 hours with normal traffic load to get relevant recommendations.

Summary

You've seen important tips here to get better performance using several stable engines used in production. Other engines exist but are not so common in production or not stable enough to figure out in this chapter.

Remember that if you have slowness on your application, and if it's due to the database, here is what you should check:

- Look out for any long requests (slow queries), and try to optimize them with the `explain` command
- Be sure you're using a good engine and have correctly tuned it
- Verify whether you're using indexes only where they are needed
- Be sure your hardware is correctly tuned for high performance
- If all these steps are alright, you should consider going ahead with the next chapters

Tuning MariaDB performance does not require you to change a lot of parameters, but only the most important ones. The rest of the performance will be achieved by tuning your schema, your indexes, and your application!

In the next chapter, we'll start discussing architectures and how to make a replication slave.

4
MariaDB Replication

MariaDB replication is a mechanism that permits us to replicate data to another instance on another host. Replication is generally used for the following reasons:

- **Scale out reads**: Replication permits scaling between several read databases to grow the read capacity
- **Providing high availability**: With multiple slaves, you have no read **Single Point Of Failure (SPOF)**
- **Data analysis**: Replication can be useful to have a replicated environment to allow querying without impacting the production environment
- **Disaster recovery**: You can have a distant copy of a master if a major issue occurs on your primary site
- **Security**: Replication can be used to add a read-only database on a DMZ for example

Replication works in an asynchronous mode, which means, if you have a low or degraded bandwidth, you will have a replication delta (slave late/with more delay) depending on your write load. The more write queries you have, the more information will need to be replicated and the faster the network line should be. In the best cases, the replication time difference could be in seconds or minutes, but in the worst cases it can be an hour or several hours.

You can replicate all the databases, selected databases, or some tables in a database.

In this chapter, we will see several ways to build slaves, how to manage them, how to avoid problems, and the advantages and possibilities of these solutions. You also have some architecture examples of slave replications to help you define a good solution for your needs.

To help you to test a replication process, here is a `Vagrantfile` that will start two MariaDB instances. The following diagram shows the architecture we're going to set up:

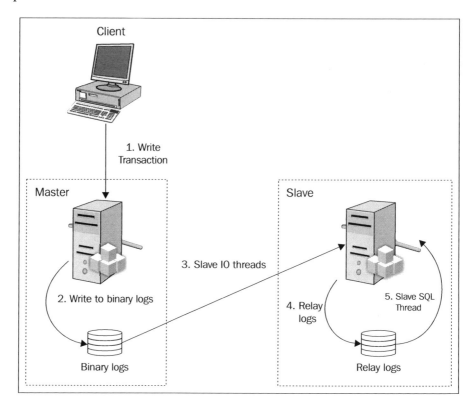

To make it simpler, we've got a dedicated network here for the replication with this information:

- Master node IP (master node): `192.168.33.31`
- Slave1 node IP (classical replication node): `192.168.33.32`
- Slave2 node IP (gtid replication node): `192.168.33.33`
- Load Balancer node IP (haproxy): `192.168.33.40`

You've noticed that the `Vagrantfile` has changed a little as we've got new roles:

- **db**: For database purposes, it installs MariaDB and the percona repository
- **lb**: This is the load balancer, it installs haproxy

How replication works

The following diagram shows how the replication process works:

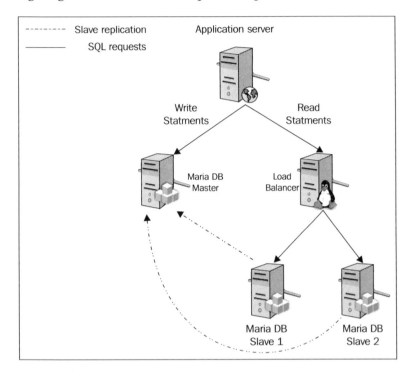

A little explanation makes it easier to understand the process:

1. A client requests a write transaction on the master host.
2. The binary logs (also called binlogs) are updated. The binary logs contain events that describe database changes.
3. The slave receives the information from the master.
4. It then appends it to its relay logs.
5. The slave SQL thread replays the statements contained in the relay logs.

There are 2 kinds of replication mechanisms:

*   **Standard replication**: This is the most common method, standard, each node has its own transaction ID
*   **Global Transaction ID (GTID) replication**: GTID permits each node to have the same transaction ID on all replicated nodes (only available from MariaDB 10)

We will see both the mechanisms and understand the advantages of GTID. In both the cases, when a network cut occurs, it is able to automatically reconnect and resume the replication (depending on the retention days).

Now, since you know a little bit more about the functional aspect, we're going to practice it. The standard replication was released on MySQL 5.0 first and is still available on MariaDB 10.

Configuring the master node

The first thing to do is to prepare the master node. We need to activate some options in its configuration file (my.cnf):

```
[mysqld]
server-id=1
bind-address = 0.0.0.0
log_bin=/var/log/mysql/mariadb-bin
```

These are the minimum options. Let's study them in detail:

- server-id: This should be a unique ID. Here, we've chosen 1 but you can choose a number up to 2^32-1.

- bind-address: This is the IP address on which the MariaDB instance should listen. By default, it is 127.0.0.1. You can bind it to 192.168.33.31 if you want to listen only on this interface. With 0.0.0.0, we want to bind on all available interfaces.

- log-bin: This is where you can store the binary logs.

Now, we are able to build a master/slave replication. There are other options that you should be aware of:

```
expire_logs_days=10
sync_binlog = 1
slave_compressed_protocol
transaction-isolation = READ COMMITTED
binlog_format = row
```

Let's see how useful these options can be:

- expire_logs_days: This is the number of days for binlogs retention. This is generally used to avoid binlogs taking all the disk space indefinitely. After 10 days (here), it is automatically flushed.

This also means if you have a delta between your master and your slave that is bigger than 10 days, you won't be able to resume the replication but you will need to do a full sync instead!

- `sync_binlog`: This will synchronize the binary logfile to the disk (flush) after each write event. Set this value to 1 to activate this functionality. This is the safest choice but also the slowest. Disable it if you need more replication performances.

- `slave_compressed_protocol`: This will use compression if the slave gets the option too. This consumes a little bit more of CPU, but makes the replication faster.

- `binlog_format`: This chooses which kind of binlog format you want (row, statement, or mixed). The row format is the best to guarantee safe replications.

Now, restart your MariaDB master instance to activate your new options.

Preparing the master node

As your master is ready to serve now, you will need a dedicated account for replication. This account will only have the replication rights. Of course, you can add more rights to this dedicated user or choose an existing user, but it's not recommended for security reasons.

So on the master, create a dedicated user (for security reasons) that is allowed to connect from the slave server (here, `192.168.33.32`):

```
MariaDB [(none)]> create user 'replication'@'192.168.33.32'
identified by 'password';
```

You should change the username and password; there is no restriction on the username.

Then, grant the replication privileges to all the databases to make it easy:

```
MariaDB [(none)]> grant replication slave on *.* to
'replication'@'192.168.33.32';
```

There are no obligations to grant privileges on all databases. You can select the restricted databases here, but other options exist to restrict the database access.

Now, reload the privileges:

```
MariaDB [(none)]> FLUSH PRIVILEGES;
```

Let's now look at the master information:

```
MariaDB [(none)]> show master status;
+--------------------+----------+--------------+------------------+
| File               | Position | Binlog_Do_DB | Binlog_Ignore_DB |
+--------------------+----------+--------------+------------------+
| mariadb-bin.000012 |      328 |              |                  |
+--------------------+----------+--------------+------------------+
1 row in set (0.00 sec)
```

The file corresponds to the `binary logs` file available in your `logbin` directory, and then the next column shows the current position in the binary log.

Configuring the slave node

If you want to have the benefits of your master options, you need to set them as well on the slave. So basically, if you want to activate the transfer compression, you need to activate it on the slave side as well:

```
[mysqld]
server-id=2
bind-address = 0.0.0.0
slave_compressed_protocol = 1
```

Now, we've set the `server-id` value as 2 here. Remember that it is important to have a unique ID here. Here are other interesting options:

```
binlog_format = row
read_only
```

The `read_only` option is used in the preceding command. To be sure that your slave won't have any changes with your master, you can disable any write operations.

Creating a slave

There are multiple ways to create a slave. Here are two of the common and best ways:

- `mysqldump`: We can create a slave with the classical `mysqldump` tool. It works well, but it could take a very long time depending on the database size and locks tables during the whole dump.

- Xtrabackup: This is a Percona open source tool. It is faster and has a very small lock table duration on InnoDB/XtraDB.

Using mysqldump

The biggest inconvenience with the mysqldump solution is that you need to lock tables during the whole dump operation. This could be really problematic during production hours. Anyway, it works quite well and this is the classical way to perform human readable dumps. So, first let's flush all the data on the disk that hasn't been written yet and lock the tables:

```
MariaDB [(none)]> flush tables with read lock;
```

Now, you're ready to dump the databases. If you want to perform a full replication with all the databases available on the master, you can run the following command:

```
> mysqldump -uroot -p --opt --routines --triggers --events --single-
transaction --master-data=2 -A > alldb.sql
```

There are a lot of options here and not all of them are needed. Anyway, to be as close as possible to the master node, it's necessary. Here is the explanation:

- --opt: This option is an all-in-one option that in fact includes the following:
    - --add-locks: This will give faster insertions on restore.
    - --create-options: This will add all the MariaDB options in the create statement.
    - --disable-keys: This helps speed up dump restore because indexes are created after and not during import.
    - --extended-insert: This uses multi-row insert to speed up import.
    - --lock-tables: This locks the tables before dumping them.
    - --quick: This is used for large tables.
    - --set-charset: This adds the charset in the dump.
    - --routines: This includes procedures and functions in the dump.
    - --triggers: This adds triggers in the dump.
    - --events: This dumps the mysql.event table as well.
    - --single-transaction: This gets a consistent state for the InnoDB engine. This option requires to be in a full InnoDB/XtraDB state to avoid flushing tables with read locks. If this is not the case, it will be useless.

- --master-data: When set to 2, this adds the master binlog file and position information as comments in the dump. When set to 1, this will execute the change master to statement on the server where the dump is imported.
  - -A: This is used to dump all the databases.

Once the preceding command is executed, release the lock on tables:

```
MariaDB [(none)]> unlock tables;
```

You can now transfer the dump to the slave server your dump (the alldb.sql file here) to start the restoration procedure.

To restore the dump on the slave, run the following command:

```
> mysql -uroot -p < alldb.sql
```

Now, you have a restored version on the slave of an x instant of the master.

Now, to be ready to start the slave, we need to get the binary logfile and position written in the dump file, if you've chosen the master-data option to be 1:

```
> grep -m 1 "^-- CHANGE MASTER" alldb.sql
-- CHANGE MASTER TO MASTER_LOG_FILE='mariadb-bin.000012',
MASTER_LOG_POS=328;
```

Using Xtrabackup

Xtrabackup is the best solution to create backups for several reasons:

- It can create dumps fast
- It locks tables for a very short time
- It can stream compressed databases

To be able to use Xtrabackup for replication purposes, we need to have Xtrabackup installed on both the master and slave server. To install it, add the repository of Percona, add a preference pinning file, and install it (already done if you're using the Vagrantfile):

```
> apt-key adv --keyserver keys.gnupg.net --recv-keys 1C4CBDCDCD2EFD2A
> add-apt-repository 'deb http://repo.percona.com/apt wheezy main'
echo 'Package: *
Pin: release o=Percona Development Team
Pin-Priority: 100' > /etc/apt/preferences.d/00percona.pref
```

```
> aptitude update
> aptitude install xtrabackup
```

To be able to boot the slave properly, be sure no MariaDB instance is running on your slave and delete all the current MariaDB `datadir` content:

```
slave1> service mysql stop
[ ok ] Stopping MariaDB database server: mysqld.
slave1> service mysql status
[info] MariaDB is stopped..
slave1> rm -Rf /var/lib/mysql/*
```

You will also need to do an SSH key exchange from the master to the slave to be able to stream the backup directly to the slave:

```
master1> ssh-copy-id 192.168.33.32
```

Replace the IP address with the slave's IP address. You can now launch the stream (via `xbstream`) backup from the master to the slave through SSH:

```
master1> innobackupex --stream=xbstream ./ | ssh root@192.168.33.32
"xbstream -x -C /var/lib/mysql/"
[...]
innobackupex: MySQL binlog position: filename 'mariadb-bin.000012',
position 328
140220 22:12:48  innobackupex: Connection to database server closed
140220 22:12:48  innobackupex: completed OK!
```

Now, the backup has been pushed on the slave server in `/var/lib/mysql`; however, it's not ready for use. We need to prepare it on the slave host using the following command:

```
slave1> innobackupex --apply-log /var/lib/mysql
[...]
InnoDB: FTS optimize thread exiting.
InnoDB: Starting shutdown...
InnoDB: Shutdown completed; log sequence number 1619478
140220 22:31:23  innobackupex: completed OK!
```

Change the right to give MariaDB user control using the following command:

```
slave1> chown -Rf mysql. /var/lib/mysql
```

You can now start the slave host with the following command:

```
slave1> service mysql start
```

Now, to be ready to start the slave, we need to get the binary logfile and position located in `/var/lib/mysql/xtrabackup_binlog_info` on the slave:

```
mariadb-bin.000012  328
```

We now have all the necessary information to start the slave! Let's do it! The `stop` and `reset` options are not required but, as a rule, it's better to do it. This is generally done when a previous slave was configured and it's required to make it work to build a new replication. Execute these commands on the slave:

```
MariaDB [(none)]> stop slave;
MariaDB [(none)]> reset slave;
MariaDB [(none)]> change master to master_host='192.168.33.31',
master_user='replication', master_password='password',
master_log_file='mariadb-bin.000012', master_log_pos=328;
MariaDB [(none)]> start slave;
```

What does the `change master` command do? It indicates to the slave the IP/DNS of the master host, the credentials for replication, and the `logbin` information.

The `logbin` information indicates the position of the slave to the master. If actions occurred on the master during the time interval of the back up and the restore operations, those actions will be replayed on the slave to elevate it at the same level of data as the master node.

The last thing to do is to replicate, from the master node, the `debian.cnf` file from `/etc/mysql/` to the slave one. Then, you have to change the password of that user with the one indicated in the `debian.cnf` file to replicate it across all nodes:

```
MariaDB [(none)]> SET PASSWORD FOR 'debian-sys-maint'@'localhost' =
PASSWORD('password');
MariaDB [(none)]> FLUSH PRIVILEGES;
```

This avoids a failed startup service on the slaves.

Checking the slave status

You can check the slave status with the following command:

```
MariaDB [(none)]> show slave status\G;
*************************** 1. row ***************************
                Slave_IO_State: Waiting for master to send event
```

```
               Master_Host: 192.168.33.31
               Master_User: replication
               Master_Port: 3306
             Connect_Retry: 60
           Master_Log_File: mariadb-bin.000012
         Read_Master_Log_Pos: 328
            Relay_Log_File: mysqld-relay-bin.000006
             Relay_Log_Pos: 617
     Relay_Master_Log_File: mariadb-bin.000012
          Slave_IO_Running: Yes
         Slave_SQL_Running: Yes
           Replicate_Do_DB:
       Replicate_Ignore_DB:
        Replicate_Do_Table:
    Replicate_Ignore_Table:
   Replicate_Wild_Do_Table:
Replicate_Wild_Ignore_Table:
                Last_Errno: 0
                Last_Error:
              Skip_Counter: 0
       Exec_Master_Log_Pos: 328
           Relay_Log_Space: 1284
           Until_Condition: None
            Until_Log_File:
             Until_Log_Pos: 0
         Master_SSL_Allowed: No
         Master_SSL_CA_File:
         Master_SSL_CA_Path:
           Master_SSL_Cert:
         Master_SSL_Cipher:
            Master_SSL_Key:
     Seconds_Behind_Master: 0
Master_SSL_Verify_Server_Cert: No
            Last_IO_Errno: 0
            Last_IO_Error:
           Last_SQL_Errno: 0
           Last_SQL_Error:
 Replicate_Ignore_Server_Ids:
          Master_Server_Id: 1
```

```
            Master_SSL_Crl:
        Master_SSL_Crlpath:
                Using_Gtid: No
                Gtid_IO_Pos:
1 row in set (0.00 sec)
```

Here there is a huge amount of interesting information:

- `Slave_IO_Running` and `Slave_SQL_Running`: If they both are set to `yes`, then the replication is ok. If one of them is not, then you'll have to correct it.

- `Last_Errno` and `Last_Error`: They indicate when a problem occurs and can notify the current SQL query what has failed the replication. You can then try to reproduce or understand it.

This is the most important information on the `show slave status` command.

The relay logs store the replication state which is updated on data changes. This works independently of the master bin logs. This helps the slave to make the correlation between binary logs and itself. It is commonly used when you want to chain slaves from other slaves.

GTID replication

GTID has been introduced in MariaDB 10 and adds a new event to each transaction in the binlog. This new event is the Global ID that gives a unique identifier across all the replicated servers. This is how it is different from the classical replication. One of the big advantages is that you can now easily change the master as you get the same transaction ID across all nodes.

The other important thing is the slave is recorded in a crash-safe way. This involves using a transactional engine like InnoDB to be fully crash-safe.

The big difference with the classical replication is that GTID of the last applied transaction is stored in the `gtid_slave_pos` file of the `mysql` database. This table is updated each time a transaction is written. If the slave crashes, it is easy for it to catch the last state position and see with the master if it matches the last transaction commit. Having the same GTID number permits us to get consistent binlogs as well.

An important thing to know is classical replication is still available to maintain backward compatibility. However, GTID replication is enabled by default on MariaDB 10!

What is GTID

We've talked about the GTID replication solution, which is the best, but what is a GTID exactly? It is composed of three separated dashed numbers like x-y-z. They are explained as follows:

- x: This is the first number, that is, the domain ID
- y: This is the second number, that is, the server ID (as classical replication)
- z: This is the third number, that is, the sequence number (increasing on each event)

Configuring the master node

The configuration of the master node is very similar to the classical replication. Nothing different on that side, so you can pick up the same configuration:

```
[mysqld]
server-id=1
bind-address = 0.0.0.0
log_bin=/var/log/mysql/mariadb-bin
expire_logs_days=10
sync_binlog = 1
slave_compressed_protocol = 1
binlog_format = row
```

However, there are new and interesting options such as gtid_strict_mode. It permits us to enforce the discipline about having the exact binlogs across all the replicated nodes using GTID. This feature makes replication debugging easier and you are strongly encouraged to activate it:

```
gtid_strict_mode=1
```

You can then check the global variable status with the following command:

```
MariaDB [(none)]> select @@global.gtid_strict_mode;
+---------------------------+
| @@global.gtid_strict_mode |
+---------------------------+
|                         1 |
+---------------------------+
1 row in set (0.00 sec)
```

Preparing the master node

Like the classical replication, to allow a node to replicate master databases, create a user and give replication rights:

```
MariaDB [(none)]> create user 'replication'@'192.168.33.33'
identified by 'password';
MariaDB [(none)]> grant replication slave on *.* to
'replication'@'192.168.33.33';
MariaDB [(none)]> FLUSH PRIVILEGES;
```

You may notice that we can plug this new GTID slave on the current master, which already has a non-GTID slave. Don't worry, it works. You can have both activated.

Then, check the current GTID position using the following command:

```
MariaDB [(none)]> SELECT @@GLOBAL.gtid_current_pos;
+---------------------------+
| @@GLOBAL.gtid_current_pos |
+---------------------------+
| 0-1-2149                  |
+---------------------------+
1 row in set (0.00 sec)
```

Configuring a GTID slave node

As a rule, the configuration of the slave doesn't change, neither from the classical replication. Do not forget to change the `server-id` value and apply the `gtid_strict_mode` option to be compliant with the master:

```
[mysqld]
server-id=3
bind-address = 0.0.0.0
slave_compressed_protocol = 1
binlog_format = row
read_only
gtid_strict_mode=1
```

Restart your slave node for the changes to take effect.

Creating a slave

Unfortunately, at the time of writing, the integration of the GTID information in the backup solutions is not fully ready yet, so you have to manually get the GTID information from the master before doing the backup.

The methods to create a slave are identical to the classical ones. So, please refer to the `mysqldump` or Xtrabackup solutions.

Starting the slave

You now have the GTID information, the backup has been restored to the new slave node, and we are ready to start it:

```
MariaDB [(none)]> stop slave;
MariaDB [(none)]> reset slave;
MariaDB [(none)]> set global gtid_slave_pos = "0-1-2149";
MariaDB [(none)]> change master to master_host='192.168.33.31',
master_user='replication', master_password='password',
master_use_gtid=slave_pos;
MariaDB [(none)]> start slave;
```

Now, the slave is starting and resuming changes since the backup was done. In comparison to the classical replication, we've changed the master position and `binlog` file with the `master_user_gtid` parameter.

Three possibilities exist for the `master_user_gtid` parameter:

- `slave_pos`: This is a safe method for the slave nodes. With this method, you can point to any other master node easily.
- `current_pos`: This method is not totally safe if you're not using `gtid_strict_mode`, as extra transactions could be inserted in the binlogs of the slave server. This parameter is generally used when a slave could be master if the master failed.
- `no`: This is used to disable GTID.

You can check the current position of the slave using the following command:

```
MariaDB [(none)]> select @@gtid_slave_pos;
+------------------+
| @@gtid_slave_pos |
+------------------+
| 0-1-2149         |
```

```
+------------------+
1 row in set (0.00 sec)
```

It should be identical to the current master position if you run the command at the same time.

Checking the slave status

The method to check a slave status doesn't change from the classical replication; however, you will see the fulfilled parameters instead:

```
MariaDB [(none)]> show slave status\G;
*************************** 1. row ***************************
               Slave_IO_State: Waiting for master to send event
                  Master_Host: 192.168.33.31
                  Master_User: replication
                  Master_Port: 3306
                Connect_Retry: 60
              Master_Log_File: mariadb-bin.0000212
          Read_Master_Log_Pos: 328
               Relay_Log_File: mysqld-relay-bin.000006
                Relay_Log_Pos: 617
        Relay_Master_Log_File: mariadb-bin.000012
             Slave_IO_Running: Yes
            Slave_SQL_Running: Yes
              Replicate_Do_DB:
          Replicate_Ignore_DB:
           Replicate_Do_Table:
       Replicate_Ignore_Table:
      Replicate_Wild_Do_Table:
  Replicate_Wild_Ignore_Table:
                   Last_Errno: 0
                   Last_Error:
                 Skip_Counter: 0
          Exec_Master_Log_Pos: 328
              Relay_Log_Space: 1284
              Until_Condition: None
               Until_Log_File:
                Until_Log_Pos: 0
```

```
            Master_SSL_Allowed: No
            Master_SSL_CA_File:
            Master_SSL_CA_Path:
              Master_SSL_Cert:
            Master_SSL_Cipher:
               Master_SSL_Key:
         Seconds_Behind_Master: 0
 Master_SSL_Verify_Server_Cert: No
                 Last_IO_Errno: 0
                 Last_IO_Error:
                Last_SQL_Errno: 0
                Last_SQL_Error:
     Replicate_Ignore_Server_Ids:
              Master_Server_Id: 1
                Master_SSL_Crl:
            Master_SSL_Crlpath:
                    Using_Gtid: Slave_Pos
                   Gtid_IO_Pos: 0-1-2149
1 row in set (0.01 sec)
```

Just as we did in the classical method, we can set the two parameters `Slave_IO_Running` and `Slave_SQL_Running` values to `Yes`, which means everything is running fine.

The `Using_Gtid` parameter indicates the replication method used. The `Gtid_IO_Pos` parameter is the current GTID position, and it should be equal to the `@@GLOBAL.gtid_current_pos` value on the master host.

Migrating from classical to GTID replication

There is no planned deprecation for the classical replication and both can be used in multiple slave replication solutions. However, it's strongly recommended to switch from classical to GTID replication to get better stability and less maintenance. To switch from the classical to the GTID, it's simple. Let's take the slave1 node to do it. First of all, we'll need to stop the slave, performing a change in the master position to take GTID instead and switch back on the server. It's as easy as that.

So, let's look at the current status of the slave:

```
MariaDB [(none)]> show slave status\G;
[...]
                    Using_Gtid: No
                   Gtid_IO_Pos:
1 row in set (0.00 sec)
```

Stop the slave and get the current GTID value on itself as the master. Send it even if it's not in GTID:

```
MariaDB [(none)]> stop slave;
MariaDB [(none)]> select @@gtid_slave_pos;
+------------------+
| @@gtid_slave_pos |
+------------------+
| 0-1-2162         |
+------------------+
1 row in set (0.00 sec)
```

Now, configure this slave position and start the slave:

```
MariaDB [(none)]> set global gtid_slave_pos = "0-1-2162";
MariaDB [(none)]> change master to master_host='192.168.33.31',
master_user='replication', master_password='password',
master_use_gtid=slave_pos;
MariaDB [(none)]> start slave;
```

Then, check whether you've correctly switched using the following command:

```
MariaDB [(none)]> show slave status\G;
[...]
              Slave_IO_Running: Yes
             Slave_SQL_Running: Yes
[...]
                 Last_SQL_Errno: 0
                 Last_SQL_Error:
[...]
                    Using_Gtid: Slave_Pos
                   Gtid_IO_Pos: 0-1-2164
1 row in set (0.00 sec)
```

That's it! We have switched from the classical to GTID replication.

Parallel replication

By default, replications are single-threaded (only one event executing at a time). This can lead to performance issues when you're using multisource replication without activating parallel replication. Since MariaDB 10, a pool of separate replication worker threads is available to apply multiple events in parallel. You can go up to 10 times faster when parallel replication is enabled.

To enable parallel replication, add this line in your MariaDB configuration file (`my.cnf`):

```
slave-parallel-threads=4
```

A `0` value means disabled and the maximum value is `16383`.

If you're going too high on this value, you may encounter a slowdown.

Other options can be used and adjusted to fine tune parallel replication:

*   `slave_parallel_max_queued`: This sets the memory limit for the SQL threads.
*   `slave_domain_parallel_threads`: This shows how many connections a master can reserve at most (at one time).
*   `binlog_commit_wait_count`: This reduces I/O on the binary log. This will help parallel replication adoption on the slave.
*   `binlog_commit_wait_usec`: This sets how many micro seconds binary logs will wait (for at least `binlog_commit_wait_count` commits) to queue for a group commit.

Load balancing read transactions

Having a single slave to switch it to master in case of problems is a good solution for high availability. However, if you need an intensive read across your database and have already optimized all the things you could do, then the solution is to build additional slaves.

The goal here is to distribute the traffic across multiple slaves for the read access and only write to the MariaDB instance that will then replicate to the slaves. Let's call this the read-only group of MariaDB: *read group*.

Your application should be able to split by itself the read and write requests. So, we can use DNS round robin for load balance against the read MariaDB instances, as this is the simplest method. However, the danger of that mechanism is that it doesn't detect failure. For example, you've got one write server and two read nodes. If you're running on one read node instead of two, your request will fail at 50 percent.

The solution to avoid this problem is to have a load balancer. You can have a physical (high cost) load balancer or you can use a software load balancer such as HAProxy. HAProxy is a very fast, low memory footprint, free, and an open source load balancer. It provides high performances and is perfect for this kind of usage. The following diagram shows the working of a load balancer:

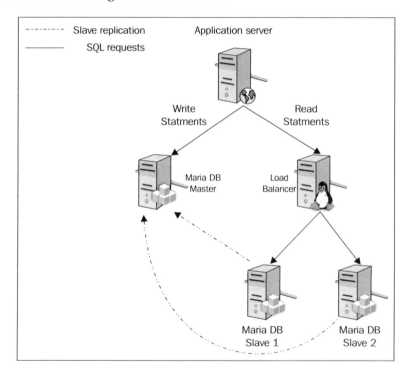

In the preceding figure, you can see the load balancer serving read servers while the write (master) server is alone. Slaves are getting information from the master.

Of course, here, you've got a SPOF on your write MariaDB instance and load balancer, but we'll see later in the book how to cover those aspects.

So to set up HAProxy in Debian wheezy, we'll need to use backports, as the package wasn't ready when wheezy was in the frozen stage.

Installing HAProxy

To install HAProxy manually, you'll need to activate the wheezy backports.
So, add the backports appropriate repository in `/etc/apt/sources.list.d/`
`wheezy-backports.list`:

```
deb http://ftp.debian.org/debian/ wheezy-backports main
deb-src http://ftp.debian.org/debian/ wheezy-backports main
```

Then install HAProxy:

```
> aptitude update
> aptitude install haproxy
```

Then, you can enable it to autostart on boot:

```
> sed -i "s/ENABLED=0/ENABLED=1/" /etc/default/haproxy
```

HAProxy is now ready to be configured.

Configuring HAProxy

First of all, we will need to create a user on the slave hosts to allow HAProxy
to perform a SQL connection. As we have multiple read hosts, if you don't want
to create a user on each slave, you can consider creating one on the master host
which will then replicate to the slaves.

So, we need to create a new user on the master node without any rights. This will
permit HAProxy to do the following:

- Connect on the instance (`tcp`)
- See if it can connect or not (MariaDB authentication)
- Close properly the connection (`tcp`)

Create the user and allow connection using the following commands:

```
MariaDB [(none)]> create user 'haproxy'@'192.168.33.40';
MariaDB [(none)]> flush privileges;
```

You can now add the HAProxy configuration, as follows, in `/etc/haproxy/haproxy.`
`cfg` (comments are included in the configuration file for better understanding):

```
global
    # log redirection (syslog)
    log /dev/log    local0
    log /dev/log    local1 notice
```

```
        # maximum of connections for haproxy
        maxconn 4096
        # chroot for security reasons
        chroot /var/lib/haproxy
        # user/group for haproxy process
        user haproxy
        group haproxy
        # act as a daemon
        daemon

defaults
        # use gloval log declaration
        log global
        # default check type
        mode    http
        # only log when closing session
        option  tcplog
        # only log failed connections
        # retry 3 times before setting node as failed
        # redispatch traffic to other servers
        option  dontlognull retries 3 option redispatch
        # maximum connection for the backend
        maxconn 1024
        # timeouts
        contimeout 5000
        clitimeout 50000
        srvtimeout 50000

# enable web check health interface on port 80
listen haproxy 0.0.0.0:80
        mode    http
        stats   enable
        # set credentials
        stats   auth admin:password

# loadbalance on slaves
listen mariadb-read-slaves 0.0.0.0:3306
        # use tcp method
        mode tcp
        # round robin mechanism
        balance roundrobin
        # tcp keepalive (pipelining) on both side (clt/srv)
        option tcpka
        # perform mariadb connection with haproxy user
        option mysql-check user haproxy
        # set all read only nodes
        # inter: interval of check in milliseconds
        server slave1 192.168.33.32:3306 check inter 1000
        server slave2 192.168.33.33:3306 check inter 1000
```

You can now start the `haproxy` process properly:

```
> service haproxy start
```

It will then listen on two interfaces as follows:

- `3306`: This is to load balance on the backend servers (MariaDB read group)
- `80`: This is the admin web interface (change the credentials for more security)

There are some options that you can change, such as the interval of check if you want something more reactive, or the number of retries before setting a slave as down. HAProxy is really powerful and can act up to the seventh layer. So, you can tune a lot of things.

Checking health

In configuration, the web health check has been added. That permits us to get a graphical interface to see the current status of all your nodes.

You can access it by using your web browser with admin/password credentials:

```
http://<loadbalancer_ip>/haproxy?stats
```

Here is a preview of what the web interface provides:

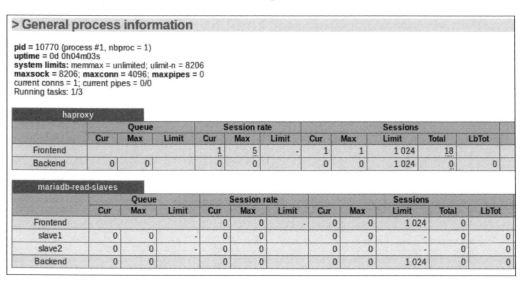

When it's green, that means everything is fine. Try to stop or kill severely (-9) a MariaDB instance, and you'll see all the traffic redirected to the only remaining host.

Testing the configuration

Testing the configuration is simple. You can use `tcpdump` to see the connections going one time on **slave1** and the second time on **slave2**, then **slave1**, then **slave2**, and so on.

So, on the load balancer, launch `tcpdump`:

```
> tcpdump -i any port 3306
```

From another machine, target the load balancer on port `3306`:

```
> nc -v 192.168.33.40 3306
```

You'll see the connections load balanced on each slave. If `tcpdump` is too verbose for you, test with the `netstat` command on the load balancer:

```
> watch -n1 'netstat -auntpl | grep 3306'
```

The following screenshot shows the output:

```
Every 1.0s: netstat -auntpl | grep 3306

tcp   0   0 0.0.0.0:3306          0.0.0.0:*            LISTEN      12977/haproxy
tcp   0   0 192.168.33.40:36761   192.168.33.33:3306   TIME_WAIT   -
tcp   0   0 192.168.33.40:36145   192.168.33.32:3306   ESTABLISHED 12977/haproxy
tcp   0   0 192.168.33.40:3306    192.168.33.33:38802  TIME_WAIT   -
tcp   0   0 192.168.33.40:36791   192.168.33.33:3306   TIME_WAIT   -
tcp   0   0 192.168.33.40:3306    192.168.33.33:38803  ESTABLISHED 12977/haproxy
tcp   0   0 192.168.33.40:36701   192.168.33.33:3306   TIME_WAIT   -
tcp   0   0 192.168.33.40:36703   192.168.33.33:3306   TIME_WAIT   -
```

Use cases and troubleshooting

Use cases are really needed for novices and for those who do not practice these kind of solutions in production. That's why you'll see schema with explanations of what could happen in production. Now, let's discuss outages and how to resolve them.

SQL errors

In a replication mode, you can encounter errors if you do not respect what has been established. A common mistake is for the privileges to be configured on a slave node and not the master.

Here is a scenario with a database as an example:

- **Master**: This is the server used as read/write
- **Slave1**: This is the server used as read only

A junior database administrator connects to the slave server as someone asked for a new database and creates a database crap. The database is present on the slave node, but not the master. Two days later, another database administrator connects on the master node because he needs to perform an urgent insertion in that database. As he doesn't see it, he creates it now and performs the database creation named crap. Everything runs fine for him and the master host.

But there is a problem! The replication falls down, as it can't execute the `create database` statement on an already existing database. In this case, it's strongly recommended to have a monitoring system as your slave server is still serving data, but outdated data! Write operations are still operating on your master node and the more the time elapses, the more outdated data you get. Here is what this error looks like:

```
MariaDB [(none)]> show slave status\G;
*************************** 1. row ***************************
               Slave_IO_State: Waiting for master to send event
                  Master_Host: 192.168.33.31
                  Master_User: replication
                  Master_Port: 3306
                Connect_Retry: 60
              Master_Log_File: mariadb-bin.000020
          Read_Master_Log_Pos: 2142
               Relay_Log_File: mysqld-relay-bin.000002
                Relay_Log_Pos: 656
        Relay_Master_Log_File: mariadb-bin.000020
             Slave_IO_Running: Yes
            Slave_SQL_Running: No
              Replicate_Do_DB:
          Replicate_Ignore_DB:
           Replicate_Do_Table:
       Replicate_Ignore_Table:
      Replicate_Wild_Do_Table:
  Replicate_Wild_Ignore_Table:
                   Last_Errno: 1007
                   Last_Error: Error 'Can't create database 'crap';
database exists' on query. Default database: 'crap'. Query: 'create
database crap'
                 Skip_Counter: 0
          Exec_Master_Log_Pos: 2021
              Relay_Log_Space: 1075
```

```
                Until_Condition: None
                 Until_Log_File:
                  Until_Log_Pos: 0
              Master_SSL_Allowed: No
              Master_SSL_CA_File:
              Master_SSL_CA_Path:
                 Master_SSL_Cert:
               Master_SSL_Cipher:
                  Master_SSL_Key:
            Seconds_Behind_Master: NULL
Master_SSL_Verify_Server_Cert: No
                  Last_IO_Errno: 0
                  Last_IO_Error:
                 Last_SQL_Errno: 1007
                 Last_SQL_Error: Error 'Can't create database 'crap';
database exists' on query. Default database: 'crap'. Query: 'create
database crap'
    Replicate_Ignore_Server_Ids:
               Master_Server_Id: 1
                 Master_SSL_Crl:
             Master_SSL_Crlpath:
                     Using_Gtid: Slave_Pos
                    Gtid_IO_Pos: 0-1-2168
1 row in set (0.00 sec)
```

You can easily correct the error. The first thing to do is to analyze the query and understand why it has failed. In general, MariaDB replication architectures are stable and don't break by themselves. Most of the time, it's a human error or a bad replication configuration from the beginning.

 Please note that replications are capable of resuming themselves in network loss, server crashing, or power cut issues.

The first thing to do is to stop the slave:

```
MariaDB [(none)]> stop slave;
```

Then, after analyzing, you've three solutions:

- **Correct**: You can correct the problem yourself and start the replication again. It won't crash anymore and perform the action. This is done using the following commands:

```
MariaDB [(none)]> drop database crap;
MariaDB [(none)]> start slave;
```

- **Skip**: You don't care about that current problem and prefer to skip it using the following commands:

```
MariaDB [(none)]> set global sql_slave_skip_counter=1;
MariaDB [(none)]> start slave;
```

    Here, we are skipping one by one the problems (=1). You can of course skip more, but it's strongly recommended to manage problems one-by-one to avoid inconsistencies!

    Then, look at the slave status and correct all the issues until everything is ok. As you've seen, it's not so complicated to correct errors; however, if you're in a very bad situation, it's preferable to lose a slave and recreate it from scratch instead of having an inconsistent slave.

- **GTID**: `skip_counter` is unfortunately not available for GTID replications. A discussion is in progress at the moment (https://mariadb.atlassian.net/browse/MDEV-4937). Take the current GTID position on the slave server and then jump to the next ID. The following command line shows an example:

```
MariaDB [(none)]> SELECT @@GLOBAL.gtid_current_pos;
+---------------------------+
| @@GLOBAL.gtid_current_pos |
+---------------------------+
| 0-1-2159                  |
+---------------------------+
MariaDB [(none)]> set global gtid_slave_pos = "0-1-2160";
MariaDB [(none)]> start slave;
```

    Now, check the slave status and increment the GTID number until it works as expected. You have to correct of course if it's a more complicated issue.

 Please note that one of the Percona toolkit tools (pt-table-checksum) is useful in these kinds of cases, when you want to be sure that the master and slave are really the same.

Analyzing binlogs

You need to read `binlog` when you analyze multiple replication errors. This will help you to understand what will be the next operation.

To read binlogs, use the following commands:

```
> cd /var/log/mysql
> mysqlbinlog mariadb-bin.000020
```

You need to choose the desired `binlog` file and you'll get GTID information with SQL requests:

```
# at 1812
#140223 18:23:48 server id 1  end_log_pos 1908    Query
thread_id=61     exec_time=0  error_code=0
SET TIMESTAMP=1393179828/*!*/;
create user 'haproxy'@'192.168.33.40'
/*!*/;
# at 1908
#140223 18:23:59 server id 1  end_log_pos 1946    GTID 0-1-2167
```

GTID – switching a slave to master and recovering

Let's take a situation where we have a master and slave replication in a GTID environment, as shown in the following diagram:

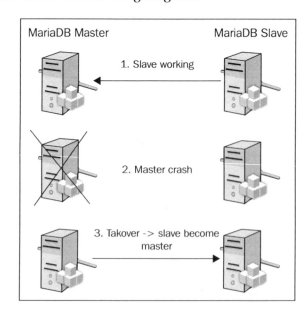

Here is the scenario. Everything is running well. We lose the master and we're doing a takeover on the slave by transforming it as the new master node. The old master node has an electric power issue. The old master is ready to start and we are going to failback to the old master node. But first of all, we need to resync the missed data on that old master.

Here is how to achieve the resolution for the preceding scenario:

1. Change your application settings to connect to the slave instead of the old master for write statements.

2. Remove the `read_only` parameter if you added it in the configuration, and restart MariaDB or do it on the fly:

```
MariaDB [(none)]> SET GLOBAL read_only=0;
```

3. Stop the slave mechanism using the following command:

```
MariaDB [(none)]> stop slave;
```

4. We will need a replication account on the slave/new master node (we shouldn't forget to remove that after the operation):

```
MariaDB [(none)]> create user 'replication'@'192.168.33.31'
identified by 'password';

MariaDB [(none)]> grant replication slave on *.* to
'replication'@'192.168.33.31';

MariaDB [(none)]> flush privileges;
```

The problem here is the old master has never been a slave. So, if we take a look at the current status of the old master, we won't have the requested information:

```
MariaDB [(none)]> select @@gtid_slave_pos;
+------------------+
| @@gtid_slave_pos |
+------------------+
|                  |
+------------------+
1 row in set (0.00 sec)
```

So, configure the old master to get the changes back:

```
MariaDB [(none)]> change master to
master_host='192.168.33.33', master_user='replication',
master_password='password', master_use_gtid=current_pos;

MariaDB [(none)]> start slave;
```

5. Now, if you check the old master, all the information is up to date!

6. Stop the current master to be sure that no connections will go to this server:

    ```
    > service mysql stop
    ```

7. Configure your application to go back to the old master.

8. On the master, stop the slave replication with the following command:

    ```
    MariaDB [(none)]> stop slave;
    ```

9. Start the ex-master to become a slave again:

    ```
    > service mysql start;
    ```

10. Perform the same operation on that node to take information back:

    ```
    MariaDB [(none)]> change master to
    master_host='192.168.33.31', master_user='replication',
    master_password='password', master_use_gtid=current_pos;

    MariaDB [(none)]> start slave;
    ```

It's done! All the operations are complete and you've finished it properly.

Summary

You saw in this chapter how to build slaves: the classical and GTID method. You now know how to optimize them, how to load balance against multiple read instances, and how to correct errors!

So much information in this chapter! It's strongly recommended to spend time to test every scenario, try to break replications, and so on, because in production it will not be so easy.

Replication is the first step of building a highly scalable system. That's why it's important to master it.

In the next chapter, we'll see how to implement those replications with more constraints, such as WAN architectures.

5
WAN Slave Architectures

In the previous chapter, we learned how to play with slave replications. You now know how it works and want to know how we could grow and geographically extend them to several regions.

You will encounter several issues in the following areas:

- The architecture of replications
- The security
- The bandwidth

We'll cover all these topics to help you understand the pros and cons of setting a lot of replications. We will see different use cases and associated solutions.

Cascade slaves

In the previous chapter, we've seen how to build several slaves from a master node. When you have a few nodes, it's not really a problem for the master node to handle them.

However, when you multiply the number of slave nodes, you'll encounter more and more I/O problems with your master node. It will be hard for it to perform write operations and give them to the slave nodes from the binary logs. So basically, you shouldn't have these kinds of architectures.

Refer to the following diagram:

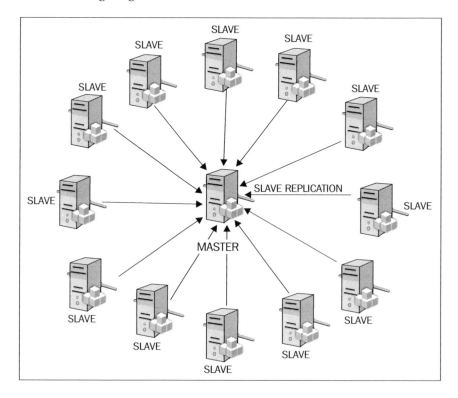

Monitor the master node properly to ensure that it is not overloaded. Of course, the number of maximum slaves depends on the load of the master node.

To resolve this kind of problem, you can perform **slave cascading**. The following diagram shows a simple solution:

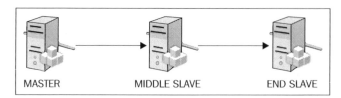

This means that you can have a master replicated on a slave and then replicated on another slave (as shown in the following diagram). This really helps in scaling with high load traffic.

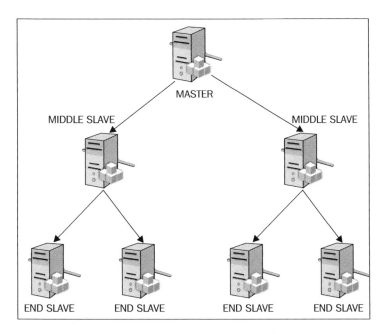

With this solution, you can scale more and minimize the replication load on the master node. To configure it, add the following line on your slave's middle node's configuration (my.cnf):

```
log_slave_updates = 1
```

The major problem in this solution is the configuration; if you lose one of the middle slaves, you lose 50 percent of your up-to-date slaves. However, all the end slaves are still accessible and you can reconfigure them to connect to another slave.

Speeding up replication performance for middle slaves

One of the things we're expecting from a slave node is to apply events from the slave relay logs to the slave database; this will make it ready to serve read requests.

However, for a middle (relay) slave server, we need not care about that. What we want from it is to transmit the information as quickly as possible to the end slave. To achieve this, we need to change how the middle slave will work.

About the master and end slave configuration, nothing changes! However, for the middle slave, here is what you need to set in addition of a classical slave configuration:

```
[mysqld]
log-bin                                      = /var/log/mysql/mysql-bin.
log
slave_compressed_protocol = 1
sync_binlog                        = 1
relay_log                           = /var/log/mysql/relay-bin
relay_log_index                   = /var/log/mysql/relay-bin.index
relay_log_info_file               = /var/log/mysql/relay-bin.info
log_slave_updates
read_only
skip-innodb
default-storage-engine        = blackhole
```

As you can see here, we're using BLACKHOLE as the default engine. This means that if there is no type of engine specified when creating a table, the BLACKHOLE engine will be set.

We're also using the `skip-innodb` option to bypass InnoDB table creation even if this is specified during table creation. In this case, the BLACKHOLE engine will be used instead.

You can now easily create new tables, even in InnoDB; the middle slave server will use BLACKHOLE, while the end slave servers will use the requested engine. That's what we wanted.

What about current tables? Can we convert the current middle slave server to BLACKHOLE tables without changing the end servers slave schema? Of course yes! You first need to specify that you don't want to replicate the commands you're going to enter to the end servers. Then, alter all tables to BLACKHOLE. The following is an example conversion with a table:

```
MariaDB [(none)]> SET sql_log_bin = 0;
MariaDB [(none)]> ALTER TABLE my_table ENGINE = 'BLACKHOLE';
MariaDB [(none)]> SET sql_log_bin = 1;
```

Once done, reactivate the `sql_log_bin`. Notice that changing the `sql_log_bin` value only takes effect during the session; other background tasks still replicate to end slave servers. That's it! Your table has only been converted to BLACKHOLE on the middle slave server and you've now increased the speed of the replication.

Restricting replications

You saw how easy it is to create a replication. However, you may not want to replicate all your databases. In your MariaDB configuration file, you can configure which databases or tables you want to replicate.

Changing this can drastically reduce the traffic load and CPU usage. For example, if you've got 1 TB of databases and you only need 20 GB from the databases on your slaves for read purposes, you don't have to replicate all the data.

Another point would be about security access. Let's say you've got MariaDB instances placed in DMZ and you don't want all your data to be replicated (such as credentials, credits card details, and confidential information). You wouldn't want to expose all your data, as they could be stolen if you're attacked and hacked. In this case, you can limit what you want to sync. Notice that it is best practice to reduce privilege restrictions if you want to add additional security.

If you take the output of a SHOW SLAVE STATUS command, you can see applied replication restrictions:

```
MariaDB [(none)]> SHOW SLAVE STATUS\G;
*************************** 1. row ***************************
               Slave_IO_State: Waiting for master to send event
                  Master_Host: 192.168.33.31
                  Master_User: replication
                  Master_Port: 3306
                Connect_Retry: 60
              Master_Log_File: mariadb-bin.000012
          Read_Master_Log_Pos: 328
               Relay_Log_File: mysqld-relay-bin.000006
                Relay_Log_Pos: 617
        Relay_Master_Log_File: mariadb-bin.000012
             Slave_IO_Running: Yes
            Slave_SQL_Running: Yes
              Replicate_Do_DB:
          Replicate_Ignore_DB:
           Replicate_Do_Table:
       Replicate_Ignore_Table:
      Replicate_Wild_Do_Table:
  Replicate_Wild_Ignore_Table:
[...]
1 row in set (0.00 sec)
```

Here it's blank everywhere, which means that there are no restrictions at all.

Now let's look at these interesting options:

- `replicate_do_db`: This is a comma-separated explicit list of database names to replicate as slave. You can see restricted databases you've set in the SLAVE STATUS command. To configure them in your MariaDB configuration file, you have to add a new line with each database you want to replicate:

```
replicate_do_db = mysql
replicate_do_db = database1
replicate_do_db = database2
[...]
```

  You also can make these changes on the fly:

```
MariaDB [(none)]> stop slave;
MariaDB [(none)]> set global replicate_do_db =
"database1,database2";
MariaDB [(none)]> start slave;
```

  Another important thing is the `mysql` database. Note that all users and accesses are stored here and it is usually a good practice to synchronize across slave.

- `replicate_do_table`: This works like the `replicate_do_db` option, but for tables. You can sync only some tables of one or multiple databases. For example, in your MariaDB configuration file, add the following:

```
replicate_do_table = database1.table1
replicate_do_table = database1.table3
replicate_do_table = database2.table8
[...]
```

  You can also change it on the fly:

```
MariaDB [(none)]> stop slave;
MariaDB [(none)]> set global replicate_do_table = "database1.
table1,database1.table3";
MariaDB [(none)]> start slave;
```

- `replicate_wild_do_table`: You saw that `replicate_do_table` is very useful. However, when you start to have a huge amount of tables, it can be a nightmare to manage. So a good solution is to use wildcards like the following on the fly:

```
MariaDB [(none)]> stop slave;
```

```
MariaDB [(none)]> set global replicate_wild_do_table = "database1.
table%,database2.%";

MariaDB [(none)]> start slave;
```

To make the changes permanent, change the configuration file in the following manner:

```
replicate_wild_do_table = "database1.table%";
replicate_wild_do_table = "database2.%";
```

Of course, there is no sense here to wildcard all tables of database2; replicate_do_db should be used instead.

- replicate_ignore_db: With replicate_do_db, you saw how to restrict replication to some databases. With replicate_ignore_db, this is inversed; it will synchronize all databases instead of those ignored. This method is generally used for instances that are usually updated with new databases. This is done to avoid manually configuring a replication database by database.

  So, to ignore database replications, use the following commands:

  ```
  MariaDB [(none)]> stop slave;

  MariaDB [(none)]> set global replicate_ignore_db =
  "database1,database2";

  MariaDB [(none)]> start slave;
  ```

  To set this permanently, add the following lines in the MariaDB configuration file:

  ```
  replicate_ignore_db = database1
  replicate_ignore_db = database2
  ```

- replicate_ignore_table: This does the opposite of what replicate_do_db does; you can select all the database tables that you want to ignore. This is generally used for temporary tables that are only locally used.

  So if you want to configure it in MariaDB configuration file, add the following lines:

  ```
  replicate_ignore_table = database1.tmp_table
  replicate_ignore_table = database2.tmp_table
  ```

  If you want to configure it on the fly, use the following commands:

  ```
  MariaDB [(none)]> stop slave;

  MariaDB [(none)]> set global replicate_ignore_table = "database1.
  tmp_table,database2.tmp_table";

  MariaDB [(none)]> start slave;
  ```

- `replicate_wild_ignore_table`: Like `replicate_wild_do_table`, you can use wildcards to ignore some tables. This means that it will replicate everything instead of the ignored tables by wildcards. Here is an example that you can add in your MariaDB configuration file:

```
replicate_wild_ignore_table = "database1.tmp_%";
replicate_wild_ignore_table = "database2.tmp_%";
```

If you want to do it on the fly:

```
MariaDB [(none)]> stop slave;
MariaDB [(none)]> set global replicate_wild_ignore_table =
"database1.tmp_%,database2.tmp_%";
MariaDB [(none)]> start slave;
```

Designing slave in multiple continents

When you want to build a geographical distant architecture, you need to think about several things:

- Should I replicate everything?
- Is write speed important?
- What is the expected read load for each site?

The following figure shows an example with a French Datacenter where we've got the master node and several slaves that distribute information to other countries (Brazil and Japan):

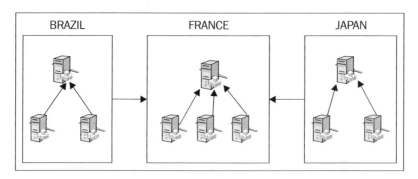

The latency and bandwidth with such distances are problematic for replication. Consider the following important information:

- **Should I replicate everything**: In the previous section, we saw how to replicate only some databases or tables and how to exclude some of them from replication. It's important to understand and know the purpose of the replication. Is this done for a site extension or is it for a full replication such as disaster recovery? If you want to build a full replication where you can completely start to recover, then you need to replicate everything! But, you should be careful with the latency and bandwidth for this kind of project. It is strongly recommended that the latency be very close to high bandwidth! If you want to have a site extension for example, simply replicate only what you need. Usually, distance implies latency. Try to optimize the latency by limiting what you need to the strict minimum.

- **Is slave lag important**: If you do not have enough bandwidth between your master and end slaves, or your middle slaves to the other end slaves, you'll get replication lags. That means you can have several minutes, or even hours of delta replication between two hosts. For example, if you get 4h for replication lag and lose the primary node, your slave will be late from 4h. That means you've lost data!!! That's why you may consider TokuDB, which uses a different mechanism, to avoid this slave lag.

- **What is the expected read load for each site**: As described in the first point, it's important to limit the latency and your needs. That's why you should avoid having several replications with high latency area. Instead, you should have one or two (for fault tolerance) replicates. Then, if you need more read scalability, you can create other local slaves (in the same area) from the current slaves. This reduces the load on the master, minimizes the used bandwidth, and gives you the possibility to scale out easily.

Be sure of what and how many replications you will perform and what are the impacts, before adding a new slave.

SSL replication

Implementing SSL on replication is an easy task. The question is: do you need SSL? In a completely local and closed network (and depending on your security restrictions of course), you generally don't need to set SSL as there is no **Man In The Middle (MITM)** possibility like with VPN.

However, in a nonrestricted, DMZ, or any opened network area, it's strongly recommended to add more security. Also, as database information is generally very important/critical, it could be very problematic if your data gets stolen. The privacy of your data is generally very important, as is the confidentiality. That's why you may think of implementing SSL replication to get uncleared traffic between multiple MariaDB hosts.

SSL will of course introduce network and CPU overhead. This parameter has to be taken into account as well. However, in some cases, like several Cloud providers, you'll have only a public IP per OS instance and you need to establish communication between two Internet-exposed MariaDB instances. It's recommended to configure your firewall to limit the source, but that is generally not enough. In such situations, you have the following two options:

- **Using a VPN to encrypt all your traffic over the Internet**: If this is done, you don't need to set up SSL inside MariaDB. However, this will be much more complicated to implement and will add other network problems. Anyway, it's an excellent solution. If, for several reasons, you need to add a VPN along with the SSL for replication, you'll get twice the amount of network and CPU overhead.

- **Using SSL replication for your front MariaDB server**: After this is done, you reduce the number of overheads in your complete infrastructure. You generally do not need SSL on the SQL backends.

The following is an illustration of what is common for good performance and security:

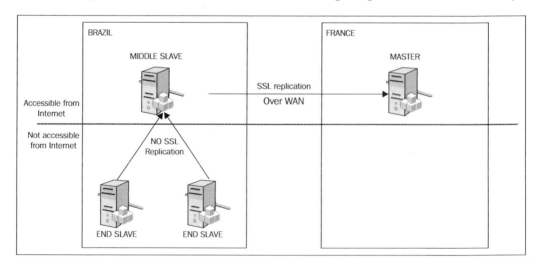

Generating certificates

You may already have a **certificate authority** (**CA**) that could deliver certificates. If that's the case, you can jump that section.

External CA providing paid certificates is useless, involved MariaDB instances are close to the same company and don't need to pay for a CRT because security is satisfied with a self-signed certificate.

An important thing to note about SSL information between server and client is that if they are too close (organization name, unit, and so on), you'll get errors and won't be able to connect.

Building your own CA

If you do not have a CA, then you need to manually generate your certificates and auto-self-sign them.

First, create a folder named `ssl` where the MariaDB configuration file is located, and then create a `ssl` folder to store all generated keys and move into that directory:

```
> mkdir -p /etc/mysql/ssl ~/ssl/{signedcerts,private}
> cd ~/ssl
```

We're now ready to generate your CA certificate. The higher the size of the private key, the higher the establish time will be. A connection with a key of 4096 bits is three times slower than without encryption. For security reasons, we've chose 4096 here:

```
> openssl genrsa 4096 > private/ca-key.pem
Generating RSA private key, 4096 bit long modulus
................................................................................
................................................................................
................................................................................
.............................................++
................................................................................
.............................................++
e is 65537 (0x10001)
> openssl req -new -x509 -nodes -days 3650 -key private/ca-key.pem -out
cacert.pem
```

You are about to be asked to enter information that will be incorporated into your certificate request.

What you are about to enter is what is called a Distinguished Name or a DN.

There are quite a few fields but you can leave some blank

```
For some fields there will be a default value,
If you enter '.', the field will be left blank.
-----
Country Name (2 letter code) [AU]:FR
State or Province Name (full name) [Some-State]:Ile de France
Locality Name (eg, city) []:Paris
Organization Name (eg, company) [Internet Widgits Pty Ltd]:Pierre Mavro
Company
Organizational Unit Name (eg, section) []:
Common Name (e.g. server FQDN or YOUR name) []:ssl.fqdn.com
Email Address []:pierre@mavro.fr
```

Adapt the fields with your data. We set the certificate validity here to 10 years to avoid recreating some too frequently.

Building your server certificate

We're now going to build the server key certificate:

```
> openssl req -newkey rsa:4096 -days 3650 -nodes -keyout private/server-
key.pem -out private/server-req.pem
Generating a 4096 bit RSA private key
......++
...............................................................................
...............................................................................
.....................................................++
writing new private key to 'private/server-key.pem'
-----
You are about to be asked to enter information that will be incorporated
into your certificate request.
What you are about to enter is what is called a Distinguished Name or a
DN.
There are quite a few fields but you can leave some blank
For some fields there will be a default value,
If you enter '.', the field will be left blank.
-----
Country Name (2 letter code) [AU]:FR
State or Province Name (full name) [Some-State]:Ile de France
Locality Name (eg, city) []:Paris
Organization Name (eg, company) [Internet Widgits Pty Ltd]:Pierre Mavro
Company
```

```
Organizational Unit Name (eg, section) []:
Common Name (e.g. server FQDN or YOUR name) []:master.fqdn.com
Email Address []:pierre@mavro.fr


Please enter the following 'extra' attributes
to be sent with your certificate request
A challenge password []:mypassword
An optional company name []:
```

This certificate is of 4096 bits. That means it is the current security standard, but will require more CPU usage on both MariaDB instances for encryption/decryption. It is up to you to find the best compromise between performance and security. As a rule, if you want security, do not choose a very light encryption or it won't be efficient and secure enough.

You now need to enter a pass phrase (challenge password). A passphrase will be asked for this certificate but you should not enter one. This will be a problem because each time a reboot of MariaDB occurs, the pass phrase will be prompted and the service won't start until you enter it. So let's remove the passphrase:

```
> openssl rsa -in private/server-key.pem -out private/server-key.pem
writing RSA key
```

We can now sign it:

```
> openssl x509 -req -in private/server-req.pem -days 3650 -CA cacert.pem
-CAkey private/ca-key.pem -set_serial 01 -out signedcerts/server-cert.pem
Signature ok
subject=/C=FR/ST=Ile de France/L=Paris/O=Pierre Mavro Company/CN=master.
fqdn.com/emailAddress=pierre@mavro.fr
Getting CA Private Key
```

Building your client certificates

Let's create our first client key certificate:

```
> openssl req -newkey rsa:4096 -days 3650 -nodes -keyout private/client-
key.pem -out private/client-req.pem
Generating a 4096 bit RSA private key
..............................................................................
..............................................................................
..............................................................................
..............................................................................
.......................................++
```

```
. . . . . . . . . . . . . . . . . . . . . . . . . . . . . . . . . . . . . . . . . . . . . . . . . . . . . . . . . . . . . . . .
. . . . . . . . . . . .++
writing new private key to 'private/client-key.pem'
-----

You are about to be asked to enter information that will be incorporated
into your certificate request.
What you are about to enter is what is called a Distinguished Name or a
DN.
There are quite a few fields but you can leave some blank
For some fields there will be a default value,
If you enter '.', the field will be left blank.
-----
Country Name (2 letter code) [AU]:FR
State or Province Name (full name) [Some-State]:Ile de France
Locality Name (eg, city) []:Paris
Organization Name (eg, company) [Internet Widgits Pty Ltd]:Pierre Mavro
Company
Organizational Unit Name (eg, section) []:
Common Name (e.g. server FQDN or YOUR name) []:middle1.fqdn.com
Email Address []:pierre@mavro.fr


Please enter the following 'extra' attributes
to be sent with your certificate request
A challenge password []:mypassword
An optional company name []:
```

We're now removing the pass phrase like on the server:

```
> openssl rsa -in private/client-key.pem -out private/client-key.pem
writing RSA key
```

And to finish, let's sign it:

```
> openssl x509 -req -in private/client-req.pem -days 3650 -CA cacert.pem
-CAkey private/ca-key.pem -set_serial 01 -out signedcerts/client-cert.pem
Signature ok
subject=/C=FR/ST=Ile de France/L=Paris/O=Pierre Mavro Company/CN=middle1.
fqdn.com/emailAddress=pierre@mavro.fr
Getting CA Private Key
```

You should now have something like the following in your folder:

```
> tree
.
|-- cacert.pem
|-- private
|    |-- ca-key.pem
|    |-- client-key.pem
|    |-- client-req.pem
|    |-- server-key.pem
|    `-- server-req.pem
`-- signedcerts
     |-- client-cert.pem
     `-- server-cert.pem

2 directories, 8 files
```

Now, you should move this `~/ssl` folder to a secure server (inaccessible from the Internet).

Checking your certificates

At any time, you can check your certificate to validate it:

```
> openssl verify -CAfile cacert.pem signedcerts/server-cert.pem
signedcerts/client-cert.pem
signedcerts/server-cert.pem: OK
signedcerts/client-cert.pem: OK
```

Configuring MariaDB for SSL

As we have our certificates now, we're ready to configure the nodes. The following are modifications required when you set up an existing replication to an SSL one.

Master SSL

On the master, take the configuration from the last chapter and add the following lines in your MariaDB configuration file (`my.cnf`):

```
[mysqld]
ssl-ca=/etc/mysql/ssl/cacert.pem
ssl-cert=/etc/mysql/ssl/server-cert.pem
ssl-key=/etc/mysql/ssl/server-key.pem
```

You now need to copy these files to your `ssl` folder (`/etc/mysql/ssl`). Then, grant privileges that require SSL (adapt with your configuration):

```
MariaDB [(none)]> grant replication slave on *.* to
'replication'@'192.168.33.33' require ssl;
MariaDB [(none)]> flush privileges;
```

Check (after having configured it) if the slave is still able to connect to the master, as we now require SSL for this MariaDB user:

```
MariaDB [(none)]>  SELECT user,host,ssl_type FROM mysql.user;
+------------------+---------------+----------+
| user             | host          | ssl_type |
+------------------+---------------+----------+
| root             | localhost     |          |
| root             | master        |          |
| root             | 127.0.0.1     |          |
| root             | ::1           |          |
| debian-sys-maint | localhost     |          |
| replication      | 192.168.33.33 | ANY      |
+------------------+---------------+----------+
```

To finish, restart MariaDB. You can check on the master node that the configuration is correct:

```
MariaDB [(none)]> SHOW VARIABLES LIKE '%ssl%';
+---------------+------------------------------+
| Variable_name | Value                        |
+---------------+------------------------------+
| have_openssl  | YES                          |
| have_ssl      | YES                          |
| ssl_ca        | /etc/mysql/ssl/ca-cert.pem   |
| ssl_capath    |                              |
| ssl_cert      | /etc/mysql/ssl/server-cert.pem |
| ssl_cipher    |                              |
| ssl_crl       |                              |
| ssl_crlpath   |                              |
| ssl_key       | /etc/mysql/ssl/server-key.pem |
+---------------+------------------------------+
9 rows in set (0.00 sec)
```

If you want to go ahead with SSL certificates, you can also change the value of `ssl_cipher`. This will allow changing the algorithm to get better performances or security.

Client SSL

The clients need to have SSL enabled in your MariaDB configuration as well:

```
[mysqld]
ssl-ca=/etc/mysql/ssl/cacert.pem
ssl-cert=/etc/mysql/ssl/client-cert.pem
ssl-key=/etc/mysql/ssl/client-key.pem
```

Then update the slave information:

```
MariaDB [(none)]> stop slave;
MariaDB [(none)]> change master to master_host='192.168.33.31', master_
user='replication', master_password='password', master_use_gtid=current_
pos, master_ssl=1, MASTER_SSL_CA='/etc/mysql/ssl/cacert.pem', MASTER_SSL_
CERT='/etc/mysql/ssl/client-cert.pem', MASTER_SSL_KEY='/etc/mysql/ssl/
client-key.pem';
MariaDB [(none)]> start slave;
```

We set the `master_ssl` option here to force SSL connectivity and the path to different SSL certificates. Do not forget to copy the certificates in the SSL directory.

You can check on the clients whether the configuration is correct:

```
MariaDB [(none)]> SHOW VARIABLES LIKE '%ssl%';
+---------------+-------------------------------+
| Variable_name | Value                         |
+---------------+-------------------------------+
| have_openssl  | YES                           |
| have_ssl      | YES                           |
| ssl_ca        | /etc/mysql/ssl/cacert.pem     |
| ssl_capath    |                               |
| ssl_cert      | /etc/mysql/ssl/client-cert.pem |
| ssl_cipher    |                               |
| ssl_crl       |                               |
| ssl_crlpath   |                               |
| ssl_key       | /etc/mysql/ssl/client-key.pem |
+---------------+-------------------------------+
9 rows in set (0.00 sec)
```

If you now use the `slave status` command, you'll get information about SSL:

```
MariaDB [(none)]> show slave status\G;
*************************** 1. row ***************************
               Slave_IO_State: Waiting for master to send event
                  Master_Host: 192.168.33.31
```

```
                       Master_User: replication
                       Master_Port: 3306
                      Connect_Retry: 60
                    Master_Log_File: mariadb-bin.000014
                Read_Master_Log_Pos: 328
                     Relay_Log_File: mysqld-relay-bin.000005
                      Relay_Log_Pos: 617
              Relay_Master_Log_File: mariadb-bin.000014
                   Slave_IO_Running: Yes
                  Slave_SQL_Running: Yes
                    Replicate_Do_DB:
                Replicate_Ignore_DB:
                 Replicate_Do_Table:
             Replicate_Ignore_Table:
            Replicate_Wild_Do_Table:
        Replicate_Wild_Ignore_Table:
                         Last_Errno: 0
                         Last_Error:
                       Skip_Counter: 0
                Exec_Master_Log_Pos: 328
                    Relay_Log_Space: 1204
                    Until_Condition: None
                     Until_Log_File:
                      Until_Log_Pos: 0
                  Master_SSL_Allowed: Yes
                 Master_SSL_CA_File: /etc/mysql/ssl/cacert.pem
                 Master_SSL_CA_Path:
                    Master_SSL_Cert: /etc/mysql/ssl/client-cert.pem
                  Master_SSL_Cipher:
                     Master_SSL_Key: /etc/mysql/ssl/client-key.pem
              Seconds_Behind_Master: 0
    Master_SSL_Verify_Server_Cert: No
                      Last_IO_Errno: 0
                      Last_IO_Error:
                     Last_SQL_Errno: 0
                     Last_SQL_Error:
          Replicate_Ignore_Server_Ids:
                   Master_Server_Id: 1
                     Master_SSL_Crl: /etc/mysql/ssl/cacert.pem
```

```
        Master_SSL_Crlpath:
              Using_Gtid: No
              Gtid_IO_Pos:
1 row in set (0.00 sec)
```

Compression options

An important option when you're in a WAN environment is the compression. We already saw it in the previous chapter. It allows compressing data across replicated nodes. Here is what you need to add in the MariaDB configuration file:

```
slave_compressed_protocol = 1
```

Summary

In this chapter, you saw how to build WAN slave architectures, what are the risks, and things that you should take care about, such as latency and security. You also saw how to limit what you want to replicate and you now understand what is essential for a WAN replication.

In the next chapter, you'll learn how to build a dual master solution.

6
Building a Dual Master Replication

In the previous chapters, you saw how to build complex slave replications. However, in all those solutions, there was a **Single Point of Failure (SPOF)**: the master node.

The solution to avoid having a single master is to build a dual master replication. It's common to have a simple dual master replication architecture. However, it's important to do things right when you're managing this kind of thing. Compared to other solutions, you can't afford to make mistakes and should be very careful with these kinds of tasks in production usage. To be as strict as possible, we're going to use cluster tools for some solutions; load balancer and features will only be available beginning with MariaDB 10.

Dual master replication and risks

A dual master replication is very simple to implement. If you know how to build a slave, you'll be able to create a dual master easily. It's in fact a slave replication on both sides. The following diagram shows dual-sided replication:

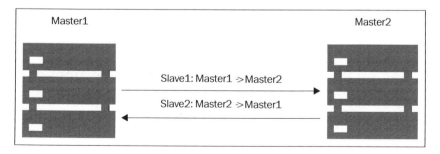

This means that in theory you can write to both MariaDB instances at the same time. However, doing so is likely to result in inconsistent data between the two hosts, breaking replication (because of PRIMARY/UNIQUE key collisions) and, worse than that, you may end up having inconsistent data between two hosts.

 Do not write on to both the masters at the same time!

The preceding tip mentions a rule that you need to follow to avoid issues in the production usages. You can minimize this kind of issue by adding the following two options in your MariaDB configuration file:

```
auto-increment-increment=2
auto-increment-offset=1
```

- This will avoid primary key collisions on the same rows of the same table:
- `auto-increment-increment`: This sets the number of masters (here 2)
- `auto-increment-offset`: This sets a unique number (taking the `server-id` is a good solution)

Technically, you need to know that it is possible to write at the same time on different tables:

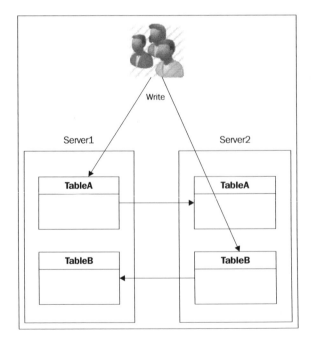

You can see the following in the preceding diagram:

- **TableA** on **Server1** is replicating to **TableA** on **Server2**
- **TableB** on **Server2** is replicating to **TableB** on **Server1**

In this instance, there is no possible issue. However, it's generally easier to maintain a replication that fully replicates all the data instead of a piece of data.

Installing and configuring a dual master

As shown in the previous chapters, you can use `Vagrantfile` to easily install MariaDB:

```ruby
# -*- mode: ruby -*-
# vi: set ft=ruby :
# Vagrantfile API/syntax version. Don't touch unless you know what
you're doing!
#
VAGRANTFILE_API_VERSION = "2"

# Insert all your Vms with configs
boxes = [
    { :name => :master1,       :role      => 'db',   :ip =>
'192.168.33.31' }, # master node 1
    { :name => :master2,       :role      => 'db',   :ip =>
'192.168.33.32' }, # master node 2
    { :name => :loadbalancer,  :role      => 'lb',   :ip =>
'192.168.33.33' }, # load balancer 1
    { :name => :loadbalancer2, :role      => 'lb',   :ip =>
'192.168.33.34' }, # load balancer 2
    { :name => :drbd1,         :role      => 'drbd', :ip =>
'192.168.33.41' }, # drbd 1
    { :name => :drbd2,         :role      => 'drbd', :ip =>
'192.168.33.42' }, # drbd 2
]

$install_common = <<INSTALL
aptitude update
DEBIAN_FRONTEND=noninteractive aptitude -y -o Dpkg::Options::="--
force-confdef" -o Dpkg::Options::="--force-confold" install python-
software-properties openntpd
INSTALL

$install = <<INSTALL
aptitude update
```

```
DEBIAN_FRONTEND=noninteractive aptitude -y -o Dpkg::Options::="--
force-confdef" -o Dpkg::Options::="--force-confold" install python-
software-properties
apt-key adv --recv-keys --keyserver keyserver.ubuntu.com
0xcbcb082a1bb943db
apt-key adv --keyserver keys.gnupg.net --recv-keys 1C4CBDCDCD2EFD2A
add-apt-repository 'deb http://ftp.igh.cnrs.fr/pub/mariadb/repo/10.0/
debian wheezy main'
add-apt-repository 'deb http://repo.percona.com/apt wheezy main'
echo 'Package: *
Pin: release o=Percona Development Team
Pin-Priority: 100' > /etc/apt/preferences.d/00percona.pref
aptitude update
DEBIAN_FRONTEND=noninteractive aptitude -y -o Dpkg::Options::="--
force-confdef" -o Dpkg::Options::="--force-confold" install mariadb-
server percona-toolkit
INSTALL


$install_lb = <<INSTALL
add-apt-repository 'deb http://ftp.fr.debian.org/debian/ wheezy-
backports main'
aptitude update
DEBIAN_FRONTEND=noninteractive aptitude -y -o Dpkg::Options::="--
force-confdef" -o Dpkg::Options::="--force-confold" install haproxy
tcpdump keepalived
sed -i "s/ENABLED=0/ENABLED=1/" /etc/default/haproxy
echo "net.ipv4.ip_nonlocal_bind = 1" >> /etc/sysctl.conf
INSTALL


$install_drbd = <<INSTALL
aptitude update
DEBIAN_FRONTEND=noninteractive aptitude -y -o Dpkg::Options::="--
force-confdef" -o Dpkg::Options::="--force-confold" install drbd8-
utils parted
echo "drbd" >> /etc/modules
INSTALL


$install_pacemaker = <<INSTALL
aptitude update
DEBIAN_FRONTEND=noninteractive aptitude -y -o Dpkg::Options::="--
force-confdef" -o Dpkg::Options::="--force-confold" install pacemaker
corosync
INSTALL


Vagrant::Config.run do |config|
  # Default box OS
```

```
  vm_default = proc do |boxcnf|
    boxcnf.vm.box      = "deimosfr/debian-wheezy"
  end

  boxes.each do |opts|
    vm_default.call(config)
    config.vm.define opts[:name] do |config|
        config.vm.customize ["modifyvm", :id, "--cpus", 2]
        config.vm.network    :hostonly, opts[:ip]
        config.vm.host_name = "%s.vm" % opts[:name].to_s
        config.vm.provision "shell", inline: $install_common
        # Install HAProxy for load balancer server or
        if opts[:role] == 'lb'
            config.vm.provision "shell", inline: $install_lb
        else
            config.vm.provision "shell", inline: $install
        end
        # Add a second drive for DRBD
        if opts[:role] == 'drbd'
            config.vm.provision "shell", inline: $install_drbd
            config.vm.provision "shell", inline: $install_pacemaker
            file_to_disk = 'drbd-disk_' + opts[:name].to_s + '.vdi'
            config.vm.customize ['createhd', '--filename', file_to_
disk, '--size', 4 * 1024]
            config.vm.customize ['storageattach', :id, '--storagectl',
'SATA', '--port', 1, '--device', 0, '--type', 'hdd', '--medium', file_
to_disk]
        end

        # Pacemaker
        if opts[:role] == 'pm'
            config.vm.provision "shell", inline: $install
            config.vm.provision "shell", inline: $install_pacemaker
        end
    end
  end
end
```

Then, you'll be able to have two nodes to start your replication. What we will see in that section is in fact a quick setup, where all used options have already been discussed in *Chapter 4, MariaDB Replication*.

First of all, we need to properly configure both MariaDB configuration files to give them the possibility to be slave and master at the same time.

The following is an example of the configuration required:

```
[mysqld]
server-id=1
bind-address = 0.0.0.0
log_bin=/var/log/mysql/mariadb-bin
expire_logs_days=10
sync_binlog = 1
slave_compressed_protocol = 1
binlog_format = row
```

 Be sure that the read_only option is not activated in your configuration file.

Do not forget to change the server-id value for both masters. As for slaves, *this value should be unique!* Once done, restart MariaDB on both nodes.

We're going to create replication users to allow the following actions:

- Replication from Master2 to Master1
- Replication from Master1 to Master2

We've got two servers here with their corresponding IP addresses.

Execute the following command lines on Master1:

```
MariaDB [(none)]> create user 'replication'@'192.168.33.32' identified by
'password';
MariaDB [(none)]> grant replication slave on *.* to
'replication'@'192.168.33.32';
MariaDB [(none)]> create user 'replication'@'192.168.33.31' identified by
'password';
MariaDB [(none)]> grant replication slave on *.* to
'replication'@'192.168.33.31';
MariaDB [(none)]> flush privileges;
```

Take a look at the current position:

```
MariaDB [(none)]> SELECT @@GLOBAL.gtid_current_pos;
+---------------------------+
| @@GLOBAL.gtid_current_pos |
+---------------------------+
| 0-1-4289                  |
+---------------------------+
```

Now, use `mysqldump` (no need to use `xtrabackup` as this is a fresh install and there is no need to lock tables as there is no activity) to make a proper replication from Master1 node to Master2. Generally, we do not need to create a dump here; however, as this is best practice, let's do it:

```
> mysqldump -uroot -p --opt --routines --triggers --events --single-
transaction --master-data=2 -A > alldb.sql
```

Transfer the dump on the Master2 node. Connect on that Master2 node and restore the SQL dump:

```
> mysql -uroot -p < alldb.sql
```

You also need to copy the `/etc/mysql/debian.cnf` configuration file from Master1 to Master2! This file contains credentials necessary for Debian usages. If you forget to copy that file, you'll encounter problems on starting and stopping the MySQL service on Master2.

Then, configure Master2 to be the slave of Master1:

```
MariaDB [(none)]> flush privileges;
MariaDB [(none)]> stop slave;
MariaDB [(none)]> reset slave;
MariaDB [(none)]> set global gtid_slave_pos = "0-1-4289";
MariaDB [(none)]> change master to master_host='192.168.33.31', master_
user='replication', master_password='password', master_use_gtid=slave_
pos;
MariaDB [(none)]> start slave;
```

You can now check the slave status of the Master2 node:

```
MariaDB [(none)]> show slave status\G;
*************************** 1. row ***************************
               Slave_IO_State: Waiting for master to send event
                  Master_Host: 192.168.33.31
                  Master_User: replication
                  Master_Port: 3306
                Connect_Retry: 60
              Master_Log_File: mariadb-bin.000018
          Read_Master_Log_Pos: 1119
               Relay_Log_File: mysqld-relay-bin.000002
                Relay_Log_Pos: 656
        Relay_Master_Log_File: mariadb-bin.000018
             Slave_IO_Running: Yes
            Slave_SQL_Running: Yes
```

```
              Replicate_Do_DB:
          Replicate_Ignore_DB:
           Replicate_Do_Table:
       Replicate_Ignore_Table:
      Replicate_Wild_Do_Table:
  Replicate_Wild_Ignore_Table:
                    Last_Errno: 0
                    Last_Error:
                 Skip_Counter: 0
          Exec_Master_Log_Pos: 1119
              Relay_Log_Space: 954
              Until_Condition: None
               Until_Log_File:
                Until_Log_Pos: 0
            Master_SSL_Allowed: No
            Master_SSL_CA_File:
            Master_SSL_CA_Path:
               Master_SSL_Cert:
             Master_SSL_Cipher:
                Master_SSL_Key:
        Seconds_Behind_Master: 0
Master_SSL_Verify_Server_Cert: No
                Last_IO_Errno: 0
                Last_IO_Error:
               Last_SQL_Errno: 0
               Last_SQL_Error:
     Replicate_Ignore_Server_Ids:
              Master_Server_Id: 1
                Master_SSL_Crl:
            Master_SSL_Crlpath:
                    Using_Gtid: Slave_Pos
                  Gtid_IO_Pos: 0-1-4289
1 row in set (0.00 sec)
```

Now we're going to set the slave replication from Master1 to Master2. As we've already got synced data, we do not need to dump all databases; it makes no sense.

So, we will simply have to get the master information *from the Master2 node*:

```
MariaDB [(none)]> SELECT @@GLOBAL.gtid_current_pos;
+---------------------------+
| @@GLOBAL.gtid_current_pos |
```

```
+---------------------------+
| 0-2-4407                  |
+---------------------------+
```

Then configure and start the slave *on the Master1 node*:

```
MariaDB [(none)]> stop slave;

MariaDB [(none)]> reset slave;

MariaDB [(none)]> set global gtid_slave_pos = "0-2-4407";

MariaDB [(none)]> change master to master_host='192.168.33.32', master_
user='replication', master_password='password', master_use_gtid=slave_
pos;

MariaDB [(none)]> start slave;
```

That's it! If you now check the status of this Master1 node, it is a slave as well.

To confirm this works well, here is a simple solution. We're going to create a database from Master1 and drop it from Master2. So, on node 1, use the following command:

```
MariaDB [(none)]> create database replication_test;
```

On Master2, use the following commands:

```
MariaDB [(none)]> show databases;
+--------------------+
| Database           |
+--------------------+
| information_schema |
| mysql              |
| performance_schema |
| replication_test   |
+--------------------+
4 rows in set (0.00 sec)
MariaDB [(none)]> drop database replication_test;
```

Now list your databases on the Master1 node; you'll see that replication_test has disappeared!

The replication works correctly on both sides!

Automatic management

One of the goals of the dual master replication mode is to avoid doing a manual intervention on both servers when an issue occurs. We want to reduce the switching time as far as possible in case a server fails. To do so, multiple solutions exist and we're going to see some of them here.

HAProxy

HAProxy was discussed in *Chapter 4, MariaDB Replication*, to load balance against multiple slaves. We're now going to see how to do so on a dual master replication. To follow the rules, we should *load balance on failover*, not on configuration. So why should we use a load balancer if we do not have to load balance? Because HAProxy is powerful, easy to install, easy to maintain, and does the job perfectly.

Now let's see what failover means. Failover means if one server goes down, it should automatically switch to the other one. This action should be automatic, that is, without any human intervention!

The following diagram shows a comfortable scenario for this kind of project:

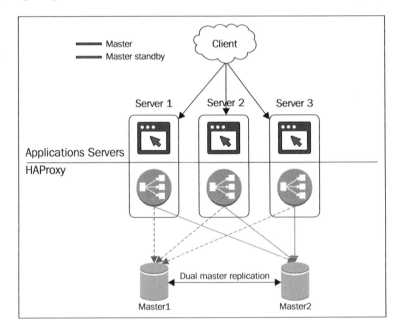

The dotted line means we are designing a current path for SQL queries from the application servers. The solid line is the backup one, as there is no load balancing at all here. As you can see, we've got a HAProxy server running on each application server. This configuration could be useful if you don't need to manage dedicated HAProxy servers (with Keepalived for example).

To install HAProxy, use the following commands:

```
> add-apt-repository 'deb http://ftp.fr.debian.org/debian/ wheezy-
backports main'
> aptitude update
> aptitude install haproxy tcpdump socat hatop
> sed -i "s/ENABLED=0/ENABLED=1/" /etc/default/haproxy
```

Then add the HAProxy user:

```
MariaDB [(none)]> create user 'haproxy'@'192.168.33.33';
MariaDB [(none)]> flush privileges;
```

Now apply that configuration file (/etc/haproxy/haproxy.cfg):

```
global
    # log redirection (syslog)
    log /dev/log        local0
    log /dev/log        local1 notice
    # maximum of connections for haproxy
    maxconn 4096
    # chroot for security reasons
    chroot /var/lib/haproxy
    # user/group for haproxy process
    user haproxy
    group haproxy
    # act as a daemon
    daemon
    # enable stats unix socket
    stats socket /var/lib/haproxy/stats mode 777 level admin

defaults
    # use gloval log declaration
    log        global
    # default check type
    mode        http
    # only log when closing session
    option        tcplog
    # only log failed connections
```

```
# retry 3 times before setting node as failed
# redispatch traffic to other servers
option      dontlognull retries 3 option redispatch
# maximum connection for the backend
maxconn 1024
# timeouts
contimeout 5000
clitimeout 50000
srvtimeout 50000

# enable web check health interface on port 80
listen haproxy 0.0.0.0:80
    mode      http
    stats   enable
    # set credentials
    stats   auth admin:password

# loadbalance on master nodes
listen mariadb-masters 0.0.0.0:3306
    # use tcp method
    mode tcp
    # tcp keepalive (pipelining) on both side (clt/srv)
    option tcpka
    # perform mariadb connection with haproxy user
    option mysql-check user haproxy
    # set all write nodes
    # inter: interval of check in milliseconds
    server master1 192.168.33.31:3306 check inter 1000
    server master2 192.168.33.32:3306 check inter 1000 backup
```

Now reload the HAProxy service.

In this configuration file, it's important to add the backup parameter at the end of the Master2 server. This parameter will indicate that we do not want to load balance against all servers, rather we'll redirect all queries to the Master1 server and automatically switch to Master2 if Master1 fails.

The major problem of that solution is *the fallback!* For instance, when you lose your Master1 node and all traffic is redirected by HAProxy to the Master2 node.

 Having a lag between the two masters will cause data inconsistencies! It is important to have no lag replication when you're using this method.

Now suppose that you have network flip-flap on the Master1 node. HAProxy will automatically fallback to the Master1 node as soon as it is available. You can adjust it by adding a new parameter called `rise`:

```
server master1 192.168.33.31:3306 check inter 1000 rise 300
```

With the rise parameter set to 300 seconds, you'll not be annoyed by network flip-flap. However, there are scenarios where you can have problems:

- Master1 crashes and reboots.
- Master2 takes the load.
- Master1 is back after 2 minutes.
- Master2 fails at the fourth minute.
- The load is not redirected to Master1! It will only switch once the 300th second is reached even if you're in the blackout!

So if you want to do that, do not set too high a number for `rise`. A value of 20 seconds is a good compromise. You should also consider having a dedicated network bonding for replication usage to reduce possible network issues.

If you want to disable auto failback, you can set the `rise` number to 99999999 (which corresponds to 15 years). Each HAProxy has to have an identical configuration file, so it's preferable to use configuration management (Ansible, Puppet, Chef, and SaltStack).

Learning about the maintenance mode

If you have a problem with one node and want to set it in maintenance mode, we can use a few methods that will be described in the next sections.

Using Unix Socket

You can use Unix Socket to set a node in the maintenance mode.

To look at the current state of the HAProxy statistics, use the following command:

```
> echo "show stat" | socat stdio /var/lib/haproxy/stats | awk -F, '{
print $1,$2,$18 }'
# pxname svname status
haproxy FRONTEND OPEN
haproxy BACKEND UP
mariadb-masters FRONTEND OPEN
mariadb-masters master1 UP
mariadb-masters master2 UP
mariadb-masters BACKEND UP
```

As you can see here, both nodes are up. Now if you want to put Master2 into maintenance mode, use the following command:

```
> echo "disable server mariadb-masters/master2" | socat stdio /var/lib/
haproxy/stats"
```

You can now check if it is in the maintenance mode:

```
> echo "show stat" | socat stdio /var/lib/haproxy/stats | awk -F, '{
print $1,$2,$18 }'
# pxname svname status
haproxy FRONTEND OPEN
haproxy BACKEND UP
mariadb-masters FRONTEND OPEN
mariadb-masters master1 UP
mariadb-masters master2 MAINT
mariadb-masters BACKEND UP
```

To enable the node again, do the following:

```
> echo "enable server mariadb-masters/master2" | socat stdio /var/lib/
haproxy/stats
```

That's it!

Using HATop

HATop is a tool that permits you to see and manage your load balancer with an **ncurses** interactive GUI.

You can set a node in maintenance and see errors and other features. To launch it, you need to have the HAProxy socket activated and then run that command:

```
> hatop -s /var/lib/haproxy/stats
```

Here is what it looks like

Using the configuration file

If you do not want to use Unix Socket but only want to use the configuration file, you also can add `disabled` to the HAProxy configuration file (`haproxy.cfg`):

```
server master2 192.168.33.32:3306 check inter 1000 backup disabled
```

Then reload the configuration:

```
> service haproxy reload
[ ok ] Reloading haproxy: haproxy.
```

If you check on the web interface, you will see Master2 in maintenance mode. Remove this parameter to pull off maintenance mode on that node.

Keepalived

Keepalived is a routing solution based on the **Virtual Router Redundancy Protocol (VRRP)** protocol. The main goal is to provide high availability. You will be able to implement a **Virtual IP (VIP)** to failover on one of the two HAProxy nodes if an issue occurs. Here is a schema of what you can do with Keepalived to avoid the HAProxy issue:

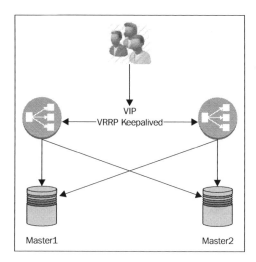

Every command and the following configuration should be achieved on both nodes to manually install Keepalived:

```
aptitude install keepalived
```

We now need to inform the kernel that we want to allow binding on non local IP on the hosts. Perform the following steps to do so:

1. Add the following line in /etc/sysctl.conf:

    ```
    net.ipv4.ip_nonlocal_bind = 1
    ```

2. Then enable it:

    ```
    > sysctl -p
    net.ipv4.ip_nonlocal_bind = 1
    ```

3. Create a configuration file named keepalived.conf under /etc/keepalived/:

    ```
    # Detect if haproxy is down
    vrrp_script check_haproxy {
        # verify the pid existence
        script "killall -0 haproxy"
        # check every 2 seconds
        interval 2
        # add 2 points of prio if OK
        weight 2
    }

    # VRRP/VIP for haproxy
    vrrp_instance haproxy_vip {
        # select the interface to monitor
        interface eth2
        state MASTER
        # set a unique ID for this route
        virtual_router_id 10
        # master: 101
        # backup: 100
        priority 100
        virtual_ipaddress {
            # set the wished VIP
            192.168.33.10
        }
        track_script {
            check_haproxy
        }
    }
    ```

Let's explain what that configuration does:

- `vrrp_script`: This will execute a script to get the return value of it. It always should return 0 to be working correctly. You can adjust the check interval if you want.

- `interface`: You need to specify the interface on which the VIP should be mounted and monitored.

- `priority`: On the primary node (you'll have to define one), set 100 and set 101 on the other node. If you set both to 100, a backup node will automatically be selected.

- `virtual_ipaddress`: Set the VIP for this service. That means all MariaDB connections will pass through that VIP, get routed to HAProxy, and finally get distributed to a MariaDB node.

Then, restart Keepalived to make the configuration active:

```
> /etc/init.d/keepalived restart
```

If you look at your logs, you will see something like the following on the master node:

```
Mar 23 13:54:04 loadbalancer Keepalived_vrrp: VRRP_Script(check_haproxy)
succeeded
Mar 23 13:54:05 loadbalancer Keepalived_vrrp: VRRP_Instance(haproxy_vip)
Transition to MASTER STATE
Mar 23 13:54:05 loadbalancer Keepalived_vrrp: VRRP_Instance(haproxy_vip)
Received lower prio advert, forcing new election
Mar 23 13:54:06 loadbalancer Keepalived_vrrp: VRRP_Instance(haproxy_vip)
Entering MASTER STATE
```

The following can be seen on the backup node:

```
Mar 23 13:54:04 loadbalancer2 Keepalived_vrrp: VRRP_Script(check_haproxy)
succeeded
Mar 23 13:54:05 loadbalancer2 Keepalived_vrrp: VRRP_Instance(haproxy_vip)
Transition to MASTER STATE
Mar 23 13:54:05 loadbalancer2 Keepalived_vrrp: VRRP_Instance(haproxy_vip)
Received higher prio advert
Mar 23 13:54:05 loadbalancer2 Keepalived_vrrp: VRRP_Instance(haproxy_vip)
Entering BACKUP STATE
```

If you check on the master host, you'll see the IP address attributed:

```
> ip a show eth2
4: eth2: <BROADCAST,MULTICAST,UP,LOWER_UP> mtu 1500 qdisc pfifo_fast
state UP qlen 1000
    link/ether 08:00:27:ec:43:e9 brd ff:ff:ff:ff:ff:ff
    inet 192.168.33.34/24 brd 192.168.33.255 scope global eth2
    inet 192.168.33.10/32 scope global eth2
```

Pacemaker or Percona Replication Manager

Pacemaker is an open source, high availability resource manager to manage clusters. It uses **Corosync** or **Heartbeat** to provide messaging and membership services.

We're going to use both these tools and we will also use a custom MariaDB/MySQL resource agent created by Percona (and contributors) for Corosync in order to make the integration very powerful. This resource agent is called **Percona Replication Manager (PRM)**.

So if you're using the `Vagrantfile` given at the beginning of the chapter, Pacemaker and Corosync will automatically be installed. However, if you need to install them manually, run the following command:

```
> aptitude install pacemaker corosync
```

By default (and it is recommended), cluster nodes use multicast to talk to each other. You may have to adapt your switch configuration to support multicast if it's not the case.

The following schema will help you to understand a little bit of what a good cluster infrastructure should look like:

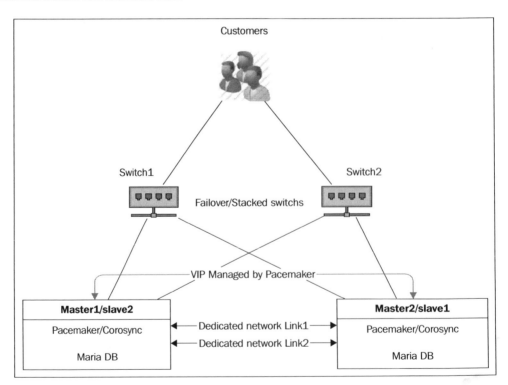

You can see two redundant switches here, both connected to both master nodes. To finish on the physical connectivity, you should consider having two cross-linked and bonded interfaces. You can also pass through a dedicated switch for this part. Do not underestimate the importance of those links. This is how the heartbeat of the cluster communicates.

That means if you lose that link, the cluster won't be able to communicate with nodes and you'll get a cluster split-brain. In that case, you'll get duplicate IP addresses on your network (caused by the VIP) with both nodes as master. This situation could be very uncomfortable to repair if data are written on both sides. You now understand why it's preferable to get a bonded link with cross cables.

The VIP is an IP that can switch from one node to another. It is collocated with the master node. With PRM, there is no dual master configuration; in face, it's a master/slave configuration with a VIP on the master node. If the master node fails, it will switch the master service and VIP to the available node and try to configure the slave once the failed node gets back online.

To communicate with all nodes, the cluster will need an authentication key. Why? Because it broadcasts to discover nodes at boot and needs to avoid registering in a bad cluster if you have multiple nodes on the same network.

Another important thing is that nodes should be able to communicate correctly all together! So, it is important to get a correct DNS name available to all nodes or a correct /etc/hosts file containing all nodes names and IPs.

Finally, you absolutely need to have your server time synchronized. *A NTP client updating your nodes is a must have!* If your servers are not time-synced, you'll get unwanted issues.

Before going ahead with Pacemaker/Corosync, you need to prepare your MariaDB instances. On a classical master/slave replication, you need a dedicated user with replication rights.

Be sure replication is working on all nodes with the correct MariaDB configuration (as seen at the beginning of the chapter) before going further.

Here you need additional users and one to test connectivity. So grant those rights using the following commands:

```
MariaDB [(none)]> grant replication client, replication slave on *.* to
replication@'192.168.33.%' identified by 'password';
```

```
MariaDB [(none)]> grant replication client, replication slave,
SUPER, PROCESS, RELOAD on *.* to replication@'localhost' identified by
'password';
```

```
MariaDB [(none)]> grant select ON mysql.user to test_user@'localhost'
identified by 'password';
```

You now need to dump the required databases with this new information and import it on the second node. There is no need to create the master/slave configuration, PRM will do this for us.

Then we're going to generate the authorization key. But before that, we need to generate entropy by using the following command:

```
> while [ 1 ] ; do tar cj /usr | md5sum >/dev/null ; done &
```

This will create an archive of /usr, creating a checksum on it and forwarding it to /dev/null to drop it. We can now generate the authkey:

```
> cd /etc/corosync
> corosync-keygen
Corosync Cluster Engine Authentication key generator.
Gathering 1024 bits for key from /dev/random.
Press keys on your keyboard to generate entropy.
Press keys on your keyboard to generate entropy (bits = 24).
Press keys on your keyboard to generate entropy (bits = 88).
Press keys on your keyboard to generate entropy (bits = 152).
[...]
Press keys on your keyboard to generate entropy (bits = 864).
Press keys on your keyboard to generate entropy (bits = 928).
Press keys on your keyboard to generate entropy (bits = 992).
Writing corosync key to /etc/corosync/authkey.
```

Then, kill the shell PID of the tar/md5 that will be used for entropy.

The authkey is generated on Master1; you now need to transfer it to Master2 in the same location (/etc/corosync/authkey) with 0400 rights.

Now, let's take a look at the configuration file in `/etc/corosync/corosync.conf`:

```
# Please read the openais.conf.5 manual page

# Backward compatibility for OpenAIS
compatibility: whitetank

totem {
    version: 2
    # How long before declaring a token lost (ms)
    token: 3000
    # How many token retransmits before forming a new configuration
    token_retransmits_before_loss_const: 10
    # How long to wait for join messages in the membership protocol
(ms)
    join: 60
    # How long to wait for consensus to be achieved before starting a
new round of membership configuration (ms)
    consensus: 3600
     # Turn off the virtual synchrony filter
    vsftype: none
    # Number of messages that may be sent by one processor on receipt
of the token
    max_messages: 20
    # Limit generated node ids to 31-bits (positive signed integers)
    clear_node_high_bit: yes
    # Disable encryption
     secauth: on
    # How many threads to use for encryption/decryption
     threads: 0
    # Optionally assign a fixed node id (integer)
    # nodeid: 1234
    # This specifies the mode of redundant ring, which may be none,
active, or passive.
     rrp_mode: none


    # Define the private/dedicated cluster binded network address and
multicast information
    interface {
        # The following values need to be set based on your environment
        ringnumber: 0
        bindnetaddr: 192.168.33.0
        mcastaddr: 226.94.1.1
        mcastport: 5405
```

```
        ttl: 1
    }
}

amf {
    mode: disabled
}

service {
    # Load the Pacemaker Cluster Resource Manager
    ver:        0
    name:       pacemaker
}

aisexec {
        user:   root
        group:  root
}

logging {
        fileline: off
        to_stderr: no
        to_logfile: no
        to_syslog: yes
    #logfile: /var/log/corosync/corosync.log
    syslog_facility: daemon
        debug: off
        timestamp: on
        logger_subsys {
                subsys: AMF
                debug: off
                tags: enter|leave|trace1|trace2|trace3|trace4|trace6
        }
}
```

We need to make some changes to the default configuration (in bold in the preceding code). Additional comments have been added to make it more understandable.

In that file, the most important thing is to define the private/dedicated network interface (bindnetaddr). Here, for simplicity, we're *using the same subnet for everything*; however, this is *not recommended for production usage*. You need to replicate that configuration to Master2 as well.

In a cluster environment, isolate to the maximum the public and private network with dedicated LAN or VLAN!

Logs are also redirected to syslog, which is the simplest way to store logs. You can also use a dedicated log file for it if you want.

Now we're going to change the Corosync/Debian default configuration to make it start at boot on both nodes. Edit the `corosync` file under `/etc/default/` and change the `START` value:

```
# start corosync at boot [yes|no]
START=yes
```

PRM works only if MariaDB/MySQL services are properly stopped. That's why we're going to disable autostart for this service on both nodes:

```
> update-rc.d -f mysql disable
```

We need to install the resource agent from Percona now on both nodes.

If you're using a classical replication, do the following:

```
> url='https://raw.githubusercontent.com/percona/percona-pacemaker-
agents/master/agents/mysql_prm'
```

If you're using a GTID replication, do the following:

```
> url='https://raw.githubusercontent.com/percona/percona-pacemaker-
agents/master/agents/mysql_prm56'
```

Now install PRM:

```
> cd /usr/lib/ocf/resource.d/
> mkdir percona
> cd percona/
> wget -O mysql -q $url
> chmod u+x mysql
```

This is just a bash script that will be called by Pacemaker/Corosync to get the correct state of a MariaDB service.

You're now ready to start Pacemaker/Corosync! Simply start the `corosync` service:

```
> /etc/init.d/corosync restart
```

You can take a look at the cluster status after a few seconds (look for the requested time for cluster creation, authentication nodes, and so on):

```
> crm status
============
Last updated: Sun Mar 23 09:51:00 2014
Last change: Sun Mar 23 08:57:46 2014 via crm_attribute on master1
Stack: openais
Current DC: master2 - partition with quorum
Version: 1.1.7-ee0730e13d124c3d58f00016c3376a1de5323cff
2 Nodes configured, 2 expected votes
0 Resources configured.
============


Online: [ master1 master2 ]
```

We can see here that we got two nodes online and configured. This is good news! We do not have any configured resources yet, but this will come.

Regarding the votes, this is a consensus mechanism to calculate the cluster state. To avoid being in a split-brain situation, you need to have the majority of the total of the nodes in your cluster, plus one. That means in a cluster of 6 nodes, you can lose 2 nodes (*6-(6/3+1)*) without any problems; your cluster will still work properly. Here we got 2 nodes, so we can add a quorum to get 3 votes. This is not the subject of the book, but if you want to avoid the split-brain case, you should consider having 3 nodes or adding a quorum device.

The configuration is empty, so we're going to update it with the `crm` command:

```
> crm configure edit
```

You should replace what you have with the following:

```
node master1 \
    attributes p_mysql_mysql_master_IP="192.168.33.31" \
    attributes standby="off"
node master2 \
    attributes p_mysql_mysql_master_IP="192.168.33.32" \
    attributes standby="off"
primitive p_mysql ocf:percona:mysql \
    params config="/etc/mysql/my.cnf"\
    pid="/var/run/mysqld/mysqld.pid" \
```

```
    socket="/var/run/mysqld/mysqld.sock" \
    replication_user="replication" \
    replication_passwd="password" \
    max_slave_lag="60" \
    evict_outdated_slaves="false" \
    binary="/usr/sbin/mysqld" \
    test_user="test_user" \
    test_passwd="password" \
    op monitor interval="5s" role="Master" OCF_CHECK_LEVEL="1" \
    op monitor interval="2s" role="Slave" OCF_CHECK_LEVEL="1" \
    op start interval="0" timeout="60s" \
    op stop interval="0" timeout="60s"
primitive writer_vip ocf:heartbeat:IPaddr2 \
    params ip="192.168.33.100" nic="eth2" \
    op monitor interval="10s" \
    meta target-role="Started"
ms ms_MySQL p_mysql \
    meta master-max="1" master-node-max="1" clone-max="2" clone-node-
max="1" notify="true" globally-unique="false" target-role="Started"
is-managed="true"
location cli-prefer-writer_vip writer_vip \
    rule $id="cli-prefer-rule-writer_vip" inf: #uname eq master1
colocation writer_vip_on_master inf: writer_vip ms_MySQL:Master
order ms_MySQL_promote_before_vip inf: ms_MySQL:promote writer_
vip:start
property $id="cib-bootstrap-options" \
    dc-version="1.1.7-ee0730e13d124c3d58f00016c3376a1de5323cff" \
    cluster-infrastructure="openais" \
    expected-quorum-votes="2" \
    no-quorum-policy="ignore" \
    stonith-enabled="false" \
    last-lrm-refresh="1395506003"
rsc_defaults $id="rsc-options" \
    resource-stickiness="INFINITY"
```

When you register and quit from Vi, the preceding will be applied automatically. If you make syntax errors or anything that could be annoying, you'll be notified and will be prompted to re-edit.

This is a huge configuration, and it would take too long to explain in detail what everything does. So we're going to concentrate on what you need to change and how it works:

- `node`: These lines are the node names of the MariaDB servers with their private/public network IP. The `p_mysql_mysql_master_IP` attributes indicate the IP to be used when a MySQL `change master` command is invoked by other nodes. You need to adapt those lines of course.

- `primitive p_mysql`: This is information related to the MariaDB instance: all the required path for socket, PID, binary path, and so on. You have to enter the replication username and password used everywhere as well. You also have to enter `test_user` credentials. Other options are for cluster monitoring.

- `primitive writer_vip`: This is the public VIP to access your MariaDB master. This VIP will be used by your applications to connect to a working instance of MariaDB. Pacemaker/Corosync will perform the task of giving you an always working version of your MariaDB master instance.

- `ms ms_MySQL`: This is where you configure the number of wanted masters and slaves. With PRM, you can have complex solutions based on MariaDB replications. Here, we just want a Failover/Fault tolerance system and do not need to set up more.

- `location cli-prefer-writer_vip`: This indicates that we prefer having the master node on Master1. This is, for example, the case when you boot the whole cluster (all nodes) at the same time.

- `colocation`: This indicates that the VIP has to be placed on the master node!

- `order`: This indicates that MariaDB should be available to work before starting the VIP.

- `property`: This is the cluster property. Here, we declare that we do not have **Shoot The Other Node In The Head (STONITH)** configured (fencing method), and there is no quorum here.

- `rsc_defaults`: We define resource stickiness here. This part is important when you have flip-flap on your servers. Suppose your Master1 has a hardware network card issue which flip-flaps the connectivity. Without this option, the master and VIP would always want to auto fail back to their preference node. As we generally do not want to have a disconnection, it's better to set the stickiness. When your first node is back to a normal state, you can manually switch to it with a `crm` command. So, to simplify, it disables the auto failback.

If you check the status, you can see it works fine:

```
> crm_mon -rA
============
Last updated: Sun Mar 23 08:57:46 2014
Last change: Sun Mar 23 08:57:46 2014 via crm_attribute on master1
Stack: openais
Current DC: master2 - partition with quorum
Version: 1.1.7-ee0730e13d124c3d58f00016c3376a1de5323cff
2 Nodes configured, 2 expected votes
3 Resources configured.
============


Online: [ master1 master2 ]


Full list of resources:

writer_vip        (ocf::heartbeat:IPaddr2):        Started master1
 Master/Slave Set: ms_MySQL [p_mysql]
     Masters: [ master1 ]
     Slaves: [ master2 ]


Node Attributes:
* Node master1:
    + master-p_mysql:0              : 1060
    + p_mysql_mysql_master_IP       : 192.168.33.31
    + readable                      : 1
* Node master2:
    + master-p_mysql:1              : 60
    + p_mysql_mysql_master_IP       : 192.168.33.32
    + readable                      : 1
```

The `-rA` option shows all/unused resources and permits to autorefresh the status.

You can switch nodes by setting one of the nodes in maintenance. Let's say we want to move all resources from Master1 to Master2:

```
> crm node standby master1
> crm node online master1
```

Now Master2 is the master and Master1 the slave:

```
> crm status
============
Last updated: Sun Mar 23 11:24:34 2014
Last change: Sun Mar 23 11:23:58 2014 via crm_attribute on master1
Stack: openais
Current DC: master2 - partition with quorum
Version: 1.1.7-ee0730e13d124c3d58f00016c3376a1de5323cff
2 Nodes configured, 2 expected votes
3 Resources configured.
============


Online: [ master1 master2 ]

 writer_vip     (ocf::heartbeat:IPaddr2):      Started master2
 Master/Slave Set: ms_MySQL [p_mysql]
     Masters: [ master2 ]
     Slaves: [ master1 ]
```

You have a working master/slave solution that is fault-tolerant on two nodes. If you want to go ahead with PRM or need more explanation, you can look at the official documentation at https://github.com/percona/percona-pacemaker-agents/blob/master/doc/PRM-setup-guide.rst.

DRBD

You may have huge traffic on your master node with a high replication lag that makes your replication unstable. First of all, try to resolve it by ensuring that you don't have any network issues and have enough bandwidth. Remember that, for a dual master replication, a fast local network is recommended (1 GB, 10 GB, or 40 GB Ethernet, or InfiniBand).

If the problem can not be resolved, you should consider having a block replication system such as **Distributed Replicated Block Device (DRBD)** instead of the dual master replication. DRBD will work along with with Pacemaker/Corosync to get automatic management. The architecture should looks like this:

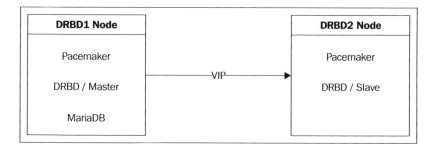

The first step is to create a Pacemaker/Corosync cluster. You can take the previous configuration for that. To prepare it, perform the following steps:

1. Install an `ntp` client.
2. Be sure the hostname's nodes are correctly accessible.
3. Generate authkey and copy it to the other node.
4. Install the `/etc/corosync/corosync.conf` configuration file.
5. Edit the `/etc/default/corosync` file.
6. Start `corosync`.

You can now install DRBD manually and load the module:

```
> aptitude install drbd8-utils
> modprobe drbd
```

Then, make it persistent by adding it to loadable modules at machine boot:

```
> echo "drbd" >> /etc/modules
```

Now, edit the global configuration (`/etc/drbd.d/global_common.conf`) and change it as follows:

```
# Global configuration
global {
    # Do not report statistics usage to LinBit
    usage-count no;
}

# All resources inherit the options set in this section
common {
    # C (Synchronous replication protocol)
    protocol C;
```

```
    startup {
        # Wait for connection timeout (in seconds)
        wfc-timeout 1 ;
        # Wait for connection timeout, if this node was a degraded
cluster (in seconds)
        degr-wfc-timeout 1 ;
    }


    net {
        # Maximum number of requests to be allocated by DRBD
        max-buffers 8192;
        # The highest number of data blocks between two write
barriers
        max-epoch-size 8192;
        # The size of the TCP socket send buffer
        sndbuf-size 512k;
        # How often the I/O subsystem's controller is forced to
process pending I/O requests
        unplug-watermark 8192;
        # The HMAC algorithm to enable peer authentication at all
        cram-hmac-alg sha1;
        # The shared secret used in peer authentication
        shared-secret "xxx";
        # Split brains
        # Split brain, resource is not in the Primary role on any
host
        after-sb-0pri disconnect;
        # Split brain, resource is in the Primary role on one host
        after-sb-1pri disconnect;
        # Split brain, resource is in the Primary role on both
host
        after-sb-2pri disconnect;
        # Helps to solve the cases when the outcome of the resync
decision is incompatible with the current role assignment
        rr-conflict disconnect;
    }


    handlers {
        # If the node is primary, degraded and if the local copy
of the data is inconsistent
        pri-on-incon-degr "echo Current node is primary, degraded
and the local copy of the data is inconsistent | wall ";
    }
```

```
disk {
        # The node downgrades the disk status to inconsistent on
io errors
        on-io-error pass_on;
        # Disable protecting data if power failure (done by
hardware)
        no-disk-barrier;
        # Disable the backing device to support disk flushes
        no-disk-flushes;
        # Do not let write requests drain before write requests of
a new reordering domain are issued
        no-disk-drain;
        # Disables the use of disk flushes and barrier BIOs when
accessing the meta data device
        no-md-flushes;
    }

    syncer {
        # The maximum bandwidth a resource uses for background re-
synchronization
        rate 500M;
        # Control how big the hot area (= active set) can get
        al-extents 3833;
    }
}
```

In this configuration, we are using Protocol C, which permits DRDB to be in synchronous mode. We also are using a disconnect mode (`after-sb*` parameters) to prevent DRBD from trying to autorepair in a split-brain scenario. It's preferable to understand why there were issues and to resume manually in some cases. As you may not be familiar with DRBD, consider using those options.

You also need to set a shared secret (choose what you want as a secret).

We are now going to configure the DRBD device:

```
resource r0 {
    # DRBD1
    on drbd1 {
        device        /dev/drbd0;
        # Disk containing the drbd partition
        disk          /dev/mapper/drbd-sql;
        # IP address of this host
        address       192.168.33.41:7788;
        # Store metadata on the same device
```

```
        meta-disk    internal;
    }
    # DRBD2
    on drbd2 {
        device      /dev/drbd0;
        disk        /dev/mapper/drbd-sql;
        address     192.168.33.42:7788;
        meta-disk   internal;
    }
}
```

You may notice that the disk is based on a device mapper. In fact, it's preferable to put the DRBD device on an LVM volume in case you want to grow the storage in future.

On your dedicated device (/dev/sdb if you used Vagrantfile), we're going to create the partition, declare the partition as LVM, and create the volume group and an LV that will take the full size of the VG (just to keep it simple). Finally, we will restart DRBD and create a filesystem on it. Launch the following commands *on both nodes*:

```
> datas_device=/dev/sdb
> parted -s -a optimal $datas_device mklabel gpt
> parted -s -a optimal $datas_device mkpart primary ext4 0% 100%
> parted -s $datas_device set 1 lvm on
> pvcreate /dev/sdb1
> vgcreate drbd /dev/sdb1
> lvcreate -l 100%FREE -n sql drbd
> /etc/init.d/drbd restart
> drbdadm create-md r0
> drbdadm up r0
```

Now, *only on the first node* (drbd1), launch the synchronization:

```
> drbdadm -- --overwrite-data-of-peer primary r0
```

You can take a look at the drbd status in the following manner:

```
> drbd-overview
  0:r0  SyncSource Primary/Secondary UpToDate/Inconsistent C r-----
   [>...................] sync'ed:  5.6% (3959900/4190044)K
```

When it's finished, it looks like this:

```
> drbd-overview
  0:r0  Connected Primary/Secondary UpToDate/UpToDate C r-----
```

Now create the filesystem:

```
> mkfs.ext4 /dev/drbd0
```

Since we are using MariaDB, we need to disable the start at boot to let Pacemaker/ Corosync manage it:

```
> update-rc.d -f drbd disable
> update-rc.d -f mysql disable
```

In the same directory, we're going to clean up some things. On the master node, do the following:

```
> /etc/init.d/mysql stop
> mv /var/lib/mysql{,.bak}
> mkdir /var/lib/mysql
> mount /dev/drbd0 /var/lib/mysql
> mv /var/lib/mysql.bak/* /var/lib/mysql/
> rmdir /var/lib/mysql.bak
> umount /var/lib/mysql
```

Then remove the content of /var/lib/mysql on the other node (drbd2):

```
> rm -Rf /var/lib/mysql
> mkdir /var/lib/mysql
```

We do not need to set a replication for MariaDB, as this will be a single instance block replicated by DRBD.

Edit the cluster configuration as shown:

```
> crm configure edit
node drbd1
node drbd2
primitive drbd_mysql ocf:linbit:drbd \
    params drbd_resource="r0" \
    op monitor interval="29s" role="Master" \
    op monitor interval="31s" role="Slave"
primitive fs_mysql ocf:heartbeat:Filesystem \
    params device="/dev/drbd0" directory="/var/lib/mysql/" fstype="ext4"
primitive ip_mysql ocf:heartbeat:IPaddr2 \
    params ip="192.168.33.200" nic="eth2"
primitive mysqld lsb:mysql
group mysql fs_mysql ip_mysql mysqld
```

```
ms ms_drbd_mysql drbd_mysql \
    meta master-max="1" master-node-max="1" clone-max="2" clone-node-
max="1" notify="true"
colocation mysql_on_drbd inf: mysql ms_drbd_mysql:Master
order mysql_after_drbd inf: ms_drbd_mysql:promote mysql:start
property $id="cib-bootstrap-options" \
    dc-version="1.1.7-ee0730e13d124c3d58f00016c3376a1de5323cff" \
    cluster-infrastructure="openais" \
    expected-quorum-votes="2" \
    stonith-enabled="false" \
    no-quorum-policy="ignore" \
    last-lrm-refresh="1395600237"
rsc_defaults $id="rsc-options" \
    resource-stickiness="100"
```

Let's see the explanation of some points:

- `drbd_resource`: Here, r0 is the DRBD resource name.
- `fm parameters`: Enter the DRBD device with a mount point and filesystem.
- `primitive vip`: Set the VIP and network interface name for DRBD communication. You can use a private dedicated network.

You're now ready to start! Start the `corosync` service and check the status:

```
> /etc/init.d/corosync start
> crm_mon -rA
============
Last updated: Sun Mar 23 20:28:12 2014
Last change: Sun Mar 23 18:43:57 2014 via crmd on drbd1
Stack: openais
Current DC: drbd1 - partition with quorum
Version: 1.1.7-ee0730e13d124c3d58f00016c3376a1de5323cff
2 Nodes configured, 2 expected votes
5 Resources configured.
============


Online: [ drbd1 drbd2 ]


Full list of resources:

 Resource Group: mysql
```

```
     fs_mysql    (ocf::heartbeat:Filesystem):      Started drbd2
     ip_mysql    (ocf::heartbeat:IPaddr2):         Started drbd2
     mysqld      (lsb:mysql):     Started drbd2
 Master/Slave Set: ms_drbd_mysql [drbd_mysql]
     Masters: [ drbd2 ]
     Slaves: [ drbd1 ]


Node Attributes:
* Node drbd1:
    + master-drbd_mysql:0              : 10000
* Node drbd2:
    + master-drbd_mysql:1              : 10000
```

How to repair a dual master replication

In a dual master replication, you can easily have issues if you do it manually without a cluster or something else.

There is not much difference between repairing a master/slave and a master/master replication. However, you should take care of one evident thing: when you're working on an issue on Master 2 for example, *you absolutely need to stop the slave replication on Master1*!

The advantage of doing this is simple; if you make mistakes on Master2, they won't be replicated on Master1. This helps you to keep your Master2 node as close as Master1 if you can correctly repair it. However, if you fail, you can recreate from a dump of your Master2 without impacting Master1 data.

That's why, in a dual master replication, the first thing to do is to stop the slave replication! If you are not sure which one to stop, it's preferable to stop all slave replications instead of modifying unwanted data.

Summary

In this chapter, you learned how to build a dual master replication and how to use high level software for high availability and load balancing. The complexity of some software such as Pacemaker/Corosync demands some practice before going live with production.

In the next chapter, we'll see additional solutions from MariaDB 10 that help to set up complex infrastructures.

7
MariaDB Multimaster Slaves

You're now familiar with slave and dual master replications. You've seen their benefits as well. However, other very interesting features are available since MariaDB 10.

Most of these features are for advanced usages. However, they could be used in a more classical way to avoid manual data manipulations (like a multimaster slave solution).

Multimaster slave replication

The multimaster slave replication, also known as multisource replication, uses the GTID mechanism to provide this feature:

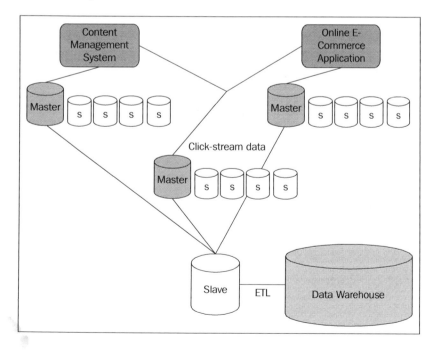

Here, for example, you have a master database with slaves for a CMS application. On the other hand, you've got a master and multiple slaves for your e-commerce application. Data could be huge and it is dispersed across several databases and tables.

In this kind of situation, when you want to aggregate data, you generally need to perform tricks with triggers. Alternatively, you need to use any other kind of complicated solution.

That's when multisource replication comes into action. From multiple master or slave databases/tables, you can build a database that will contain data from multiple databases/tables. This is very useful to get all data you want as up-to-date as possible without huge amounts of work.

So if you need to aggregate data easily without needing an **Extract-Transform-Load (ETL)**, use multisource replication. You'll then be able to send that data to your data warehouse or Big Data analytics with an ETL for example or Hadoop; the limitation for multisource replication is 64 hosts.

Setting up a multisource replication

To make it simple, let's start with two masters with different content and a slave that will take the full content of both MariaDB instances:

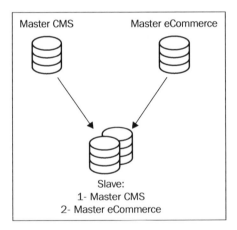

The following is the technical information required by the schema:

- Master1: 192.168.33.31
- Master2: 192.168.33.32
- Slave1: 192.168.33.33

If you do not put on any restrictions, then unless you *really* know what you are doing, all database names must be unique across servers! You'll get a slave replication issue in that case.

You can use a `Vagrantfile` with the following content for this situation:

```ruby
# -*- mode: ruby -*-
# vi: set ft=ruby :
# Vagrantfile API/syntax version. Don't touch unless you know what
you're doing!
#
VAGRANTFILE_API_VERSION = "2"


# Insert all your Vms with configs
boxes = [
    { :name => :master1,        :role     => 'db',    :ip =>
'192.168.33.31' }, # master node 1
    { :name => :master2,        :role     => 'db',    :ip =>
'192.168.33.32' }, # master node 2
    { :name => :slave1,         :role     => 'db',    :ip =>
'192.168.33.33' }, # slave1
]


$install_common = <<INSTALL
aptitude update
DEBIAN_FRONTEND=noninteractive aptitude -y -o Dpkg::Options::="--
force-confdef" -o Dpkg::Options::="--force-confold" install python-
software-properties openntpd
INSTALL


$install = <<INSTALL
aptitude update
DEBIAN_FRONTEND=noninteractive aptitude -y -o Dpkg::Options::="--
force-confdef" -o Dpkg::Options::="--force-confold" install python-
software-properties
apt-key adv --recv-keys --keyserver keyserver.ubuntu.com
0xcbcb082a1bb943db
apt-key adv --keyserver keys.gnupg.net --recv-keys 1C4CBDCDCD2EFD2A
add-apt-repository 'deb http://ftp.igh.cnrs.fr/pub/mariadb/repo/10.0/
debian wheezy main'
add-apt-repository 'deb http://repo.percona.com/apt wheezy main'
echo 'Package: *
Pin: release o=Percona Development Team
```

```
Pin-Priority: 100' > /etc/apt/preferences.d/00percona.pref
aptitude update
DEBIAN_FRONTEND=noninteractive aptitude -y -o Dpkg::Options::="--
force-confdef" -o Dpkg::Options::="--force-confold" install mariadb-
server percona-toolkit
INSTALL


Vagrant::Config.run do |config|
  # Default box OS
  vm_default = proc do |boxcnf|
    boxcnf.vm.box       = "deimosfr/debian-wheezy"
  end

  boxes.each do |opts|
    vm_default.call(config)
    config.vm.define opts[:name] do |config|
        config.vm.network    :hostonly, opts[:ip]
        config.vm.host_name = "%s.vm" % opts[:name].to_s
        config.vm.provision "shell", inline: $install_common
        config.vm.provision "shell", inline: $install
    end
  end
end
```

On both the master nodes, use the following minimal MariaDB configuration:

```
[mysqld]
server-id=1
gtid_strict_mode=1
bind-address = 0.0.0.0
log_bin=/var/log/mysql/mariadb-bin
expire_logs_days=10
sync_binlog = 1
slave_compressed_protocol = 1
binlog_format = row
```

> You should take care about server IDs. All master nodes should
> have different IDs. If it's not the case, you'll get into trouble if you
> try to replicate from the multisource slave back to your master.

On both the master nodes, create the user that will be allowed to replicate data:

```
MariaDB [(none)]> CREATE USER 'REPLICATION'@'192.168.33.33' IDENTIFIED BY
'PASSWORD';

MariaDB [(none)]> GRANT REPLICATION SLAVE ON *.* TO
'REPLICATION'@'192.168.33.33';

MariaDB [(none)]> FLUSH PRIVILEGES;
```

On the slave node, add the following configuration in the configuration file:

```
[mysqld]
server-id=3
gtid_strict_mode=1
bind-address = 0.0.0.0
slave_compressed_protocol = 1
binlog_format = row
read_only
```

Do not forget to restart all MariaDB services after applying configuration changes. You're ready to get the GTID position on both masters. Let's do it for Master1:

```
MariaDB [(none)]> SELECT @@GLOBAL.GTID_CURRENT_POS;

+--------------------------+
| @@GLOBAL.gtid_current_pos |
+--------------------------+
| 0-1-2145                 |
+--------------------------+
```

Now take a look on the slave connection name. You will find it empty because no replication is set up yet:

```
MariaDB [(none)]> SELECT @@DEFAULT_MASTER_CONNECTION;

+----------------------------+
| @@default_master_connection |
+----------------------------+
|                            |
+----------------------------+
```

We're now ready to set up the default master connection. To do this, you need to inform MariaDB that you want to create a replication on a specific master node, with two new parameters.

The first parameter is used to give a name to that replication:

```
MariaDB [(none)]> SET @@DEFAULT_MASTER_CONNECTION='MASTER1';
```

The selected replication indicates where we're currently working on `master1`. You can verify this:

```
MariaDB [(none)]> SELECT @@DEFAULT_MASTER_CONNECTION;
+-----------------------------+
| @@default_master_connection |
+-----------------------------+
| master1                     |
+-----------------------------+
```

 In our case, to avoid any misunderstanding, it is strongly recommended that you set the default master connection name equal to the hostname. In a larger infrastructure with several slaves, you may consider naming it with the project name (here `'cms'` or `'e-commerce'`).

The second new parameter is in the `change master` command. You need to set the name of the replication you want to take action on. Here, we're still on Master1, so do the following:

```
MariaDB [(none)]> SET GLOBAL GTID_SLAVE_POS = "0-1-2145";
```

```
MariaDB [(none)]> CHANGE MASTER 'MASTER1' TO MASTER_HOST='192.168.33.31',
MASTER_USER='REPLICATION', MASTER_PASSWORD='PASSWORD', MASTER_USE_
GTID=SLAVE_POS;
```

The Master1 node is configured on the slave but not yet started. Let's finish the slave configuration for Master2:

```
MariaDB [(none)]> SET @@DEFAULT_MASTER_CONNECTION='MASTER2';
```

```
MariaDB [(none)]> SET GLOBAL GTID_SLAVE_POS = "0-1-2145";
```

```
MariaDB [(none)]> CHANGE MASTER 'MASTER2' TO MASTER_HOST='192.168.33.32',
MASTER_USER='REPLICATION', MASTER_PASSWORD='PASSWORD', MASTER_USE_
GTID=SLAVE_POS;
```

As now we've finished setting up the replication for both masters, we could start all at once:

```
MariaDB [(none)]> START ALL SLAVES;
```

Then, take a look at the current messages:

```
MariaDB [(none)]> SHOW WARNINGS;
+-------+------+-------------------------+
| Level | Code | Message                 |
+-------+------+-------------------------+
| Note  | 1937 | SLAVE 'master2' started |
| Note  | 1937 | SLAVE 'master1' started |
+-------+------+-------------------------+
2 rows in set (0.00 sec)
```

There's also a command to take a look at all slave statuses at once:

```
MariaDB [(none)]> SHOW ALL SLAVES STATUS\G ;
*************************** 1. row ***************************
              Connection_name: master1
              Slave_SQL_State: Slave has read all relay log; waiting for
the slave I/O thread to update it
               Slave_IO_State: Waiting for master to send event
                  Master_Host: 192.168.33.31
[...]
             Slave_IO_Running: Yes
            Slave_SQL_Running: Yes
[...]
               Gtid_Slave_Pos: 0-1-2145
*************************** 2. row ***************************
              Connection_name: master2
              Slave_SQL_State: Slave has read all relay log; waiting for
the slave I/O thread to update it
               Slave_IO_State: Waiting for master to send event
                  Master_Host: 192.168.33.32
[...]
             Slave_IO_Running: Yes
            Slave_SQL_Running: Yes
[...]
               Gtid_Slave_Pos: 0-1-2145
2 rows in set (0.00 sec)
```

The multimaster slave replication is now running! You can test it by creating a database on Master1; it will appear on the Slave1 node. Create a database on Master2 and it will also appear on Slave1. You need to be careful about database duplication, or it will break one of the replications and you'll need to repair it.

One last thing, which we have already discussed, is that you should be really sure about the replication you're working on (@@DEFAULT_MASTER_CONNECTION) before making changes! Double check each time!

Other options

Like classical replication options, you can apply a replication's restrictions on a per-slave basis:

- `replicate_do_db`, `replicate_do_table`
- `replicate_ignore_db`, `replicate_ignore_table`
- `replicate_wild_do_table`, `replicate_wild_ignore_table`

Similar to how we used the `start` option, you can stop all your slaves at once:

```
MariaDB [(none)]> STOP ALL SLAVES;
```

When you want to reset a replication status, you need to indicate on which replication you want to do it:

```
MariaDB [(none)]> RESET SLAVE 'MASTER1';
```

Summary

Since the beginning of the book, you've seen a lot of replication methods and usages. You're now familiar with read replications and dual masters. But what if the problem is not reads but writes? That's the subject of the next chapter—Galera Cluster.

8
Galera Cluster – Multimaster Replication

In the previous chapters, we saw solutions such as slave / multislave / master replications, slave with cluster, and load balancers, but there were no solutions that could provide several write replications. This is where Galera Cluster comes into the picture, bringing that and other features that will be discussed in detail in this chapter.

Galera Cluster is a synchronous multimaster solution created by Codership. It's a patch for MySQL and MariaDB with its own commands and configuration. On MariaDB, it has been officially promoted as the **MariaDB Cluster**.

Galera Cluster provides certification-based replication. This means that each node certifies the replicated write set against other write sets. You don't have to worry about data integrity, as it manages it automatically and very well. Galera Cluster is a young product, but is ready for production.

If you have already heard of MySQL Cluster, don't be confused; this is not the same thing at all. MySQL Cluster is a solution that has not been ported to MariaDB due to its complexity, code, and other reasons. MySQL Cluster provides availability and partitioning, while Galera Cluster provides consistency and availability. Galera Cluster is a simple yet powerful solution.

How Galera Cluster works

The following are some advantages of Galera Cluster:

- **True multimaster**: It can read and write to any node at any time
- **Synchronous replication**: There is no slave lag and no data is lost at node crash
- **Consistent data**: All nodes have the same state (same data exists between nodes at a point in time)
- **Multithreaded slave**: This enables better performance with any workload
- **No need of an HA Cluster for management**: There are no master-slave failover operations (such as Pacemaker, PCR, and so on)
- **Hot standby**: There is no downtime during failover
- **Transparent to applications**: No specific drivers or application changes are required
- **No read and write splitting needed**: There is no need to split the read and write requests
- **WAN**: Galera Cluster supports WAN replication

Galera Cluster needs at least three nodes to work properly (because of the notion of quorum, election, and so on). You can also work with a two-node cluster, but you will need an arbiter (hence three nodes). The arbiter could be used on another machine available in the same LAN of your Galera Cluster, if possible.

The multimaster replication has been *designed for InnoDB/XtraDB*. It doesn't mean you can't perform a replication with other storage engines!

If you want to use other storage engines, you will be limited by the following:

- They can only write on a single node at a time to maintain consistency.
- Replication with other nodes may not be fully supported.
- Conflict management won't be supported.
- Applications that connect to Galera will only be able to write on a single node (IP/DNS) at the same time.

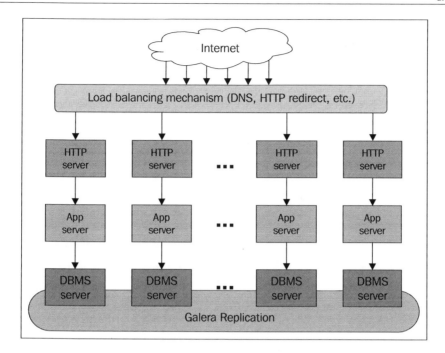

As you can see in the preceding diagram, HTTP and App servers speak directly to their respective DBMS servers without wondering which node of the Galera Cluster they are targeting.

Usually, without Galera Cluster, you can use a cluster software such as Pacemaker/ Corosync to get a VIP on a master node that can switch over in case a problem occurs. No need to get PCR in that case; a simple VIP with a custom script will be sufficient to check whether the server is in sync with others is enough.

Galera Cluster uses the following advanced mechanisms for replication:

- **Transaction reordering**: Transactions are reordered before commitment to other nodes. This increases the number of successful transaction certification pass tests.

- **Write sets**: This reduces the number of operations between nodes by writing sets in a single write set to avoid too much node coordination.

- **Database state machine**: Read-only transactions are processed on the local node. Write transactions are executed locally on shadow copies and then broadcasted as a read set to the other nodes for certification and commit.

- **Group communication**: High-level abstraction for communication between nodes to guarantee consistency (gcomm or spread).

To get consistency and similar IDs between nodes, Galera Cluster uses GTID, similar to MariaDB 10 replication. However, it doesn't use the MariaDB GTID replication mechanism at all, as it has its own implementation for its own usage.

Galera Cluster limitations

Galera Cluster has limitations that prevent it from working correctly.

 Do not go live in production if you haven't checked that your application is in compliance with the limitations listed.

The following are the limitations:

- Galera Cluster only fully supports InnoDB tables. TokuDB is planned but not yet available and MyISAM is partially supported.

- Galera Cluster uses primary keys on all your tables (mandatory) to avoid different query execution orders between all your nodes. If you do not do it on your own, Galera will create one. The delete operation is not supported on the tables without primary keys.

- Locking/unlocking tables and lock functions are not supported. They will be ignored if you try to use them.

- Galera Cluster disables query cache.

- XA transactions (global transactions) are not supported.

- Query logs can't be directed to a table, but can be directed to a file instead.

- Other less common limitations exist (please refer to the full list if you want to get them all: `http://galeracluster.com/documentation-webpages/limitations.html`) but in most cases, you shouldn't be annoyed with those ones.

The basics of installation and configuration

In this section, we will discuss the basics of the installation and configuration. As there are a lot of options and things to understand, we'll concentrate first on how to get something working in a simple way. Then, we'll see configuration options in more detail.

To avoid confusion, we'll use InnoDB exclusively in this configuration.

Installation

If you want to test it with Vagrant, you can use the following `Vagrantfile` here:

```ruby
# -*- mode: ruby -*-
# vi: set ft=ruby :
# Vagrantfile API/syntax version. Don't touch unless you know what
you're doing!
#
VAGRANTFILE_API_VERSION = "2"

# Insert all your Vms with configs
boxes = [
    { :name => :galera1, :role => 'gc', :ip => '192.168.33.31' }, #
galera cluster node 1
    { :name => :galera2, :role => 'gc', :ip => '192.168.33.32' }, #
galera cluster node 2
    { :name => :galera3, :role => 'gc', :ip => '192.168.33.33' }, #
galera cluster node 3
    { :name => :garb,    :role => 'gc', :ip => '192.168.33.34' }, #
galera quorum
    { :name => :lb,      :role => 'lb', :ip => '192.168.33.40' }, #
load balancer
    { :name => :galera4, :role => 'gc', :ip => '192.168.33.41' }, #
galera DR cluster node 1
    { :name => :galera5, :role => 'gc', :ip => '192.168.33.42' }, #
galera DR cluster node 2
    { :name => :galera6, :role => 'gc', :ip => '192.168.33.43' }, #
galera DR cluster node 3
]

$install_common = <<INSTALL
aptitude update
DEBIAN_FRONTEND=noninteractive aptitude -y -o Dpkg::Options::="--
force-confdef" -o Dpkg::Options::="--force-confold" install python-
software-properties openntpd
INSTALL

$install = <<INSTALL
```

```
apt-key adv --recv-keys --keyserver keyserver.ubuntu.com
0xcbcb082a1bb943db
apt-key adv --keyserver keys.gnupg.net --recv-keys 1C4CBDCDCD2EFD2A
add-apt-repository 'deb http://mirrors.linsrv.net/mariadb/repo/10.0/
debian wheezy main'
add-apt-repository 'deb http://repo.percona.com/apt wheezy main'
echo 'Package: *
Pin: release o=Percona Development Team
Pin-Priority: 100' > /etc/apt/preferences.d/00percona.pref
aptitude update
DEBIAN_FRONTEND=noninteractive aptitude -y -o Dpkg::Options::="--
force-confdef" -o Dpkg::Options::="--force-confold" install percona-
toolkit mariadb-galera-server galera rsync xinetd
INSTALL


$install_lb = <<INSTALL
add-apt-repository 'deb http://ftp.fr.debian.org/debian/ wheezy-
backports main'
aptitude update
DEBIAN_FRONTEND=noninteractive aptitude -y -o Dpkg::Options::="--
force-confdef" -o Dpkg::Options::="--force-confold" install haproxy
tcpdump keepalived
sed -i "s/ENABLED=0/ENABLED=1/" /etc/default/haproxy
echo "net.ipv4.ip_nonlocal_bind = 1" >> /etc/sysctl.conf
INSTALL


Vagrant::Config.run do |config|
  # Default box OS
  vm_default = proc do |boxcnf|
    boxcnf.vm.box       = "deimosfr/debian-wheezy"
  end

  boxes.each do |opts|
    vm_default.call(config)
    config.vm.define opts[:name] do |config|
        config.vm.customize ["modifyvm", :id, "--cpus", 2]
        config.vm.network    :hostonly, opts[:ip]
        config.vm.host_name = "%s.vm" % opts[:name].to_s
        config.vm.provision "shell", inline: $install_common
        # Install HAProxy for load balancer server or
        if opts[:role] == 'lb'
            config.vm.provision "shell", inline: $install_lb
        else
```

```
config.vm.provision "shell", inline: $install
config.vm.customize ["modifyvm", :id, "--memory", 768]
        end
    end
  end
end
```

The manual ways to install Galera Cluster are discussed next.

1. We need at least three servers to make it work, so ensure that you have them. On all servers, we'll need to have a MariaDB repository to be configured as the Galera Cluster is packaged inside:

   ```
   > apt-get install python-software-properties
   > apt-key adv --recv-keys --keyserver keyserver.ubuntu.com
   0xcbcb082a1bb943db
   > add-apt-repository 'deb http://ftp.igh.cnrs.fr/pub/mariadb/
   repo/10.0/debian wheezy main'
   > apt-get update
   ```

2. Now we're ready to install Galera Cluster:

   ```
   > aptitude install mariadb-galera-server galera
   ```

3. We will also need servers to be time-synced. That's why we'll install an NTP server:

   ```
   > aptitude install openntpd
   ```

4. We also need to get rsync for a method of data synchronization that we'll see later in this chapter:

   ```
   > aptitude install rsync
   ```

You can also install Xtrabackup as there is an interesting solution with it!

Configuration files

To be clear, the configuration will be split into two files:

* The classical my.cnf file
* Specific Galera Cluster configuration

If not split, the Galera Cluster configuration needs to be in the [mysqld] (ini) statement. However, to make it clear, we're going to use a dedicated file for Galera. This will permit us to override some options in the classical my.cnf configuration, thereby ensuring that we're in compliance with Galera Cluster requirements.

MariaDB configuration

Edit the MariaDB configuration file and be sure those options are enabled and correctly set in /etc/mysql/my.cnf:

```
[mysqld]
bind-address                = 0.0.0.0
datadir                     = /var/lib/mysql
innodb_buffer_pool_size     = 10G
innodb_log_file_size        = 100M
innodb_file_per_table
innodb_flush_log_at_trx_commit = 2
```

Ensure that you've properly adjusted all of these values and that this configuration is the same on all Galera nodes.

> If you don't run the same configuration on all servers, you may have replication errors.

Galera configuration

Now we're going to talk about the biggest part of the configuration file. For Galera, we're going to create a dedicated file for this purpose and override all MariaDB configurations that are mandatory for Galera to avoid a non-understandable situation.

So create a configuration file (/etc/mysql/conf.d/galera.cnf) with the following content:

```
# Galera-specific config file.

[mysqld]
# Galera Cluster
wsrep_provider = /usr/lib/galera/libgalera_smm.so
wsrep_cluster_name='mariadb_cluster'
wsrep_node_name=galera1
wsrep_node_address="192.168.33.31"
wsrep_cluster_address = 'gcom://192.168.33.31,192.168.33.32,192.168.33.33'
wsrep_retry_autocommit = 0
wsrep_sst_method = rsync
wsrep_provider_options="gcache.size = 512M; gcache.name = /tmp/galera.cache; gcache.page_size = 100M"
wsrep_slave_threads=16
```

```
#wsrep_replication_myisam = 1
#wsrep_sst_receive_address = <x.x.x.x>
#wsrep_notify_cmd="script.sh"
```

There are a lot of options here; we're going to see why they will be of interest to us:

- `wrep_provider`: This is the path where the Galera plugin is located. This allows the loading of Galera Cluster when MariaDB boots.

- `wsrep_cluster_name`: This is the name of the cluster. It's generally used when you have multiple servers in the same network subnet. This is to prevent unwanted nodes from joining the wrong cluster.

- `wsrep_node_name`: This is the unique current node name. You should absolutely avoid getting the same node name on several configurations. This helps a lot in diagnosing an issue.

- `wsrep_node_address`: If you're using a dedicated and private network for Galera communication (strongly recommended), you can set this option. Otherwise, use the public IP of your current node. Like the previous option, this should also be unique.

- `wsrep_cluster_address`: This is a list of the cluster's members. That means all the listed nodes will be masters and part of Galera Cluster.

- `wsrep_provider_options`: This allows enabling additional options. The following are the additional options that we're using:

  - `gcache.size`: This is a dedicated cache for Galera. It is buffered on disk cache and should be smaller than the database size. It is used to store replication requests when they come, apply them, and so on. You need to grow it on high traffic load if you want all your nodes to be at the same page every time. Otherwise, you won't be in a full synchronization mode.

  - `gcache.name`: This is the name and the path where `gcache` is to be stored. You can use a dedicated SSD disk to get better performance.

  - `gcache.page_size`: This is the size of the page files in the page storages.

- `wsrep_retry_autocommit`: When a conflict is detected, this options allows setting the number of retries to commit before failure.

- `wsrep_sst_method`: This is the transfer method between nodes. Others also exist; we'll see them in detail later. Rsync is the fastest method.

- `wsrep_slave_threads`: This defines how many threads to use for applying slave write sets.

- `wsrep_replication_myisam`: This permits you to activate MyISAM replication. But as there is no transaction with MyISAM, you should avoid it.

- `wsrep_sst_receive_address`: This permits you to force an IP and is generally used in situations where you reach other servers through a VIP and the remote servers don't see this server coming with the correct IP address.

- `wsrep_notify_cmd`: This executes a script on each Galera event. It could be used when a node is not a cluster member anymore; this script will be launched and will send an e-mail.

Now the MariaDB options should be overridden:

```
# Other MariaDB options
binlog_format = ROW
innodb_autoinc_lock_mode = 2
innodb_flush_log_at_trx_commit = 2
innodb_locks_unsafe_for_binlog = 1
query_cache_size = 0
```

The following options should be overridden:

- `binlog_format`: This defines the log format

- `innodb_autoinc_lock_mode`: This changes how a lock mechanism should be used

- `innodb_flush_log_at_trx_commit`: This optimizes performance but can be dangerous if there is a power outage on a whole Galera Cluster (data may be lost)

- `query_cache_size`: This disables query cache

First boot

The first boot is very important and you should start the first node with the following parameter:

```
--wsrep_cluster_address='gcomm://'
```

The `gcomm` parameter specifies which nodes are in the cluster. However, the first time, we should specify one. By adding an empty line, it promotes a new cluster.

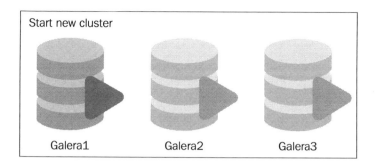

Start new cluster — Galera1, Galera2, Galera3

Here we can see that **Galera1** has started as a new cluster while the others are shut down for the moment.

Then, we'll start other nodes and they will automatically register and integrate the cluster.

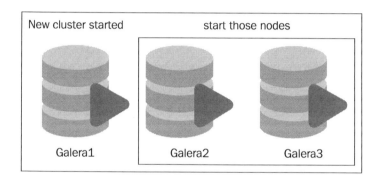

New cluster started / start those nodes — Galera1, Galera2, Galera3

We can now start the other nodes as the first one has started.

The first thing to do is to stop the current running MariaDB instances:

```
> service mysql stop
```

Then we'll create a new cluster:

```
> service mysql start --wsrep_cluster_address='gcomm://'
```

Never use an empty gcomm parameter to join a cluster; otherwise, you may break the current cluster status.

If you look at the logs, you should see something like this:

```
Apr 15 21:06:46 galera1 mysqld: 140415 21:06:46 [Note] WSREP: Flow-
control interval: [16, 16]
Apr 15 21:06:46 galera1 mysqld: 140415 21:06:46 [Note] WSREP: New
cluster view: global state: bc0dfb32-c4e1-11e3-855c-56855ec795da:0,
view# 3: Primary, number of nodes: 1, my index: 0, protocol version 2
Apr 15 21:06:46 galera1 mysqld: 140415 21:06:46 [Note] WSREP: wsrep_
notify_cmd is not defined, skipping notification.
Apr 15 21:06:46 galera1 mysqld: 140415 21:06:46 [Note] WSREP: REPL
Protocols: 5 (3, 1)
Apr 15 21:06:46 galera1 mysqld: 140415 21:06:46 [Note] WSREP: Assign
initial position for certification: 0, protocol version: 3
Apr 15 21:06:46 galera1 mysqld: 140415 21:06:46 [Note] WSREP: Service
thread queue flushed.
Apr 15 21:06:51 galera1 mysqld: 140415 21:06:51 [Note]
WSREP:  cleaning up d7e02f49-c4e1-11e3-82d1-02ff8a9aaf54
(tcp://192.168.33.32:4567)
```

You can connect and check the current status:

```
MariaDB [(none)]> SHOW STATUS LIKE 'wsrep_%';
+---------------------------+-------------------   --------------+
| Variable_name             | Value                              |
+---------------------------+-------------------   --------------+
[...]
| wsrep_local_state_comment | Synced                             |
[...]
| wsrep_incoming_addresses  | 192.168.33.31:3306                 |
| wsrep_cluster_conf_id     | 3                                  |
| wsrep_cluster_size        | 1                                  |
| wsrep_cluster_state_uuid  | bc0dfb32-c4e1-11e3-855c-56855ec795da |
| wsrep_cluster_status      | Primary                            |
| wsrep_connected           | ON                                 |
[...]
| wsrep_ready               | ON                                 |
+---------------------------+------------------------------------+
46 rows in set (0.00 sec)
```

Here is important information to know the status of the cluster:

- `wsrep_local_state_comment`: This gives the current status of the node. Here are the possible values:
    - `Joining`: The node is currently joining the cluster
    - `Donor/Desynced`: The node is in `Donor` mode (replicating data to another node) or not up-to-date with other nodes
    - `Joined`: The node has joined the cluster
    - `Synced`: The node is a cluster's member

- `wsrep_cluster_size`: This gives the number of node members in the Galera Cluster.

- `wsrep_cluster_state_uuid`: This is the unique cluster ID. All nodes should have the same UUID to be sure they are connected to each other.

- `wsrep_cluster_conf_id`: This is the configuration ID that should be the same on all nodes to be sure their configurations are on the same page.

- `wsrep_cluster_status`: This indicates the current status of the replication for a node. The statuses can be any of the following:
    - **Primary**: The node is in a master state
    - **Non-primary**: The node is not a master
    - **Disconnected**: The node is not connected to a cluster

- `wsrep_connected`: This indicates network connectivity for replication.

- `wsrep_ready`: This indicates the node is ready and is able to handle SQL transactions.

As the first node is ok, the new cluster is created. Do not forget to change node name and IP in the Galera configuration for Galera2 and Galera3 nodes.

Then, to integrate them in the cluster, simply start MariaDB:

```
> service mysql start
```

You may wonder how do they know how to integrate the cluster? The answer is simple—`wsrep_cluster_address`. Each address will be tested in the written order. That's why both nodes will integrate by contacting the first node.

When integrated, you should see the following status:

```
MariaDB [(none)]> SHOW STATUS LIKE 'wsrep_%';
+-----------------------------+---------------------------------------+
| Variable_name               | Value                                 |
+-----------------------------+---------------------------------------+
[...]
| wsrep_local_state           | 4                                     |
| wsrep_local_state_comment   | Synced                                |
[...]
| wsrep_incoming_addresses    | 192.168.33.32:3306,192.168.33.33:3306,192.1
68.33.31:3306              |
| wsrep_cluster_conf_id       | 5                                     |
| wsrep_cluster_size          | 3                                     |
| wsrep_cluster_state_uuid    | bc0dfb32-c4e1-11e3-855c-56855ec795da  |
| wsrep_cluster_status        | Primary                               |
| wsrep_connected             | ON                                    |
[...]
| wsrep_ready                 | ON                                    |
+-----------------------------+---------------------------------------+
46 rows in set (0.00 sec)
```

When a node is joining, you should see something like this in the logs of Galera1 in `/var/log/syslog`:

```
mysqld: #011group UUID = bc0dfb32-c4e1-11e3-855c-56855ec795da
mysqld: 140416 18:30:55 [Note] WSREP: Flow-control interval: [28, 28]
mysqld: 140416 18:30:55 [Note] WSREP: New cluster view: global state:
bc0dfb32-c4e1-11e3-855c-56855ec795da:0, view# 5: Primary, number of
nodes: 3, my index: 2, protocol version 2
mysqld: 140416 18:30:55 [Note] WSREP: wsrep_notify_cmd is not defined,
skipping notification.
mysqld: 140416 18:30:55 [Note] WSREP: REPL Protocols: 5 (3, 1)
mysqld: 140416 18:30:55 [Note] WSREP: Assign initial position for
certification: 0, protocol version: 3
mysqld: 140416 18:30:55 [Note] WSREP: Service thread queue flushed.
mysqld: 140416 18:30:57 [Note] WSREP: Node 1.0 (galera3) requested
state transfer from '*any*'. Selected 0.0 (galera2)(SYNCED) as donor.
mysqld: 140416 18:30:59 [Note] WSREP: 0.0 (galera2): State transfer to
1.0 (galera3) complete.
mysqld: 140416 18:30:59 [Note] WSREP: Member 0 (galera2) synced with
group.
```

```
mysqld: 140416 18:31:01 [Note] WSREP: 1.0 (galera3): State transfer
from 0.0 (galera2) complete.
mysqld: 140416 18:31:01 [Note] WSREP: Member 1 (galera3) synced with
group.
ntpd[2376]: peer 88.191.228.138 now valid
```

You can now test by creating a database on any node; it will be automatically replicated to others.

Now all nodes are aware of the others (even the Galera1 node) and you can check it easily using the following command:

```
MariaDB [(none)]> SHOW STATUS LIKE 'wsrep_%';
[...]
| wsrep_incoming_addresses    | 192.168.33.32:3306,192.168.33.33:3306,19
2.168.33.31:3306 |
```

The last thing to do is to replicate the `debian.cnf` under `/etc/mysql/` from one node to the other nodes. Then, you have to change the password of that user with the one indicated in the `debian.cnf` file to replicate it across all nodes:

```
MariaDB [(none)]> SET PASSWORD FOR 'debian-sys-maint'@'localhost' =
PASSWORD('password');

MariaDB [(none)]> FLUSH PRIVILEGES;
```

Usages and understandings

There are a lot of configuration options, and some of them depend on your needs. We'll see here what choices we have, what is the best for your needs, and how to use them.

Transfer methods

Several transfer methods exist and all have their pros and cons. Why should you change it? This is simple; when you need to integrate a node in a current cluster, a running node is designed to change state and become a Donor. The Donor will be the dedicated node to transfer data to the new node.

 When a node is in the Donor mode, transactions are locked on that node until it finishes the transfer of data.

Depending on the transfer method you choose, it will be more or less faster to create a new node. Here is what a Donor looks like when it is in Donor mode:

```
MariaDB [(NONE)]> SHOW global STATUS LIKE 'wsrep%stat%';
+-----------------------------+-------------------------------------+
| Variable_name               | VALUE                               |
+-----------------------------+-------------------------------------+
| wsrep_local_state_uuid      | bc0dfb32-c4e1-11e3-855c-56855ec795da |
| wsrep_local_state           | 2                                   |
| wsrep_local_state_comment   | Donor/Desynced                      |
| wsrep_cluster_state_uuid    | bc0dfb32-c4e1-11e3-855c-56855ec795da |
| wsrep_cluster_status        | PRIMARY                             |
+-----------------------------+-------------------------------------+
5 ROWS IN SET (0.00 sec)
```

 If you're not using a load balancer in front of your Galera Cluster, you will need to remove the donor node from it to avoid issues. Then, when it will change its state, you can reintegrate it in the Cluster.

There are two kinds of data transfer:

- **State Snapshot Transfer (SST)**: This is the way to create full backups
- **Incremental State Transfer (IST)**: This is the way to transfer the missing data

All replication mechanisms cannot do both SST and IST.

Using mysqldump

The `mysqldump` solution can perform an SST but not IST data transfer, which means on large databases, an SST could take several days if you integrate a new node in the cluster. However, this method doesn't require any additional tools to work.

You need to create a user to make it work:

```
MariaDB [(NONE)]> CREATE USER 'sst_user'@'%' IDENTIFIED BY 'sst_
password';
MariaDB [(NONE)]> GRANT ALL ON *.* TO 'sst_user'@'%' IDENTIFIED BY 'sst_
password';
MariaDB [(NONE)]> FLUSH PRIVILEGES;
```

Then, in the Galera configuration (`galera.cnf`), you need to enter these credentials:

```
wsrep_sst_auth = 'sst_user:sst_password'
```

Then, when you add a new node in the cluster, the SST method will be applied. The major problem of that solution is if you have already got a node in the cluster, but it was down for a certain amount of time, so it won't be able to resume the replication and get missing data back. *It will do an SST transfer instead of an IST transfer* when you integrate the node in the cluster.

Using Xtrabackup

Xtrabackup is a fast (but not the fastest) solution to perform SST and IST transfers. The advantage of Xtrabackup is the required lock time, which is the lowest possible. However, the replication takes time but is faster than the `mysqldump` solution.

First of all, you need to install Xtrabackup (already done if you're using `Vagrantfile`):

```
> apt-key adv --keyserver keys.gnupg.net --recv-keys 1C4CBDCDCD2EFD2A
> add-apt-repository 'deb http://repo.percona.com/apt wheezy main'
echo 'Package: *
Pin: release o=Percona Development Team
Pin-Priority: 100' > /etc/apt/preferences.d/00percona.pref
> aptitude update
> aptitude install xtrabackup
```

Then configure your SST method in the Galera configuration (`galera.cnf`):

```
wsrep_sst_method = xtrabackup
```

Using rsync

The `rsync` method is the fastest way to do IST and SST transfers. It will lock a transaction on the donor node for a longer duration as compared to Xtrabackup.

You need to install `rsync`:

```
> aptitude install rsync
```

Then, you need to declare this method in your Galera configuration file (`galera.cnf`):

```
wsrep_sst_method = rsync
```

Dedicating a donor node

You may want to dedicate a node as a Donor. This can simplify some backup processes or any other task that requires changing a synced node in the donor node.

You can, for example, configure Galera3 to be in the donor node in the Galera configuration file (`galera.cnf`):

```
wsrep_sst_donor=galera3
```

You can change it on the fly if you want (for example, if you've lost Galera3):

```
MariaDB [(NONE)]> set global wsrep_sst_donor=galera2;
```

Starting after a complete blackout

With the basic configuration, you can see how Galera Cluster works. If you try to kill a node and restart it, it will automatically rejoin the cluster and get missing data from other nodes.

If you have a power outage on your Galera Cluster, you will need to do it manually. It is unfortunately not a perfect solution to boot your cluster, with or without all nodes. I hope a feature will be included in the future versions to make this automated.

However, there are some interesting options to help you configure a node to boot in a specific situation:

- `pc.wait_prim=no`: This waits for a primary component for an indefinite time (request `mysqldump` as an SST replication method)
- `pc.bootstrap=1`: This bootstraps the primary node (avoid starting the node with an empty `'gcomm://'` value

The content in the Galera configuration file (`galera.cnf`) on all your servers should look like the following:

```
gcomm://galera1?pc.waitprim=no&pc.bootstrap=1,galera2,galera3
```

So when all the servers are started at the same time and no one is declared as primary, Galera1 will take the lead and others will automatically join. *This configuration only works with mysqldump as the wsrep_sst_method value.* It doesn't work with rsync or Xtrabackup.

Consensus clustering and maintenance

In a classic method of consensus clustering, when you're losing the majority ($N/2+1$) of your nodes, the cluster will completely fail. This is how a cluster like Galera works.

When you want to perform maintenance on your servers hosting Galera, you can shut down all your nodes instead of one and Galera will still be working. Why? Because you didn't lose your servers! You gracefully shut them down. This is the difference here; Galera automatically recalculates the total node size to make the cluster always available even with only one node!

Garb – the quorum solution

If you want to start building a Galera Cluster but do not have enough machines to build the full infrastructure yet, you can use **Garb**. It can also be used when you lose a node, you back up a node, or where the required nodes in the cluster is minimal:

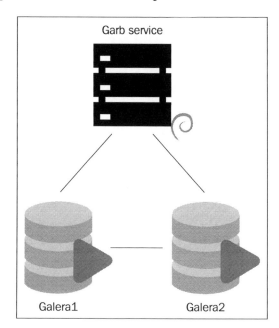

This will provide an extra fake node to avoid a split-brain or a broken cluster.

If you're using the Vagrant file, there is a given node for Garb usage called `garb`. You can test it on that node.

The Garb configuration is an easy task. You need to edit the configuration file in /etc/default/garb:

```
# Copyright (C) 2012 Coedership Oy
# This config file is to be sourced by garb service script.
# A space-separated list of node addresses (address[:port]) in the
cluster
GALERA_NODES="192.168.33.31:4567 192.168.33.32:4567
192.168.33.33:4567"

# Galera Cluster name, should be the same as on the rest of the nodes.
GALERA_GROUP="mariadb_cluster"

# Optional Galera internal options string (e.g. SSL settings)
# see http://www.codership.com/wiki/doku.php?id=galera_parameters
# GALERA_OPTIONS=""

# Log file for garbd. Optional, by default logs to syslog
# LOG_FILE= ""
```

To make it work, you need to uncomment and fill the following fields:

- GALERA_NODES: Specify each node of the cluster with the port delimited by a space character
- GALERA_GROUP: Include the name of the wsrep_cluster_name of the Galera Cluster (you've entered it in galera.cnf configuration file)

Now, configure it to boot automatically when the server starts and start the daemon now:

```
> update-rc.d -f garb defaults
> service garb start
```

Now if you look at a Galera node, you'll find a new size in the cluster:

```
MariaDB [(none)]> SHOW STATUS LIKE 'wsrep_cluster_size';
+--------------------+-------+
| Variable_name      | Value |
+--------------------+-------+
| wsrep_cluster_size | 4     |
+--------------------+-------+
1 row in set (0.00 sec)
```

Performance tuning

Some tuning can be done to get better performance. But as usual, this depends on your current requirement; you should only consider tuning Galera when you've been running for at least 24 hours with the traffic you're expecting.

Parallel slave threads

Parallel slave threads can give better performances (this is not guaranteed but will not be bad), so activating them is a good thing.

A correct calculation of this is to take four threads per physical core. So if you have eight cores on your current node, update this setting in the Galera configuration file (`galera.cnf`):

```
wsrep_slave_threads=32
```

You should avoid setting this to a value more than the `wsrep_cert_deps_distance` value.

Gcache size

Gcache size is something important to get good performance. We will see here how to calculate at minimum the size of Gcache corresponding to your usage.

Using `mysqldump` as a transfer method will require getting a bigger Gcache size. This is mainly because the `mysqldump` method only supports SST and not IST.

So, to know the minimum Gcache size you should use, you need to calculate the write rate by getting `wsrep_received_bytes` with interval times.

Here is the formula:

(received_bytes_value2 - received_bytes_value1) / (time2 - time1)

Designing redundant architectures

Galera Cluster is fantastic for getting as many master or slave nodes as possible. However, if you have a high traffic, you can dedicate some nodes as read only as well.

Read and write nodes

The problem of having dedicated nodes for read purposes is the time taken to synchronize all nodes. The more Galera nodes you have, the more you need time to replicate data. Even if it's super fast, this is to be expected.

So what kinds of solutions exist? You can mix classical/GTID replication and Galera Cluster. This way, you can dedicate as many read servers as you want connected to a Galera node to get a very fast read access. Also, you can have a Galera Cluster to get a fast and redundant write cluster. In that case, you do not have SPOF. Here is an example of kind of infrastructure:

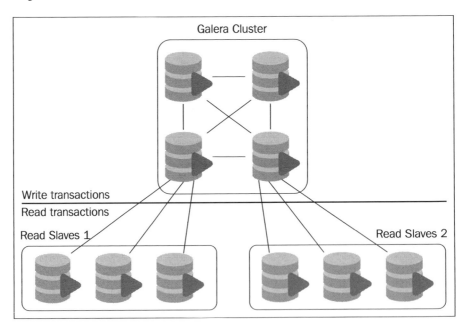

Load balanced architecture

In the previous chapters, we saw how to load balance on several MariaDB slave nodes with HAProxy, and it works pretty well. Also, HAProxy knows how to speak with MariaDB nodes.

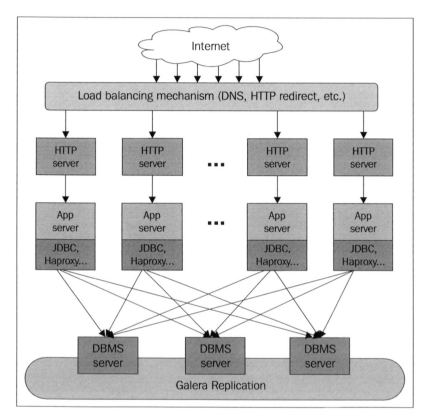

However, it doesn't know how to speak with Galera nodes and we will help it to do this. First of all, install HAProxy:

```
> add-apt-repository 'deb http://ftp.fr.debian.org/debian/ wheezy-
backports main'
> aptitude update
> aptitude install haproxy
> sed -i "s/ENABLED=0/ENABLED=1/" /etc/default/haproxy
```

Then, include the following configuration in `/etc/haproxy/haproxy.cfg`:

```
global
    # log redirection (syslog)
    log /dev/log    local0
    log /dev/log    local1 notice
    # maximum of connections for haproxy
    maxconn 4096
    # chroot for security reasons
    chroot /var/lib/haproxy
    # user/group for haproxy process
    user haproxy
    group haproxy
    # act as a daemon
    daemon
    # enable stats unix socket
    stats socket /var/lib/haproxy/stats mode 777 level admin

defaults
    # use gloval log declaration
    log    global
    # default check type
    mode    http
    # only log when closing session
    option    tcplog
    # only log failed connections
    # retry 3 times before setting node as failed
    # redispatch traffic to other servers
    option    dontlognull retries 3 option redispatch
    # maximum connection for the backend
    maxconn 2000
    # timeouts
    contimeout 5000
    clitimeout 50000
    srvtimeout 50000

# enable web check health interface on port 80
listen haproxy 0.0.0.0:80
    mode    http
    stats    enable
    # set credentials
    stats    auth admin:password
```

```
# loadbalance on Galera
listen galera-nodes 0.0.0.0:3306
    # use tcp method
    mode tcp
    # round robin mechanism
    balance roundrobin
    # tcp keepalive (pipelining) on both side (clt/srv)
    option tcpka
    # perform http request
    option httpchk
    # set all read only nodes
    # inter: interval of check in milliseconds
    server galera1 192.168.33.31:3306 check port 9200 inter 2000 rise
3 fall 3
    server galera2 192.168.33.32:3306 check port 9200 inter 2000 rise
3 fall 3
    server galera3 192.168.33.33:3306 check port 9200 inter 2000 rise
3 fall 3
```

Here, we're simply asking to do a HTTP request and HAProxy will check the HTTP return code on port 9200.

Now, on a Galera node, create a dedicated user for HAProxy check:

```
MariaDB [(none)]> CREATE USER 'galera_check'@'127.0.0.1' IDENTIFIED BY
'password';

MariaDB [(none)]> FLUSH PRIVILEGES;
```

Adapt the user and password as you want. Then, *on all Galera nodes you will need to add this script in* /usr/bin/galera_check:

```
> wget -O /usr/bin/galera_check https://raw.githubusercontent.com/
severalnines/haproxy/master/mysqlchk.sh.galera
```

Then, update the beginning of the script with the same credentials you just created:

```
#!/bin/bash
[...]
MYSQL_HOST="127.0.0.1"
MYSQL_PORT="3306"
MYSQL_USERNAME="galera_check"
MYSQL_PASSWORD="password"
MYSQL_OPTS="-N -q -A"
[...]
```

The preceding script has been created by Severalnines (http://www.severalnines.com) and has been adapted for Debian. This script will be used by xinetd when the port 9200 will be targeted. So create a xinted configuration in /etc/xinetd.d/xinetd_galera:

```
service mysqlchk
{
        flags            = REUSE
        socket_type      = stream
        port             = 9200
        wait             = no
        user             = nobody
        server           = /usr/bin/galera_check
        log_on_failure  += USERID
        disable          = no
        only_from        = 0.0.0.0/0
        per_source       = UNLIMITED
}
```

 A better thing would be to allow only HAProxy IPs instead of everybody (0.0.0.0).

Add the following information to your /etc/services nodes:

```
> echo -e "galera_check\t9200/tcp\t\t\t# galera_check" >> /etc/services
```

To finish up, change the rights and restart services on all Galera nodes:

```
> chmod 755 /usr/bin/galera_check
> service xinetd restart
```

On the load balancer server, restart the HAProxy service and you should see all Galera nodes up and running:

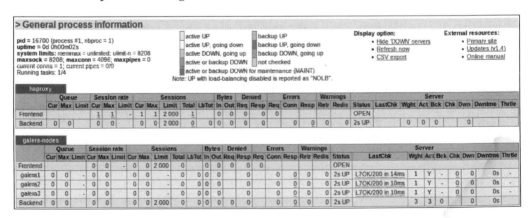

WAN replication

Suppose you want to have a Galera Cluster distributed across several countries. Let's say: France, Germany, Great Britain, and Spain:

The biggest problems here are the latency and possible timeouts as we are not in a local environment. Even if we duplicate each WAN line, add redundancy, and so on, we are not as safe as in a LAN environment.

That's why some options exist to change/grow timeout parameters. The following are the options you can add to the `wsrep` provider:

```
wsrep_provider_options = "evs.keepalive_period = PT3S; evs.inactive_
check_period = PT10S; evs.suspect_timeout = PT30S; evs.inactive_
timeout = PT1M; evs.install_timeout = PT1M"
```

The explanations are as follows:

- `evs.keepalive_period`: This describes how often keepalive beacons will be emitted (3 seconds).

- `evs.inactive_check_period`: This describes how often the check of peer inactivity will occur (10 seconds).

- `evs.suspect_timeout`: This is the inactivity period when the node will be considered as dead by other nodes. If all nodes validate it, it will be pulled off the cluster (30 seconds).

- `evs.inactive_timeout`: This is the inactivity limit where the node will be set as dead (1 minute). The `evs.suspect_timeout` value can bypass this.

- `evs.install_timeout`: This is the timeout on waiting for install message acknowledgments.

You can, of course, grow those values if you think that your network bandwidth is not as performant and stable as it should be.

Disaster recovery

Galera is a synchronized replication between all of its nodes while classical/GTID replication is asynchronous. You can mix both replications to get a **disaster recovery (DR)** solution, as shown in the following diagram:

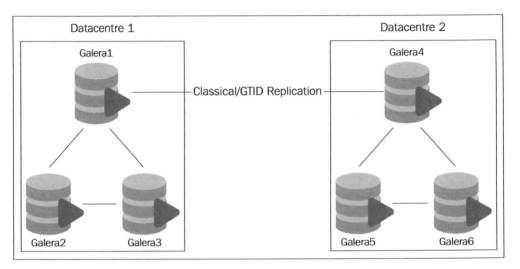

Here, we got both advantages:

- Galera Cluster is synced between all nodes
- The DR doesn't reduce the speed of the master cluster

Here is how to set up this kind of architecture:

1. You need to set up the first Galera Cluster.
2. Build your DR Galera Cluster.
3. Sync data between a master node on Galera to a designated slave node on Galera DR.
4. Create a dual master replication (without any VIP or cluster software to avoid complicated split-brain).

In this chapter, you learned how to create a Galera Cluster, so create both kinds Galera clusters.

 Do not forget to change the Galera Cluster name.

Then, you need to adapt the MariaDB configuration to enable classical/GTID replication. The thing to understand here is that as Galera nodes in a cluster are identical, the MariaDB configuration should be identical as well. So the following is the configuration for the first Galera Cluster:

```
server-id               = 1
auto_increment_increment = 2
log_bin                 = /var/log/mysql/mariadb-bin
log_bin_index           = /var/log/mysql/mariadb-bin.index
sync_binlog             = 1
expire_logs_days        = 10
max_binlog_size         = 100M
log_slave_updates       = 1
```

You should apply it on all nodes of your Galera Cluster. Do not change the value of server-id on the same cluster, it should remain the same.

To finish up, apply the same configuration on the other Galera Cluster and do not forget to change the server-id.

Then, as usual for classical/GTID replication, you need to create a dedicated user and password for replication purposes. Now, select one node on each Galera Cluster and configure each one with the change master command:

```
MariaDB [(none)]> GRANT REPLICATION SLAVE ON *.* TO
'replication'@'192.168.33.%';

MariaDB [(none)]> FLUSH PRIVILEGES;

MariaDB [(none)]> CHANGE MASTER TO MASTER_HOST='192.168.33.XX', MASTER_
USER='replication', MASTER_PASSWORD='password', MASTER_LOG_FILE='mariadb-
bin.0000XX', MASTER_LOG_POS=XXX;

MariaDB [(none)]> START SLAVE;
```

Now the configuration is finished and everything should be working properly.

If a problem occurs on the first datacenter, you can easily switch to the other one. Delta data will automatically replicate to the master Galera Cluster when it is available.

Tests and issues

Galera Cluster is a great and powerful solution. However, issues could happen and we're going to see here how to resolve them.

First of all, and as always, look at the logs (syslog by default); important information is written there and most of the time the problem will be explicit!

Paused replication

Sometimes, during a very high load write demand, the Cluster may stop replicating during this phase. Generally, this is not a good situation and you should avoid this kind of query as much as possible.

One solution can be to use an intermediate software layer to avoid it, for example, a **Advanced Message Queuing Protocol (AMQP)** software such as RabbitMQ or ZeroMQ. The setup of this kind of tool is out of the scope of this book.

To detect the paused time replication, you need to look at the flow control status. If it's equal to 1, that means the replication is paused; if it's 0, then it's ok:

```
MariaDB [(none)]> SHOW STATUS LIKE 'wsrep_%';
+--------------------------------+----------------------------------------+
| Variable_name                  | Value                                  |
+--------------------------------+----------------------------------------+
[...]
| wsrep_flow_control_paused      | 0.000000                               |
```

There's a tool named **galera-status** developed by one of my colleagues (https://github.com/fridim) from eNovance; this tool helps to know the status of a Galera Cluster and has a nice presentation. You can get the tool using the following command:

```
> wget https://raw.githubusercontent.com/fridim/galera-status/master/
galera-status
> chmod 755 galera-status
```

When you launch it, you will have something like the following:

```
galera-node:~# galera-status
                    NODE STATUS

          cluster status:   Primary
            cluster size:   3
                   Ready:   ON
               connected:   ON
           state comment:   Synced

REPLICATION HEALTH (the lower the better)

      fraction replication pause:   0.000000
              flow control sent:   0
        local send queue average:   0.000000
     local receive queue average:   0.000000

CLUSTER INTEGRITY (should be the same on all nodes)

   local state UUID: 7ed26467-98a0-11e2-0800-d5517890c3f2
   cluster conf ID: 49
```

Break Galera

One of the first things you want to test when you've set up a Galera Cluster is the failure of nodes. Let's see an example on how to test it.

From a node (for example Galera2), run the following command:

```
> watch -n1 "mysql -e \"SHOW STATUS LIKE 'wsrep_cluster_size'\""
Variable_name    Value
wsrep_cluster_size      4
```

This will show you the number of current connected nodes. Then, kill `mysqld` of another node (if you can perform insertions at that time, it would benefit us for testing purposes), let's say Galera1:

```
> pkill -9 mysqld
```

You should see the number of the cluster size reduced to 3. That's fine. Continue to insert data on the other nodes and start Galera1:

```
> service mysqld start
```

It should integrate the cluster automatically and get the delta data back. That's it!

Split-brain

A split-brain can occur if you loose more than a half of your cluster nodes. This could be problematic if you absolutely need to get it working, even in a degraded mode.

So if you really want to activate the cluster in a degraded state, you should first search the most up-to-date node by launching the following command on each active node:

```
MariaDB [(none)]> SHOW STATUS LIKE 'wsrep_last_committed';
```

When you've found the node with the highest value, reset the quorum on this node using the following command:

```
MariaDB [(none)]> SET GLOBAL wsrep_provider_options='pc.bootstrap=1';
MariaDB [(none)]> SET GLOBAL wsrep_provider_options='pc.ignore_quorum=0';
```

This will make this node the new master; all nodes will synchronize with this one and you'll recover your cluster and get it up and running.

 When you fully recover your Galera Cluster, do not forget to roll back those values.

Summary

In this chapter, we've seen how to set up a synchronous replication with Galera Cluster. This is an advanced step in classical/GTID replications. You can now start to build scalable solutions and some usages.

In the next chapter, we'll see another scaling solution with Spider, also called sharding.

Spider – Sharding Your Data

9

Spider is a specific engine made for MySQL/MariaDB. It has been integrated in MariaDB 10 which makes it one of the new and major features. It's a specific storage engine dedicated to shard data across several MariaDB servers.

It should act as a proxy to be able to work properly:

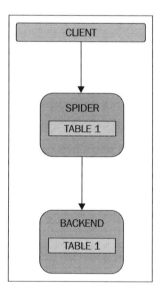

You can see in the preceding diagram that a client is talking directly to Spider to get access to its backend table content.

However, the goal of Spider is to shard your data across multiple backend servers, as illustrated in the following diagram:

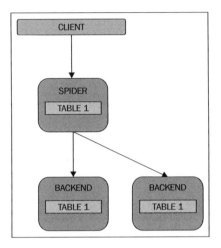

Sharding will split your data on several servers to speed up read and write queries. However, in this case, we need to replicate our shards to avoid data loss, as shown in the following diagram:

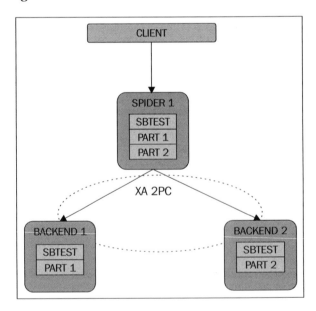

Spider monitors itself to produce SQL errors when one of the backend tables is not available. As you can see, there are three Spider servers here to avoid a split-brain (classical cluster-consensus).

 When Spider creates a table, the table links to a remote table that can be of any storage engine type.

Let's study the Spider features now:

- **Table link**: With Spider, available tables on multiple MariaDB servers are accessible like on a single table instance
- **XA transaction**: XA transactions are supported to be able to synchronize or update data over multiple MariaDB instances
- **Table partitioning**: This can create a partition table on multiple servers
- **Speed**: Spider uses several servers instead of one to boost the performance

In this chapter, you'll see an introduction to the Spider engine. Let's introduce some basics to understand an infrastructure that is based on Spider:

- **Data node**: This acts as the data storage node
- **Spider node**: This lies at the entrance of user access (load balance, failover, and so on)
- **Monitoring node**: This monitors data nodes for high availability

The preceding three roles are independent and can be separated.

Configuring Spider

As in other chapters, `Vagrantfile` is included to create an architecture sample to help you test different scenarios in this chapter:

```
# -*- mode: ruby -*-
# vi: set ft=ruby :
# Vagrantfile API/syntax version. Don't touch unless you know what
you're doing!
#
VAGRANTFILE_API_VERSION = "2"

# Insert all your Vms with configs
boxes = [
```

```
        { :name => :spider1, :role => 'db', :ip => '192.168.33.31' }, #
spider node 1
        { :name => :backend1,  :role => 'db', :ip => '192.168.33.41' }, #
shard 1
        { :name => :backend2,  :role => 'db', :ip => '192.168.33.42' }, #
shard 2
]

$install_common = <<INSTALL
aptitude update
DEBIAN_FRONTEND=noninteractive aptitude -y -o Dpkg::Options::="--
force-confdef" -o Dpkg::Options::="--force-confold" install python-
software-properties openntpd
INSTALL

$install = <<INSTALL
mkfs.ext4 -F /dev/sdb
mkdir -p /var/lib/mysql
echo "/dev/sdb    /var/lib/mysql           ext4     noatime,nodiratime,
discard        0       0" >> /etc/fstab
mount /var/lib/mysql
aptitude update
DEBIAN_FRONTEND=noninteractive aptitude -y -o Dpkg::Options::="--
force-confdef" -o Dpkg::Options::="--force-confold" install python-
software-properties
apt-key adv --recv-keys --keyserver keyserver.ubuntu.com
0xcbcb082a1bb943db
apt-key adv --keyserver keys.gnupg.net --recv-keys 1C4CBDCDCD2EFD2A
add-apt-repository 'deb http://ftp.igh.cnrs.fr/pub/mariadb/repo/10.0/
debian wheezy main'
add-apt-repository 'deb http://repo.percona.com/apt wheezy main'
echo 'Package: *
Pin: release o=Percona Development Team
Pin-Priority: 100' > /etc/apt/preferences.d/00percona.pref
aptitude update
DEBIAN_FRONTEND=noninteractive aptitude -y -o Dpkg::Options::="--
force-confdef" -o Dpkg::Options::="--force-confold" install percona-
toolkit mariadb-server sysbench htop tmux vim
INSTALL

$install_lb = <<INSTALL
add-apt-repository 'deb http://ftp.fr.debian.org/debian/ wheezy-
backports main'
aptitude update
```

```
DEBIAN_FRONTEND=noninteractive aptitude -y -o Dpkg::Options::="--
force-confdef" -o Dpkg::Options::="--force-confold" install haproxy
tcpdump keepalived
sed -i "s/ENABLED=0/ENABLED=1/" /etc/default/haproxy
echo "net.ipv4.ip_nonlocal_bind = 1" >> /etc/sysctl.conf
INSTALL

Vagrant::Config.run do |config|
  # Default box OS
  vm_default = proc do |boxcnf|
    boxcnf.vm.box        = "deimosfr/debian-wheezy"
  end

  boxes.each do |opts|
    vm_default.call(config)
    config.vm.define opts[:name] do |config|
        config.vm.customize ["modifyvm", :id, "--cpus", 2]
        config.vm.network    :hostonly, opts[:ip]
        config.vm.host_name = "%s.vm" % opts[:name].to_s
        config.vm.provision "shell", inline: $install_common
        # Install HAProxy for load balancer server or
        if opts[:role] == 'lb'
            config.vm.provision "shell", inline: $install_lb
        else
            config.vm.customize ["modifyvm", :id, "--memory", 1024]
            file_to_disk = 'mdb-disk_' + opts[:name].to_s + '.vdi'
            config.vm.customize ['createhd', '--filename', file_to_
disk, '--size', 10 * 1024]
            config.vm.customize ['storageattach', :id, '--storagectl',
'SATA', '--port', 1, '--device', 0, '--type', 'hdd', '--medium', file_
to_disk]
            config.vm.provision "shell", inline: $install
        end
    end
  end
end
```

The first thing to do on Spider is to enable it on Spider's host. It is not activated by default on MariaDB 10; however, it is built-in. To enable it, new tables and procedures have to be created. A SQL file is given to make all the prerequisites to activate it. You simply have to load it:

```
> mysql < /usr/share/mysql/install_spider.sql
```

You can now check if it is activated:

```
> mysql -e 'SELECT engine, support FROM information_schema.engines;'
+--------------------+---------+
| engine             | support |
+--------------------+---------+
|  SPIDER            | YES     |
|  MRG_MyISAM        | YES     |
|  MyISAM            | YES     |
|  BLACKHOLE         | YES     |
|  CSV               | YES     |
|  PERFORMANCE_SCHEMA | YES    |
|  ARCHIVE           | YES     |
|  InnoDB            | DEFAULT |
|  FEDERATED         | YES     |
|  Aria              | YES     |
|  MEMORY            | YES     |
+--------------------+---------+
```

We're now ready to create our first shard and use backend servers.

Creating your first shard

You're now ready to create your first shard! It is not a complicated thing. In previous chapters, we talked about load balancers like HAProxy. This is a quite similar usage here as Spider will proxy (and of course split) data to several backend servers.

We will start with a simple setup:

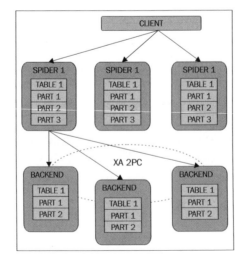

As you can see, a Spider server (`spider1/192.168.33.31`) will split data across our first backend (`backend1/192.168.33.41`) and the second backend (`backend2/192.168.33.42`).

The first thing to do is to create a Spider user to allow it to write on the backend servers. *On all backends,* create a Spider user with all rights to make it simple (more restricted rights are strongly recommended of course):

```
MariaDB [(none)]> create user 'spider_user'@'192.168.33.31' identified by
'password';
MariaDB [(none)]> grant all privileges on *.* to 'spider_
user'@'192.168.33.31' identified by 'password';
MariaDB [(none)]> flush privileges;
```

Change the password to a better one. On all backends, we now have to create the same identical database with the same structure.

> It is mandatory to get the same database and table structures on your backends (where Spider has to split your data).

Create a backend database **on all servers**:

```
MariaDB [(none)]> CREATE DATABASE backend;
```

> It is strongly recommended to have a primary key on your physical tables to avoid errors with some Spider functions such as `spider_copy_tables`.

Now insert the following table *on all backends*:

```
MariaDB [(none)]> CREATE TABLE backend.sbtest (
  id int(10) unsigned NOT NULL AUTO_INCREMENT,
  k int(10) unsigned NOT NULL DEFAULT '0',
  c char(120) NOT NULL DEFAULT '',
  pad char(60) NOT NULL DEFAULT '',
  PRIMARY KEY (id),
  KEY k (k)
) ENGINE=InnoDB;
```

As you can see, we used the InnoDB engine on the backends! You can use any engine you want on backends (Aria, TokuDB, and so on). Only the Spider servers require the Spider engine.

We've now finished with backends! Let's configure the Spider engine now *on the* spider1 *server*. First off all, you need to teach your Spider engine how to communicate with backends:

```
MariaDB [(none)]> CREATE SERVER backend1
   FOREIGN DATA WRAPPER mysql
OPTIONS(
   HOST '192.168.33.41',
   DATABASE 'backend',
   USER 'spider_user',
   PASSWORD 'password',
   PORT 3306
);
MariaDB [(none)]> CREATE SERVER backend2
   FOREIGN DATA WRAPPER mysql
OPTIONS(
   HOST '192.168.33.42',
   DATABASE 'backend',
   USER 'spider_user',
   PASSWORD 'password',
   PORT 3306
);
```

 CREATE SERVER is a MySQL/MariaDB feature and not a Spider-specific feature. Spider will just use it.

As you can see, we're doing both here, creating backends and registering the credentials/information connections. You can at any time check which databases are sharded with their defined backends using the following command:

```
MariaDB [(none)]> select Db,Server_name,Host,Username,Password,Port from
mysql.servers;
```

Db	Server_name	Host	Username	Password	Port
backend	backend1	192.168.33.41	spider_user	password	3306
backend	backend2	192.168.33.42	spider_user	password	3306

```
2 rows in set (0.00 sec)
```

We can easily see here the `backend` database sharding its data to server `backend1` and `backend2`. On the backends, we created a table with the InnoDB engine; we're now going to create the same table but with the Spider engine rather than InnoDB:

```
MariaDB [(none)]> CREATE TABLE backend.sbtest
(
  id int(10) unsigned NOT NULL AUTO_INCREMENT,
  k int(10) unsigned NOT NULL DEFAULT '0',
  c char(120) NOT NULL DEFAULT '',
  pad char(60) NOT NULL DEFAULT '',
  PRIMARY KEY (id),
  KEY k (k)
) ENGINE=spider COMMENT='database "backend", table "sbtest"'
 PARTITION BY KEY (id)
(
 PARTITION pt1 COMMENT = 'srv "backend1"',
 PARTITION pt2 COMMENT = 'srv "backend2"'
);
```

You must have noticed that while specifying table structure, we also indicated Spider connection parameters in the comments. Let's explain them:

- `Engine`: We specified Spider as the engine to be used and have added a comment to help you understand the information related to it. Some users like to add all connection parameters in the comment field. It is up to you to see what you want to add inside comments.

- `Partition by key`: We ask Spider to shard with the `id` column of the table. Here, you can also define the column on which you want to make your shard.

- `Partition`: This parameter lets us select which available backend should be used to store data.

You can now check your table configuration using the following command:

```
MariaDB [(none)]> SELECT
db_name,table_name,link_id,server,tgt_table_name,link_status FROM
mysql.spider_tables;
+----------+-------------+---------+----------+----------------+-------------+
| db_name  | table_name  | link_id | server   | tgt_table_name | link_status |
+----------+-------------+---------+----------+----------------+-------------+
| backend  | sbtest#P#pt1 |      0 | backend1 | sbtest         |           1 |
| backend  | sbtest#P#pt2 |      0 | backend2 | sbtest         |           1 |
+----------+-------------+---------+----------+----------------+-------------+
2 rows in set (0.01 sec)
```

```
+---------+---------------+----------+----------+-----------------+----+
| backend | sbtest#P#pt1  |      0   | backend1 | sbtest          | 1  |
| backend | sbtest#P#pt2  |      0   | backend2 | sbtest          | 1  |
+---------+---------------+----------+----------+-----------------+----+
```

2 rows in set (0.01 sec)

We can see here the backend database on sbtest table, which replicates the first partition (pt1) to the first backend (backend1) and the second partition (pt2) to the second backend (backend2).

Now it's play time! You may recognize the name and table structure of sbtest which is the default table used by the sysbench tool. The sysbench tool will help us insert random data into a temporary table and then we will insert them into the Spider table. From the spider1 server, create a temporary table:

MariaDB [(none)]> create database sysbench;

Let's generate some data in this newly created database:

> sysbench --test=oltp --db-driver=mysql --mysql-table-engine=innodb --mysql-user=root --mysql-password='' --mysql-host=localhost --mysql-port=3306 --oltp-table-size=1000000 --mysql-db=sysbench prepare

Now, let's inject this temporary data inside the Spider engine:

MariaDB [(none)]> insert into backend.sbtest (id,k,c,pad) select * from sysbench.sbtest;

Query OK, 1000000 rows affected (14.59 sec)

Records: 1000000 Duplicates: 0 Warnings: 0

That's it! It works like a charm.

Let's count on all servers how many lines we've got:

MariaDB [(none)]> select count(*) from backend.sbtest;

You should see something like the following number of entries:

- spider1: 1000000
- backend1: 603585
- backend2: 396415

You must have noticed that the sum of backend1 and backend2 is equal to spider1.

Now if you look at the content of the sbtest table on backend1, you'll see unpaired IDs at the beginning of table, while you'll see paired IDs on backend2.

Sharding replication

You've now seen what sharding is, how it works, and have understood the concept, but how to deal with high availability? If you remember, in the previous chapters we talked about replication, and the most advanced among them is Galera Cluster.

The first idea you may have is to combine multiple technologies such as Galera to make a scalable (sharded) and highly available architecture such as the following:

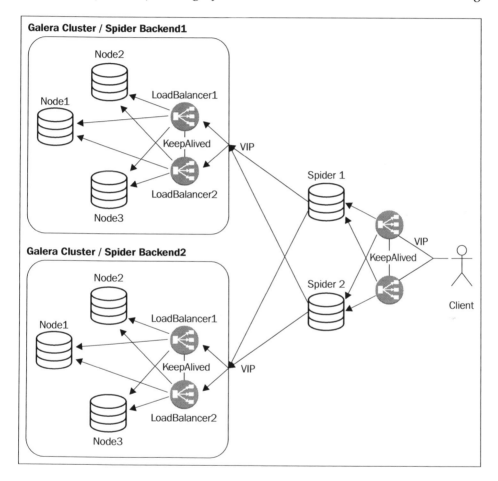

This is a good solution—one of the best. However, the price of this architecture may be very high and even more if you want a lot of shards. So what kind of other solutions do we have?

Spider, by default, embeds a replication mechanism. That means each shard could have its own shard replicated to another node. Let's try this.

Creating replicated shards

First of all, you need data to add. We will reuse the data generated by sysbench (in the sysbench database). If you do not have those data, launch the sysbench tool again.

Then, create a replication database on all backends:

```
MariaDB [(none)]> create database backend_replication;
```

If you already have data, you have to copy them to the other host; if not, you can skip this section. Run the following commands on the Spider1 host:

```
> mysqldump --host=192.168.33.41 --user=spider_user --password=password
backend sbtest | mysql --host=192.168.33.42 --user=spider_user
--password=password backend_replication
> mysqldump --host=192.168.33.42 --user=spider_user --password=password
backend sbtest | mysql --host=192.168.33.41 --user=spider_user
--password=password backend_replication
MariaDB [(none)]> DROP TABLE backend.sbtest;
```

Here, we are dumping the sbtest table in the backend database:

- From the backend1 server to the backend2 server in the backend_replication database
- From the backend2 server to the backend1 server in the backend_replication database

This is to get a copy of a shard on the other host (as replication on the same host makes no sense). To finish up, drop the sbtest table as we need to recreate a new Spider configuration.

Now, declare two new hosts on the spider1 server that will be dedicated to replication:

```
CREATE SERVER backend1_replication
  FOREIGN DATA WRAPPER mysql
OPTIONS(
  HOST '192.168.33.41',
  DATABASE 'backend_replication',
  USER 'spider_user',
  PASSWORD 'password',
  PORT 3306
);
CREATE SERVER backend2_replication
  FOREIGN DATA WRAPPER mysql
```

```
OPTIONS(
  HOST '192.168.33.42',
  DATABASE 'backend_replication',
  USER 'spider_user',
  PASSWORD 'password',
  PORT 3306
);
```

Then, declare the new table using the Spider engine and with the replication information in the comment fields:

```
CREATE TABLE backend.sbtest
(
  id int(10) unsigned NOT NULL AUTO_INCREMENT,
  k int(10) unsigned NOT NULL DEFAULT '0',
  c char(120) NOT NULL DEFAULT '',
  pad char(60) NOT NULL DEFAULT '',
  PRIMARY KEY (id),
  KEY k (k)
) ENGINE=spider COMMENT='wrapper "mysql", table "sbtest"'
 PARTITION BY KEY (id)
(
 PARTITION pt1 COMMENT = 'srv "backend1 backend2_replication", mbk "2",
mkd "2", msi "3306", link_status "0 0"',
 PARTITION pt2 COMMENT = 'srv "backend2 backend1_replication", mbk "2",
mkd "2", msi "3306", link_status "0 0"'
);
```

In the comment fields, we can see the following:

- backend1: This server manages the backend2_replication database on the same host.

- backend2: This server manages the backend1_replication database on the same host.

- mbk (Monitoring Background Kind) and mkd (Monitoring Kind): These are set to value 2 which means it will monitor the table without the WHERE clause.

- msi: This option does a basic monitoring on the MariaDB TCP port.

- link_status: This gives instructions on the status each time an ALTER TABLE statement will run without any changes. It is set to 0 to disable it.

You can now take a look at the Spider table configuration host:

```
MariaDB [(none)]> SELECT db_name,table_name,link_id,server,tgt_table_name,link_status FROM mysql.spider_tables;
+---------+------------+---------+----------------------+----------------+-------------+
| db_name | table_name | link_id | server               | tgt_table_name | link_status |
+---------+------------+---------+----------------------+----------------+-------------+
| backend | sbtest#P#pt1 |     1 | backend2_replication | sbtest         |           1 |
| backend | sbtest#P#pt1 |     0 | backend1             | sbtest         |           1 |
| backend | sbtest#P#pt2 |     0 | backend2             | sbtest         |           1 |
| backend | sbtest#P#pt2 |     1 | backend1_replication | sbtest         |           1 |
+---------+------------+---------+----------------------+----------------+-------------+
4 rows in set (0.00 sec)
```

As you can see, we've got two new entries corresponding to the replicated shards. The link_status set to 1 indicates the shards are in a normal state, a value of 2 indicates a recovery mode, 3 means abnormal, and lastly 0 means we do not want to make changes.

Spider HA monitoring

To avoid errors when you're losing a node, Spider includes high availability monitoring. That means if a shard is lost, it still will be able to answers queries as it will use the replicated shard instead. In that configuration, there is no SPOF and we created a sharding configuration (more read/write performances) plus high availability (fault tolerance).

To set this Spider monitoring up, you have to declare the Spider node as a monitoring node:

```
MariaDB [(none)]> CREATE SERVER mon
  FOREIGN DATA WRAPPER mysql
OPTIONS(
  HOST '192.168.33.31',
  DATABASE 'backend',
  USER 'spider_user',
  PASSWORD 'password',
  PORT 3306
);
```

Once again, you need to adapt the options according to your needs. You will be able to see it appearing in the server table:

```
MariaDB [(none)]> select Server_name from mysql.servers where Server_name
= 'mon';
+-------------+
| Server_name |
+-------------+
| mon         |
+-------------+
1 row in set (0.00 sec)
```

Now we're going to activate the monitoring:

```
MariaDB [(none)]> INSERT INTO mysql.spider_link_mon_servers VALUES
('%','%','%',3306,'mon',NULL,NULL,NULL,NULL,NULL,NULL,NULL,NULL,NULL
,NULL,0,NULL,NULL);
```

We're asking the Spider to monitor any Spider registered databases and any table. The configuration is now done. If a node fails, it will automatically switch the node's shard connections to the other available shards.

The monitoring node shouldn't be a SPOF. That's why it's strongly recommended to add more Spider monitoring nodes with a load balancer on top of it.

Recovering data after server failure

Spider monitoring is now set up and we have sharding and replication ready on the server; let's now test it to see if it works as expected. An easy test is to create a simple shell script that will try to request data inside shards and on Spider:

```
#!/bin/bash

spider1='mysql'
backend1='mysql --host=192.168.33.41 --user=spider_user
--password=password'
backend2='mysql --host=192.168.33.42 --user=spider_user
--password=password'

echo -e "\n##### data spider1 #####"
$spider1 -e 'select count(*) from backend.sbtest;'
$spider1 -e 'select * from backend.sbtest where id < 10 LIMIT 4;'
```

```
echo -e "\n##### data backend1 #####"
$backend1 -e 'select count(*) from backend.sbtest;'
$backend1 -e 'select * from backend.sbtest LIMIT 3;'

echo -e "\n##### data backend2 #####"
$backend2 -e 'select count(*) from backend.sbtest;'
$backend2 -e 'select * from backend.sbtest LIMIT 3;'
```

Of course, you need to adapt this to your needs. However, if you launch it, you can see everything works as expected:

```
##### data spider1 #####
+----------+
| count(*) |
+----------+
| 1000000 |
+----------+
+----+---+---+----------------------------------------------------+
| id | k | c | pad                                                |
+----+---+---+----------------------------------------------------+
| 1  | 0 |   | qqqqqqqqqqwwwwwwwwwweeeeeeeeeerrrrrrrrrrtttttttttt |
| 2  | 0 |   | qqqqqqqqqqwwwwwwwwwweeeeeeeeeerrrrrrrrrrtttttttttt |
| 3  | 0 |   | qqqqqqqqqqwwwwwwwwwweeeeeeeeeerrrrrrrrrrtttttttttt |
| 4  | 0 |   | qqqqqqqqqqwwwwwwwwwweeeeeeeeeerrrrrrrrrrtttttttttt |
+----+---+---+----------------------------------------------------+

##### data backend1 #####
+----------+
| count(*) |
+----------+
| 603585 |
+----------+
+----+---+---+----------------------------------------------------+
| id | k | c | pad                                                |
+----+---+---+----------------------------------------------------+
| 1  | 0 |   | qqqqqqqqqqwwwwwwwwwweeeeeeeeeerrrrrrrrrrtttttttttt |
| 3  | 0 |   | qqqqqqqqqqwwwwwwwwwweeeeeeeeeerrrrrrrrrrtttttttttt |
| 5  | 0 |   | qqqqqqqqqqwwwwwwwwwweeeeeeeeeerrrrrrrrrrtttttttttt |
+----+---+---+----------------------------------------------------+
```

```
##### data backend2 #####
+----------+
| count(*) |
+----------+
|   396415 |
+----------+
+----+---+---+--------------------------------------------------+
| id | k | c | pad                                              |
+----+---+---+--------------------------------------------------+
|  2 | 0 |   | qqqqqqqqqqwwwwwwwwwweeeeeeeeeerrrrrrrrrrtttttttttt |
|  4 | 0 |   | qqqqqqqqqqwwwwwwwwwweeeeeeeeeerrrrrrrrrrtttttttttt |
|  6 | 0 |   | qqqqqqqqqqwwwwwwwwwweeeeeeeeeerrrrrrrrrrtttttttttt |
+----+---+---+--------------------------------------------------+
```

If you now stop the MariaDB service on `backend1` and launch the Spider test script again, you'll see something like the following:

```
##### data spider1 #####
+----------+
| count(*) |
+----------+
|  1000000 |
+----------+
+----+---+---+--------------------------------------------------+
| id | k | c | pad                                              |
+----+---+---+--------------------------------------------------+
|  1 | 0 |   | qqqqqqqqqqwwwwwwwwwweeeeeeeeeerrrrrrrrrrtttttttttt |
|  2 | 0 |   | qqqqqqqqqqwwwwwwwwwweeeeeeeeeerrrrrrrrrrtttttttttt |
|  3 | 0 |   | qqqqqqqqqqwwwwwwwwwweeeeeeeeeerrrrrrrrrrtttttttttt |
|  4 | 0 |   | qqqqqqqqqqwwwwwwwwwweeeeeeeeeerrrrrrrrrrtttttttttt |
+----+---+---+--------------------------------------------------+
```

```
##### data backend1 #####
ERROR 2003 (HY000): Can't connect to MySQL server on '192.168.33.41' (111
"Connection refused")
ERROR 2003 (HY000): Can't connect to MySQL server on '192.168.33.41' (111
"Connection refused")

...
```

You can see from the preceding output that the `backend1` server is not accessible; however, the Spider server still returns paired and unpaired IDs as it automatically uses the `spider1` replication available on the `backend2` server.

Now if you look at `spider_tables`, you will notice that the `link_status` has changed:

```
MariaDB [(none)]> SELECT db_name,table_name,link_id,server,tgt_table_name,link_status FROM mysql.spider_tables;
+---------+--------------+---------+----------------------+----------------+-------------+
| db_name | table_name   | link_id | server               | tgt_table_name | link_status |
+---------+--------------+---------+----------------------+----------------+-------------+
| backend | sbtest#P#pt1 |       1 | backend2_replication | sbtest         |           1 |
| backend | sbtest#P#pt1 |       0 | backend1             | sbtest         |           3 |
| backend | sbtest#P#pt2 |       0 | backend2             | sbtest         |           1 |
| backend | sbtest#P#pt2 |       1 | backend1_replication | sbtest         |           3 |
+---------+--------------+---------+----------------------+----------------+-------------+
4 rows in set (0.00 sec)
```

Our running `backend2` gets a `link_status` equal to `1`, while the stopped `backend1` server is not available anymore and sets its `link_status` value equal to `3`.

What will happen when `backend1` comes back online? Unfortunately it will not synchronize diff data and come back online by itself. At the moment, since Spider is a new concept, it is not mature enough to do it on its own. However, such mechanisms are planned in the roadmap. Manual actions are required to recover when a server is up after a failure.

The first thing to do is to inform Spider that we're going to make changes on main shards located on the server that failed. For that, we are going to set those shards in maintenance mode.

The main shard that was not accessible was `backend1`. That's why we're going to set it in maintenance mode:

```
ALTER TABLE backend.sbtest
ENGINE=spider COMMENT='wrapper "mysql", table "sbtest"'
 PARTITION BY KEY (id)
(
 PARTITION pt1 COMMENT = 'srv "backend1 backend2_replication"  mbk "2",
mkd "2", msi "3306", link_status "2 0"',
 PARTITION pt2 COMMENT = 'srv "backend2 backend1_replication"  mbk "2",
mkd "2", msi "3306", link_status "0 0"'
);
```

It may be a little bit confusing, but in fact you need to set a link status for each shard. In the first line, the backend1 shard set its value to 2 while backend2_replication set its value to 0. We can't stop all shards on a single partition (here pt1); Spider denies it. So we're going to process the recovery of backend1 first, then you'll need to do the same operation for backend2_replication.

Now we're going to copy the working shard tables to the failed one. Launch the following command:

```
MariaDB [(none)]> select spider_copy_tables('backend.
sbtest#P#pt2','1','0');

+------------------------------------------------------+
| spider_copy_tables('backend.sbtest#P#pt2','1','0')   |
+------------------------------------------------------+
|                                                  1   |
+------------------------------------------------------+

1 row in set (2 min 14.61 sec)
```

A little bit of explanation is required here. Here we've taken the first partition (pt2) of the sbtest table in the backend database, selected the shard with the link_id equal to 1, and the destination link ID (0). As you can see, it could take a while synchronizing the data.

Now, you can set back the Spider configuration to be in the correct configuration:

```
ALTER TABLE backend.sbtest
ENGINE=spider COMMENT='wrapper "mysql", table "sbtest"'
 PARTITION BY KEY (id)
(
 PARTITION pt1 COMMENT = 'srv "backend1 backend2_replication"  mbk "2",
mkd "2", msi "3306", link_status "1 0"',
 PARTITION pt2 COMMENT = 'srv "backend2 backend1_replication"  mbk "2",
mkd "2", msi "3306", link_status "0 0"'
);
```

You're now done with backend1. You need to perform the same operation for backend2_replication to get back in a fully working sharding replication mode.

Performance tuning

The first thing you may have noticed is the slowness involved by the network in a sharding mode. This is absolutely normal, you can't expect to have the same speed compared to one local server if your requests are basic. So how to deal with those problems? Let's see how.

Spider parameters

Spider includes a large set of parameters by default. Like most of the engines, you can change the default parameters to speed up the query time.

The bgs mode

One of the most important settings is `spider_bgs_mode`. By default, it is disabled to optimize memory usage. However, you can change its value if your Spider servers have enough RAM to support it. If you change the default value, you can perform a read query in parallel when the plan prunes multiple partitions.

To change it, you can do the following on the fly in your current session:

```
MariaDB [(none)]> set spider_bgs_mode=2;
```

Otherwise, you can activate it for your all your sessions in your MariaDB configuration file (`/etc/mysql/my.cnf`):

```
[mysqld]
spider_bgs_mode=2;
```

The connection recycle mode

To make Spider recycle by all sessions:

```
MariaDB [(none)]> spider_conn_recycle_mode=1;
```

To make it persistent, add this in your MariaDB configuration:

```
[mysqld]
spider_conn_recycle_mode=1;
```

Statistics tables

You can gain up to 10 percent additional performance when enabling Independent Storage Engine Statistics because they are used by the optimizer:

```
MariaDB [(none)]> set global use_stat_tables='preferably';
```

To make to persistent, add it in your MariaDB configuration:

```
[mysqld]
use_stat_tables='preferably';
```

Remote SQL logs

Logs can be sent to remote backends; by default, they are on the Spider server with MariaDB logs. This can be good for security reasons (avoids log loss); however, this is not good for performance. You should disable it:

```
MariaDB [(none)]> spider_remote_sql_log_off=1;
```

To make it persistent, add the following in your MariaDB configuration:

```
[mysqld]
spider_remote_sql_log_off=1;
```

Number of shards

Will the number of shards and backends change the performance? Yes! The number of shards can change the performance of the solution. For example, having a big shard is generally not the best solution. It's like having a big table.

With MariaDB, when you have a big table, it is common to use table partitioning because you can gain a lot of performance for write statements with that technique. With Spider, it's quite the same; if you think your tables will be too big, then you have to shard them more.

Creating more shards can easily help you reduce the wait time by half during a long query. When you're requesting through Spider, multiple backends can work quickly on small queries and then Spider aggregates it to reply to the client. As the small queries are made on multiple servers, the working time of your backends are smaller than if it was on a single server. That's why having small shards with many backends is the best way to get better performance.

Summary

In this chapter, you learned how to shard data. It was difficult (because the product is young) to cover all the aspects of Spider regarding performance and features in this chapter; however, if you want to go ahead, you have to look at Direct SQL (Map Reduce on remote backend) with UDF functions.

Spider is a newly introduced technology in MariaDB, and this chapter was an introduction to it. Spider covers a lot of missing aspects, but surely will evolve faster in the coming years (as it was recently introduced in MariaDB).

10
Monitoring

Monitoring is one of the most important things to do when you have MariaDB in production. It helps to be proactive and avoid having performance issues. Monitoring can alert you when the usage approaches its limits, which could otherwise cause service disruption.

A lot of monitoring tools exist; some of them are closed source with a paid license, while others are free and/or open source. In this chapter, we will focus on one of the better known free solutions: **Nagios**. Why? In fact for the following reasons:

- It's free for download and use (core version only)
- It's been a popular software for a long time (more than 10 years)
- It's one of the most popular monitoring tools
- It's very stable for production
- Plugins can be written in any language
- Plugins can be easily reused on other projects (Shinken, Naemon, Sensu, and so on)

We're now going to see how to use Nagios depending on your architecture. In addition, we'll see what you can monitor and what is essential or optional.

By default, Nagios is embedded in Debian packages—a list of plugins. However, there is none for MariaDB. That's why we will need to use an additional package to get additional plugins.

Here is what you need to use packages:

```
> aptitude install nagios3 nagios-plugins
```

We won't see here how Nagios works, because it would be too long to explain and several books already cover that subject. Instead, we're going to cover what are the monitoring plugins for MariaDB and how to use them.

There is an important thing to take into account—having a dedicated user for monitoring!

> Monitoring does not need a write access. It needs privileges such as SELECT or PROCESS replication clients and others, based on the plugin. You should not use monitoring with more privileges than necessary (for example, with root user!).

Single instance

On a single instance (that's also available for replication and Galera), you can check several things.

First of all, you can check that your MariaDB instance is responding correctly:

```
> /usr/lib/nagios/plugins/check_mysql

Uptime: 141  Threads: 19  Questions: 298  Slow queries: 0  Opens: 55
Flush tables: 2  Open tables: 39  Queries per second avg: 2.113
```

This check creates a basic connection to your MariaDB instance and gives additional information.

If you really want to have a smaller check, you can simply make a connection and then disconnect.

> Do not simply do create a TCP connection.

Avoid creating a TCP connection (with the check_tcp plugin) because creating a TCP connection will keep the SQL connection open. The problem is that you can reach the maximum SQL connection limit simply because of monitoring. You can avoid this problem using mysql_check because it properly disconnects the SQL session before closing the TCP connection.

Another check exists that permits us to manually check other parameters (as follows). To do it, you will need to specify a mode:

- connection-time: This is the time to connect to the server
- uptime: This is the time the server has been running
- threads-connected: This is the number of currently open connections
- threadcache-hitrate: This is the hit rate of the thread-cache

- threads-created: This is the number of threads created per sec
- threads-running: This is the number of currently running threads
- threads-cached: This is the number of currently cached threads
- connects-aborted: This is the number of aborted connections per sec
- clients-aborted: This is the number of aborted connections (because the client died) per second

There are other options to check **MyISAM** or **InnoDB** engine statuses. To get the full list, launch the following command:

```
> /usr/lib/nagios/plugins/check_mysql_health
```

For some of those modes, you can set a warning and critical threshold. For example, for the number of connected threads, you can set a warning and a critical alarm.

Let's say we want to be warned when the number of connected threads reach 50 and get critical alerts when the number of connections reaches more than 80. We'll use the following command to do so:

```
> /usr/lib/nagios/plugins/check_mysql_health --mode threads-connected
--warning 50 --critical 80
OK - 1 client connection threads | threads_connected=1;50;80
```

All these options are very interesting. However, this is more dependent on system health and not on the stored data.

That's why another script exists and informs you, for example, if a query returns the correct number of rows. A very simple and useless (in most cases, but here is just used for demonstration) check would be to count the number of created users and alerts on a warning and critical threshold. We're using COUNT for that:

```
> /usr/lib/nagios/plugins/check_mysql_query -q "select count(*) from
mysql.user" -w 2 -c 6
QUERY WARNING: 'select count(*) from mysql.user' returned 5.000000
```

Here, we've asked for warning if more than two users are present, and if more than six users are present in a critical state.

It can be useful, for example, if you're using a temporary table to store elements before preprocessing them. To ensure that this table doesn't grow until there is no space left on the server, you can use this check to get notified. This will inform you that the processing tools are working properly.

Replication

With `check_mysql`, there is a simple way to know the replication status with an additional argument:

```
> /usr/lib/nagios/plugins/check_mysql -S
Uptime: 143  Threads: 19  Questions: 302  Slow queries: 0  Opens: 55
Flush tables: 2  Open tables: 39  Queries per second avg: 2.111 Slave IO:
Yes Slave SQL: Yes Seconds Behind Master: 0
```

This will inform you about slave I/O and SQL status (the most important information).

The other information is `Seconds Behind Master`, which denotes the delta between the master and the slave. This is an all-in-one check and may be enough for your needs.

However, you may want to set thresholds to `Seconds Behind Master` or disable it. Here it is not possible, but you can use the `check_mysql_health` check instead.

The following are some interesting options:

- `slave-lag`: This is the value of `Seconds Behind Master`
- `slave-io-running`: This gives information regarding the running slave I/O (copying binlog from master host)
- `slave-sql-running`: This gives information regarding the running slave SQL (playing binlog copied by the I/O thread)

As you know, `slave-io` and `slave-sql` are mandatory to be sure the slave is working fine. However, `slave-lag` is the option we were searching for!

You can define the warning and critical delta you are comfortable with. Remember that depending on your bandwidth, distance, and activity, the lag may be more or less important. It generally takes time to find the best value (depending on your network/activity architecture) and it may generate unwanted alerts (because of slow queries/network link issues and so on).

Galera Cluster

On Galera, you know that there are a lot of options and things to check to ensure that the nodes are working fine.

Percona made a script for Nagios to manage all essentials parameters and to ensure that Galera Cluster is working fine. In fact, it was able to parse the result of the Galera SHOW STATUS LIKE `'wsrep_%'` and look at if it finds a matched string or not.

To install the script, you need to have the Percona repository set correctly and then you can install the package:

```
> apt-key adv --keyserver keys.gnupg.net --recv-keys 1C4CBDCDCD2EFD2A
> add-apt-repository 'deb http://repo.percona.com/apt wheezy main'
> echo 'Package: *
Pin: release o=Percona Development Team
Pin-Priority: 100' > /etc/apt/preferences.d/00percona.pref
> aptitude update
> aptitude install percona-nagios-plugins
```

The plugins will be installed under `/usr/lib64/nagios/plugins`.

First of all, what you generally want to do is to check the cluster size, to be sure all your nodes are here. Let's say we have three Galera Cluster nodes, as we saw in *Chapter 8, Galera Cluster – Multimaster Replication*. What we really want to know is whether our Galera Clusters are in a good state, and not really the number of nodes. So once again, we're going to play with warning and critical threshold. The following is an example:

```
> /usr/lib64/nagios/plugins/pmp-check-mysql-status -x wsrep_cluster_size
-C '<=' -w 2 -c 1
OK wsrep_cluster_size = 3 | wsrep_cluster_size=3;2;1;0;
```

You can see here we've got a three-node cluster. The warning alert will be raised when only two nodes remain, whereas a critical alert will be raised when a single node remains. You need to adjust those parameters depending on your cluster size and the performances you're expecting.

Another interesting check is to know the state of a specific node. It's good to know how your cluster goes, but it's interesting to know which server is part or not part of the cluster. Here is the code to do so:

```
> /usr/lib64/nagios/plugins/pmp-check-mysql-status -x wsrep_cluster_
status -C == -T str -c non-Primary
OK wsrep_cluster_status (str) = Primary | wsrep_cluster_
status=Primary;;non-Primary;0;
```

We can see here that the current node is in a primary state, which means it is part of the cluster.

Yet another check is to know if the node is properly synced. It may be important to know when a node is in Donor mode or Unsynced. Here is the code to check it:

```
> /usr/lib64/nagios/plugins/pmp-check-mysql-status -x wsrep_local_state_
comment -C '!=' -T str -w Synced

OK wsrep_local_state_comment (str) = Synced | wsrep_local_state_
comment=Synced;;Synced;0;
```

The final important check is to know the flow control status. A flow control can be paused, which means data is not up-to-date on this host; this can be caused by several things (big write load, donor mode, and so on). To avoid having that bad surprise, you can add a check to warn if that value goes over 10 percent, and be critical over 80 percent:

```
> /usr/lib64/nagios/plugins/pmp-check-mysql-status -x wsrep_flow_control_
paused -w 0.1 -c 0.8

OK wsrep_flow_control_paused = 0.000000 | wsrep_flow_control_
paused=0.000000;0.1;0.8;0;
```

Here, we can see that everything is ok as we're at 0.000000.

Other monitoring solutions

Monitoring generally means being alerted. However, monitoring can also be graphing, historical data, log centralization, log correlation altering, and so on. We're going to see some free and open source solutions here that can be useful, in addition to Nagios.

In the following sections, we won't dive deep into existing solutions, as that could cover several dedicated books; however, you will see what is the key to good monitoring and what solutions exist.

Graphs

Using graphs to view history is very important. It helps to know what happened in the past and what the evolution of MariaDB was (or any other component).

For example, it can be interesting to have an idea of the number of threads during a year. It can help to understand if an application is usually updated, how is it evolving, and if modifications have to be made on the application side or on the MariaDB architecture side.

The most popular solution is called **Cacti**, which uses RRD to graph data. You can find it at `http://www.cacti.net/`. It's a web-based solution based on SNMP or other kinds of custom scripts. The following is an example of what a graph looks like:

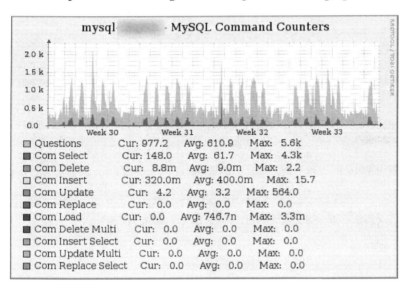

Another solution is **PNP4Nagios**. It is a Nagios-based solution. By default, Nagios checks return data that will be processed by Nagios itself for status and alerting. In addition, other information can be passed at the end of the checks, which is called **performance data**. The performance data are metrics that permit PNP4Nagios to automatically graph.

This is an easy-to-setup solution when you've got performance data on all your checks. The disadvantage is that not every check gets performance data. As checks are open source, you can edit them to implement performance data (`http://nagios.sourceforge.net/docs/3_0/perfdata.html`). PNP4Nagios is a web-based solution as well:

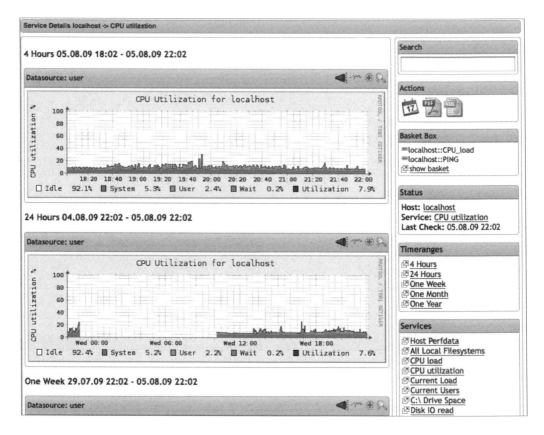

As you can see, it uses RRDTool to produce graphs and could be well integrated in the Nagios interface. **Munin** is another solution. The advantage of this one is that it automatically detects software on your system and will graph the basic metrics. Of course you can add checks that can be automatically detected and graphed with Munin. The following is what a graph looks like with Munin:

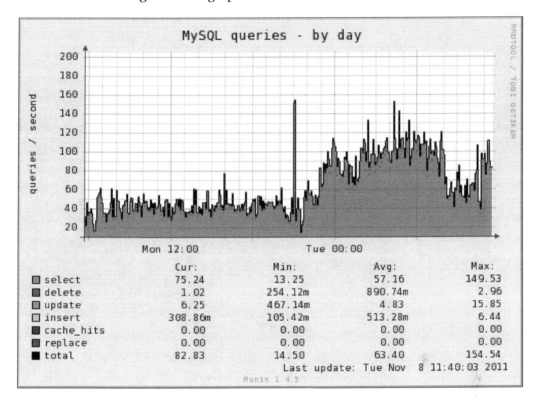

The last solution in the following bullet list is required if you've got a huge infrastructure and need more than that. For example, if you need more real-time information, a scalable solution, and high-level performance information on your running MariaDB instances, you can use the following:

- **Graphite**: This is a scalable real-time graphing GUI solution (http://graphite.wikidot.com/)

- **Collectd**: This is a very fast tool for gathering statistics (http://collectd.org/)

- **Statd**: This is a frontend proxy for Graphite (https://github.com/etsy/statsd)

Graphite is of course the most complicated one to set up, but the most advanced one compared to others:

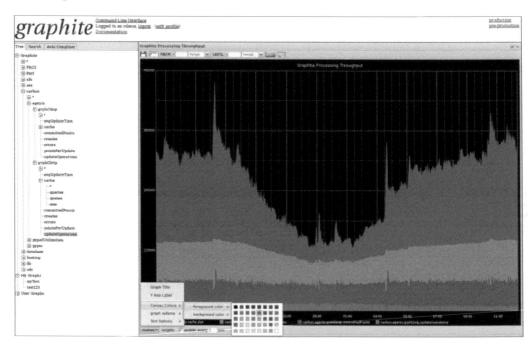

Logs

Logs are important! They are really important when you start having a replication or Galera Cluster. It is simpler to centralize logs in order to compare them easily between two nodes.

The simplest solution consists of forwarding syslog (syslog, rsyslog, syslog-ng, and so on) to a centralized server. You can store then in raw files or you can add them in a MariaDB backend and take a look at it with a web interface such as `php-syslog-ng/Logzilla`:

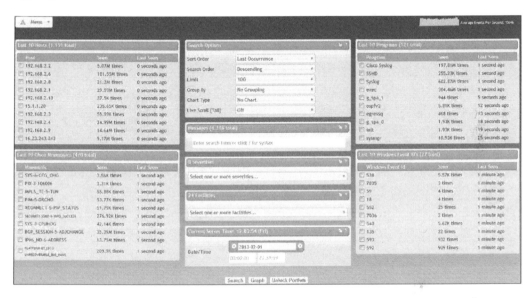

If you need a more powerful solution with high scalability and very fast search, you need to take a look at the following:

- **Logstash/Flume/Fluentd**: These are log collectors that can be used through syslog or a logfile. Then they distribute to Elasticsearch.

- **Elasticsearch**: This is a distributed, real-time search/analytics engine. It gives a full-text search solution based on Lucene.

- **Kibana**: This is a web interface for Elasticsearch.

This solution requires extra space for Elasticsearch indexes, so you really need more than the occupied space by the logs.

Summary

In this chapter, we saw how to monitor solutions for your MariaDB instances. We also saw other methods to monitor and see performance status, and we finally saw log solutions.

In the next chapter, we'll talk about one very important thing—backup.

11
Backups

In the previous chapter, we saw how to monitor MariaDB instances and statistics for performance. This is very important, but one of the most important things that cannot be forgotten is backups.

There are several ways to create backups. Each one has their pros and cons of course. Some of them are related to the technology you're using while others depend on your constraints.

We saw some of those tools in the previous chapters, but they were for specific cases. We're going to see them here in a broader perspective that will help you choose the most convenient one that suits your needs.

To make it simpler, here is a `Vagrantfile` that will install and configure a lot of things for you:

```ruby
# -*- mode: ruby -*-
# vi: set ft=ruby :
# Vagrantfile API/syntax version. Don't touch unless you know what
you're doing!
#
VAGRANTFILE_API_VERSION = "2"

# Insert all your Vms with configs
boxes = [
    { :name => :backup,        :role     => 'db',    :ip =>
'192.168.33.31' },
]

$install = <<INSTALL
aptitude update
```

```
DEBIAN_FRONTEND=noninteractive aptitude -y -o Dpkg::Options::="--
force-confdef" -o Dpkg::Options::="--force-confold" install python-
software-properties openntpd
apt-key adv --recv-keys --keyserver keyserver.ubuntu.com
0xcbcb082a1bb943db
apt-key adv --keyserver keys.gnupg.net --recv-keys 1C4CBDCDCD2EFD2A
add-apt-repository 'deb http://ftp.igh.cnrs.fr/pub/mariadb/repo/10.0/
debian wheezy main'
add-apt-repository 'deb http://repo.percona.com/apt wheezy main'
echo 'Package: *
Pin: release o=Percona Development Team
Pin-Priority: 100' > /etc/apt/preferences.d/00percona.pref
aptitude update
DEBIAN_FRONTEND=noninteractive aptitude -y -o Dpkg::Options::="--
force-confdef" -o Dpkg::Options::="--force-confold" install mariadb-
server percona-toolkit
INSTALL


Vagrant::Config.run do |config|
  # Default box OS
  vm_default = proc do |boxcnf|
    boxcnf.vm.box        = "deimosfr/debian-wheezy"
  end

  boxes.each do |opts|
    vm_default.call(config)
    config.vm.define opts[:name] do |config|
        config.vm.network   :hostonly, opts[:ip]
        config.vm.host_name = "%s.vm" % opts[:name].to_s
        file_to_disk = 'osd-disk_' + opts[:name].to_s + '.vdi'
        config.vm.customize ['createhd', '--filename', file_to_disk,
'--size', 8 * 1024]
        config.vm.customize ['storageattach', :id, '--storagectl',
'SATA', '--port', 1, '--device', 0, '--type', 'hdd', '--medium', file_
to_disk]
        config.vm.provision "shell", inline: $install
    end
  end
end
```

Using mysqldump

mysqldump is the default backup method that comes with MariaDB. It is an old and popular method. Here is an example of a classical dump with some options:

```
> mysqldump -uroot -p -P3306 --opt --routines --triggers --events
--single-transaction --master-data=2 -A > alldb.sql
```

Here is the explanation:

- -u: This is the username.
- -p: This is the password (leave it empty if you want to be prompted).
- -P: This is the port number.
- --opt: This is an all-in-one option. It includes the following:
  - --add-drop-table: This will add the drop queries before creating a new table
  - --add-locks: This gives faster insertions on restore
  - --create-options: This adds all MariaDB options in the create statement
  - --disable-keys: This speeds up the restore because indexes are created after and not during import
  - --extended-insert: This uses multirow inserts to speed up the import
  - --lock-tables: This locks tables before dumping them
  - --quick: This is used for large tables
  - --set-charset: This adds the charset in the dump
- --routines: This includes procedures and functions in the dump.
- --triggers: This adds triggers in the dump.
- --events: This adds mysql.event in the dump.
- --single-transaction: This gets a consistent state for the InnoDB engine.
- --master-data: This, when set to 2, adds the master binlog file and position information in the dump.
- -A: This is used to dump all databases. You can specify a database name instead if you don't want to dump everything.

`mysqldump` works very well with most engines. It is generally used to back up small to medium databases. A big advantage is its simplicity. Being easy to use, it remains one of the best and most commonly used methods.

To restore a dump in a specified database, use the following command:

```
> mysql -uroot -p database < dump.sql
```

Here, we imported the SQL dump file into the database named database.

The major problem is the time and the CPU consumption. When you create a backup, it dumps in the entire contents of a database in SQL format, for example, in file. Creating it is cost effective, and restoring can take a while as well on big databases.

Compression

`mysqldump` doesn't provide compression by default, and the compression will increase the CPU usage of the server. The final size of the dump can be reduced by a factor of 10 and more.

Let's try 7-Zip! First of all, install it:

```
> aptitude install p7zip-full
```

Now, we can create a dump and pipe the output to 7z to compress on the fly:

```
> mysqldump -u$user -p$password --opt --add-drop-table --routines
--triggers --events --single-transaction --master-data=2 database_name |
7z a -t7z -mx=9 -si dump.sql.7z
```

All `mysqldump` options were explained, so let's now focus on the `7z` command:

- `-a`: This appends or creates a new filename.
- `-t`: This sets the compression algorithm. 7z is one of the best, as it performs compressions in a relatively short time.
- `-mx`: This is the compression level, ranging from `1` (lower) to `9` (higher). The lower you compress, the faster it is; the higher you compress, the slower it will be.
- `-si`: This reads data from `stdin` (the piping of `mysqldump` command).
- `dump.sql.7z`: This is the output name and path where the compressed dump is stored.

Compression is an important solution that needs to be taken into account if you're low on disk space availability. However, the additional time required for backup and CPU usage should be taken into account if you're running it on a production server.

When you want to restore a backup, you will need to uncompress it first and then restore it. Of course, you can do it on the fly:

```
> 7z x -so dump.sql.7z | mysql  database_name
```

Using mysqlhotcopy

mysqlhotcopy is a little bit less known; however, it is faster than mysqldump and is available with standard MariaDB. The limitation of this tool is that it only works for MyISAM and Archive tables.

To back up locally, use the following command:

```
> mysqlhotcopy user password /var/lib/mysql/my_database --allowold -
keepold
```

Here is the explanation of the options:

- allowold: This will rename a backup directory as _old if the already exists
- Keepold: This prevents the previous backup from getting removed
- /var/lib/mysql/my_database: This sets the path to your production database

If you want to send the backup to a distant server, use the following command:

```
> mysqlhotcopy --user=user --password=pass user user@host:/home/mon_
backup --allowold --keepold
```

mysqlhotcopy locks tables while performing backups and then unlocks them once done. It doesn't back up in the SQL format, rather it backs up files. If you have a huge amount of data, even though if it's faster than mysqldump, it will lock your tables during the backup time; this could take too much of the acceptable time.

When you want to restore the backup, you need to perform the following steps:

1. Stop MariaDB.
2. Copy backups and paste them in the datadir of MariaDB.
3. Restore writes on it with correct permissions.
4. Start MariaDB.

This is easy but requires a shut down of the MariaDB instance.

LVM

Logical volume manager (LVM) allows you to create a quick snapshot that can be used for backups. Apart from that, you can perform migration with easy rollback. This is a little bit out of the scope of this chapter, but as it is quick and could be very useful, we'll discuss it.

LVM is not a MariaDB tool, but a device mapper solution providing snapshot solutions. If you're using advanced filesystems such as ZFS or BTRFS, you can also use the snapshot feature to create backups.

Snapshot

To make a usable MariaDB `datadir` snapshot, you first need to lock your tables:

```
MariaDB [(none)]> flush tables with read lock;
```

Now we're sure there will be no changes on our instance. Let's create the snapshot on the system:

```
> lvcreate --snapshot -n snap_mariadb -L 2G /dev/data/mariadb
```

Here is a list of used commands:

- `--snapshot`: This indicates we want to create an LVM snapshot
- `-n`: This is the name of the snapshot
- `-L`: This is the size of the snapshot
- `/dev/data/mariadb`: This is the logical volume path

Now you can release locked tables:

```
MariaDB [(none)]> unlock tables;
```

To know what happens when you create a LVM snapshot, you first need to know that a new volume is attached to the logical volume. LVM in fact works with an exception table that traces modified blocks (also called **Copy on Write**). When a block tends to be modified on the logical source volume, it is then copied to the snapshot and modified.

 If you didn't reserve enough space for your snapshot, don't worry; you can resize it with the `lvresize` command.

No changes are made on the logical source volume. So the table is modified to inform the changes occurred on those blocks. On the next access, the file will be read from the snapshot to get the latest changes.

Removing snapshots

Let's say you've created a snapshot, made modifications on your database, and want to keep them because it works the way you want.

You can keep the logical source volume and remove the snapshot:

```
> lvremove /dev/data/snap_mariadb
```

It's ok now, there is no snapshot anymore; your data is all up to date.

Rollback

Now let's suppose that the changes that you made are bad and you don't want it anymore. What you want is to rollback to your previous working version. We're going to use the merge option:

```
> lvconvert --merge /dev/data/snap_mariadb
  Can't merge over open origin volume
  Merging of snapshot snap_mariadb will start next activation.
```

Merging won't be done on the fly as the volume is already used. You will need to reactivate LVM for that partition. This will involve a downtime. You need to proceed in the following order:

1. Stop MariaDB.
2. Unmount the logical volume.
3. Deactivate the logical volume.
4. Activate the logical volume.
5. Mount the logical volume.
6. Start MariaDB.
7. Ok, now you're ready to do perform merging:

   ```
   > service mysql stop || exit 1
   > umount /var/lib/mysql
   > lvchange -an /dev/data/mariadb
   > lvchange -ay /dev/data/mariadb
   > mount /var/lib/mysql
   > service mysql start
   ```

That's it. If you now look in the `/dev/mapper` folder, you won't see any snapshot anymore.

Backup

Backing up is now an easy task when you've created the snapshot. However, be sure you've allowed enough space for the snapshot during the backup time to avoid resizing it during the backup.

It is very easy to create a backup with LVM. However, it won't be a SQL dump (logical dump), but binary dump files will be copied instead. How does it work? When you're creating a snapshot, you are using another logical volume for the changes. However, the logical source volume is still available for read operations and it doesn't change at all. You can then mount it and copy the data of your MariaDB files.

Now, suppose you want to use the LVM snapshot to create your backups. Here is how to technically achieve it using the previous command:

```
MariaDB [(none)]> flush tables with read lock;
> lvcreate --snapshot -n snap_mariadb -L 2G /dev/data/mariadb
MariaDB [(none)]> unlock tables;
```

The snapshot is ready; let's mount the logical source volume somewhere, copy the data to a backup folder, and remove the snapshot:

```
> mount -o ro /dev/data/snap_mariadb /mnt
> mkdir /backups
> rsync –az –delete /mnt/* /backups
> umount /mnt
> lvremove /dev/data/snap_mariadb
```

That's it! You've now got a consistent backup easily created. When you want to restore, you will just have to replace (when MariaDB is stopped) the `datadir` files from the backup to your MariaDB instance path (`/var/lib/mysql` by default).

Xtrabackup

`Xtrabackup` is the best solution to create backups for several reasons:

- It's fast in creating a backup
- It's fast in restoring a backup
- It locks a table for a very short time

- It can stream compressed databases
- It can perform incremental backups
- It allows you to compress your backups
- It allows you to encrypt your backups

In most cases, it's a better solution to backup, as it is very fast and doesn't need to lock the tables for a long time (only a few milliseconds). However, you need to take care about what you're backing up, as Xtrabackup only backs up InnoDB/XtraDB and MyISAM engines.

To install Xtrabackup, we saw in the previous chapters that you need to first configure the Percona repository and then install Xtrabackup.

Full backup

We'll see here how to create the first backup which will be a full backup. You can start creating it by running the following command:

```
> innobackupex --rsync --compress --compress-threads=$(grep
-c '^processor' /proc/cpuinfo) --use-memory=1G --user=username
--password=pass --databases=dbname /mnt
innobackupex: Backup created in directory '/mnt/2014-05-24_17-17-38'
innobackupex: MySQL binlog position: filename 'mariadb-bin.000014',
position 328
140524 17:17:41  innobackupex: Connection to database server closed
140524 17:17:41  innobackupex: completed OK!
```

You do not need to specify the database name if you want to back up all the databases. We're using some additional parameters in this command:

- `rsync`: This is used to speed up the process (that involves having the rsync binary installed on your server).
- `compress`: This adds the compression.
- `compress-threads`: This is the number of threads used for compression. You can replace this with a defined number or let grep automatically count how many cores you've got on your server.
- `use-memory`: This value is set to accelerate Xtrabackup jobs.
- `/mnt`: This parameter tells where to store the backups. Here, we want to back up in `/backups`, which will create a folder with the date of the day with the hour of backup (for example, `/mnt/2014-05-24_17-17-38`).

If you prefer transferring your backup directly to another host, you can use the
xbstream option:

```
> innobackupex --stream=xbstream ./ | ssh root@192.168.33.32 "xbstream -x
-C /mnt/"
```

Incremental backup

Incremental backup is a very nice feature that can save a lot of disk space. To work
with incremental backups, the first thing you need to have is a full backup:

```
> innobackupex --rsync /mnt
[...]
innobackupex: Backup created in directory '/mnt/2014-05-24_17-17-38'
innobackupex: MySQL binlog position: filename 'mariadb-bin.000014',
position 328
140524 17:17:41  innobackupex: Connection to database server closed
140524 17:17:41  innobackupex: completed OK!
```

Everything ran fine here. Now we're ready to start an incremental backup:

```
> innobackupex --rsync --incremental-basedir=/mnt/2014-05-24_17-17-38/
--incremental /mnt/
[...]
innobackupex: Backup created in directory '/mnt/2014-05-24_17-18-25'
innobackupex: MySQL binlog position: filename 'mariadb-bin.000014',
position 328
140524 17:18:28  innobackupex: Connection to database server closed
140524 17:18:28  innobackupex: completed OK!
```

The following are the explanations of the parameters used:

- --incremental-basedir: This sets the path of the full backup directory
- --incremental: This sets the path where to store the incremental backup

Now if you take a look at the size of the backup's folders, you'll find the following:

```
> du -sh /mnt/*
14M     /mnt/2014-05-24_17-17-38
1.2M    /mnt/2014-05-24_17-18-25
```

Note that the first line corresponds to the full (biggest size) and the second line to the
incremental backup (smallest size). We are good!

Restoring from a full backup

Perform the following steps to restore from a full backup:

1. If you've created a compressed backup, you first need to decompress it. Launch the following command with the path of the full backup:

   ```
   > innobackupex --decompress /mnt/2014-05-24_17-17-38
   ```

2. To restore a backup, you first need to prepare your backup to be restored. Select the path of your full backup:

   ```
   > innobackupex --apply-log /mnt/2014-05-24_17-17-38
   [...]
   InnoDB: Starting shutdown...
   InnoDB: Shutdown completed; log sequence number 1867798
   140524 17:35:33  innobackupex: completed OK!
   ```

3. To restore the full backup, stop MariaDB and remove the current content of the database:

   ```
   > service mysql stop
   > rm -Rf /var/lib/mysql/*
   ```

4. You can now ask to restore using the copy-back parameter as an argument and the path of the full backup in the last parameter:

   ```
   > innobackupex --copy-back /mnt/2014-05-24_17-17-38/
   innobackupex: Starting to copy InnoDB log files
   innobackupex: in '/mnt/2014-05-24_17-17-38'
   innobackupex: back to original InnoDB log directory '/var/lib/
   mysql'
   innobackupex: Copying '/mnt/2014-05-24_17-17-38/ib_logfile1' to '/
   var/lib/mysql/ib_logfile1'
   innobackupex: Copying '/mnt/2014-05-24_17-17-38/ib_logfile0' to '/
   var/lib/mysql/ib_logfile0'
   innobackupex: Finished copying back files.
   140524 17:58:22  innobackupex: completed OK!
   ```

5. To finish, restore rights and start MySQL:

   ```
   > chown -R mysql. /var/lib/mysql
   > service mysql start
   ```

Restoring from an incremental backup

Perform the following steps to restore from an incremental backup:

1. Like for the full backup, the first thing to do is to prepare the full backup, but this time with a new option (`redo-only`):

    ```
    > innobackupex --apply-log --redo-only /mnt/2014-05-24_17-17-38
    [...]
    InnoDB: Starting shutdown...
    InnoDB: Shutdown completed; log sequence number 1867798
    140524 18:56:38  innobackupex: completed OK!
    ```

2. Now you need to merge the incremental backup to the full backup:

    ```
    > innobackupex --apply-log --incremental-dir=/mnt/2014-05-24_17-18-25/ /mnt/2014-05-24_17-17-38
    [...]
    140524 19:05:21  innobackupex: completed OK!
    ```

3. Then, as seen earlier, you need to prepare the backup for restore:

    ```
    > service mysql stop
    > rm -Rf /var/lib/mysql/*
    ```

4. Then restore the backup:

    ```
    > innobackupex --copy-back /mnt/2014-05-24_17-17-38/
    > chown -R mysql. /var/lib/mysql
    > service mysql start
    ```

You've now seen all the common ways to use Xtrabackup.

Galera backup

Backup of Galera is not a complicated task; it just requires organization. This is simply because when you're doing a backup, your node goes in Donor mode. Using Xtrabackup will reduce the Donor mode time as compared to a classical dump and helps in quickly integrating a new node.

If you want to back up a Galera node with `mysqldump`, it is strongly recommended to use a load balancer (such as HAProxy) to move out the cluster node that provides data for backups. If you put in place what has been seen in *Chapter 8, Galera Cluster – Multimaster Replication*, there won't be any problem. When a node is in Donor mode, it will automatically be removed from the load balancer and will automatically be reintegrated while it gets finished and synced.

If you have no special constraints and can use Xtrabackup, it's better. To create a backup, you need to add a new option dedicated for Galera Cluster, which will create a `xtrabackup_galera_info` file with Galera information inside. If you do not use it, you won't be able to create incremental backups. So, to backup, perform the following steps:

```
> innobackupex --rsync --galera-info /mnt
```

To restore, there is nothing much to do; proceed like a classical MariaDB instance:

```
> service mysql stop
> rm -Rf /var/lib/mysql/*
> innobackupex --copy-back /mnt/2014-05-24_17-17-38/
> chown -R mysql. /var/lib/mysql
```

However, to start it, you will need to set the UUID state at the moment of the backup. This will integrate the node in the Galera Cluster. The following is how to do it:

1. If you now take a look at `xtrabackup_galera_info`, you will see the local node UUID state:

   ```
   > cat /mnt/2014-05-24_17-17-38/xtrabackup_galera_info
   5c9f6a1b-cd43-11e3-ad13-22007f7479c5:688
   ```

2. To finish, integrate the cluster in the following manner:

   ```
   > service mysql start --wsrep_cluster_
   address='gcomm://192.168.33.31' --wsrep_start_position="5c9f6a1b-
   cd43-11e3-ad13-22007f7479c5:688 "
   ```

You need to specify a working node of the current Galera Cluster (`wsrep_cluster_address`) and set the UUID position with the `wsrep_start_position` parameter previously taken in the `xtrabackup_galera_info` file.

> Remember that when you integrate a node in a Galera Cluster, a delta copy has to be created, so a node will be set as Donor during integrating. This will permit the new node to get the delta between the backup and the current state. It will then be up-to-date, synced, and the donor node will remain synced as well.

It is possible to predict this kind of thing by forcing the donor node. This will permit to move out the load balancer, such as a node, defining it as Donor and integrating back in the load balancer once its job has finished. You can force a node to be the main donor node using the following command:

```
MariaDB [(none)]> SET global wsrep_sst_donor='192.168.33.31';
```

Summary

Backup is something important, and several methods exist for it. There is no best solution; there are many backup tools and you generally have to choose one that fits your needs. Other tools exist that have not been covered because of their license, price, or maturity level. The MariaDB world is growing very fast and new solutions are going to emerge, bringing more simplicity and features.

Index

E

Elasticsearch 255
Error-Correcting Code memory (ECC memory) 13
explain command 42, 43, 93
Extract-Transform-Load (ETL) 184

F

FederatedX 36
filesystem optimization
  filesystem options 23-25
first boot, Galera Cluster
  performing 200-205
first shard
  creating 228-232
flush method, InnoDB 85
flush method, TokuDB 88
full backup
  about 265
  restoring from 267
functionalities
  disabled, for Intel 16
Fusion-io direct acceleration cards 12

G

Galera1 201
Galera backup 268, 269
Galera Cluster
  about 191, 248, 249
  advanced mechanisms 193
  advantages 192
  configuration 194
  configuration files 197
  first boot, performing 200-205
  installing 195
  installing manually 197
  issues, resolving 219
  limitations 194
  nodes, testing 221
  performance tuning 211
  redundant architectures, designing 212
  starting 208
  tests 219
  usages 205
  working 192, 193

Galera Cluster, advantages
  consistent data 192
  hot standby 192
  multithreaded slave 192
  synchronous replication 192
  transparent to applications 192
  true multimaster 192
  WAN 192
Galera Cluster configuration
  Galera configuration file, creating 198
  MariaDB configuration file, editing 198
Galera Cluster, usages
  consensus clustering 209
  donor node, dedicating 208
  Garb, using 209, 210
  maintenance, performing 209
  transfer methods 205
Galera configuration file
  creating 198
  gcache.name 199
  gcache.page_size 199
  gcache.size 199
  MariaDB options, overriding 200
  wrep_provider 199
  wsrep_cluster_address 199
  wsrep_cluster_name 199
  wsrep_node_address 199
  wsrep_node_name 199
  wsrep_notify_cmd 200
  wsrep_provider_options 199
  wsrep_replication_myisam 200
  wsrep_retry_autocommit 199
  wsrep_slave_threads 199
  wsrep_sst_method 199
  wsrep_sst_receive_address 200
GALERA_GROUP 210
GALERA_NODES 210
Garb
  about 209
  configuration file, editing 210
  using 209, 210
Gcache size 211
global statistics 66
Global Transaction ID. See GTID
graph
  about 251
  using 251, 254

Thank you for buying
MariaDB High Performance

About Packt Publishing

Packt, pronounced 'packed', published its first book "*Mastering phpMyAdmin for Effective MySQL Management*" in April 2004 and subsequently continued to specialize in publishing highly focused books on specific technologies and solutions.

Our books and publications share the experiences of your fellow IT professionals in adapting and customizing today's systems, applications, and frameworks. Our solution based books give you the knowledge and power to customize the software and technologies you're using to get the job done. Packt books are more specific and less general than the IT books you have seen in the past. Our unique business model allows us to bring you more focused information, giving you more of what you need to know, and less of what you don't.

Packt is a modern, yet unique publishing company, which focuses on producing quality, cutting-edge books for communities of developers, administrators, and newbies alike. For more information, please visit our website: www.packtpub.com.

About Packt Open Source

In 2010, Packt launched two new brands, Packt Open Source and Packt Enterprise, in order to continue its focus on specialization. This book is part of the Packt Open Source brand, home to books published on software built around Open Source licenses, and offering information to anybody from advanced developers to budding web designers. The Open Source brand also runs Packt's Open Source Royalty Scheme, by which Packt gives a royalty to each Open Source project about whose software a book is sold.

Writing for Packt

We welcome all inquiries from people who are interested in authoring. Book proposals should be sent to author@packtpub.com. If your book idea is still at an early stage and you would like to discuss it first before writing a formal book proposal, contact us; one of our commissioning editors will get in touch with you.

We're not just looking for published authors; if you have strong technical skills but no writing experience, our experienced editors can help you develop a writing career, or simply get some additional reward for your expertise.

Pentaho Data Integration Beginner's Guide

Second Edition

ISBN: 978-1-78216-504-0   Paperback: 502 pages

Get up and running with the Pentaho Data Integration tool using this hands-on, easy-to-read guide

1. Manipulate your data by exploring, transforming, validating, and integrating it.

2. Learn to migrate data between applications.

3. Explore several features of Pentaho Data Integration 5.0.

4. Connect to any database engine, explore the databases, and perform all kinds of operations on databases.

Pentaho Data Integration 4 Cookbook

ISBN: 978-1-84951-524-5   Paperback: 352 pages

Over 70 recipes to solve ETL problems using Pentaho Kettle

1. Manipulate your data by exploring, transforming, validating, integrating, and more.

2. Work with all kinds of data sources such as databases, plain files, and XML structures, among others.

3. Use Kettle in integration with other components of the Pentaho Business Intelligence Suite.

Please check **www.PacktPub.com** for information on our titles